TEXTS
OF
IDENTITY

INQUIRIES IN SOCIAL CONSTRUCTION

Series editors
Kenneth J. Gergen and John Shotter

This series is designed to enable scholars across the disciplines and across national boundaries to participate in an emerging dialogue which many believe presages a major shift in the western intellectual tradition.

Besides raising uncertainties in older assumptions about knowledge and the self, this wide-reaching dialogue has given 'voice' to a range of new subjects: the social construction of personal identities; the role of power in the social making of meanings; the role of rhetoric and narrative in establishing sciences; the centrality of everyday activities. Their shared concern is cultural critique and renewal. Among the protagonists in this lively dialogue are sociologists of science, psychologists, communications theorists, cyberneticists, ethnomethodologists, literary theorists, feminists, and social historians.

Inquiries in Social Construction affords a vehicle for exploring this new consciousness, for investigating the problems raised, and the implications for society. It does so by focusing upon a common theme across the debates: the extent to which abilities and processes, formerly located in individuals, are now seen as products of human community.

Also in this series

The Social Construction of Lesbianism
Celia Kitzinger

Rhetoric in the Human Sciences
edited by Herbert W. Simons

TEXTS
OF
IDENTITY

EDITED BY
JOHN SHOTTER
and
KENNETH J. GERGEN

SAGE Publications
London · Newbury Park · New Delhi

Preface, Introduction and arrangement © John Shotter and Kenneth J. Gergen 1989
Chapter 1 © Edward E. Sampson 1989
Chapter 2 © Rom Harré 1989
Chapter 3 © B.R. Slugoski and G.P. Ginsburg 1989
Chapter 4 © Ian Parker 1989
Chapter 5 © Kenneth J. Gergen 1989
Chapter 6 © Celia Kitzinger 1989
Chapter 7 © Khachig Tölölyan 1989
Chapter 8 © Nikolas Rose 1989
Chapter 9 © John Shotter 1989
Chapter 10 © Katharine Young 1989
Chapter 11 © David Holt 1989
Chapter 12 © Kevin Murray 1989
Chapter 13 © Margaret Wetherell and Jonathan Potter 1989
Chapter 14 © Kurt W. Back 1989

First published 1989

SAGE Publications Ltd
28 Banner Street
London EC1Y 8QE

SAGE Publications Inc
2111 West Hillcrest Drive
Newbury Park, California 91230

SAGE Publications India Pvt Ltd
C-236 Defence Colony
New Delhi 110 024

British Library Cataloguing in Publication Data

Texts of identity.— (Inquiries in social
  construction series; v. 2).
  1. Man. Identity – Sociological
  perspectives
  I. Shotter, John II. Gergen, Kenneth J.
  (Kenneth Jay), *1934–* III. Series
  302

  ISBN 0-8039-8172-4
  ISBN 0-8039-8173-2 Pbk

Library of Congress catalog card number 88-062098

Printed in Great Britain by Billing and Sons Ltd, Worcester.

Contents

Notes on Contributors

Kurt W. Back is James B. Duke Professor of Sociology at Duke University, North Carolina. His long term interest has been in the nature of the encounter movement in America, and he is the author of *Beyond Words: the story of sensitivity training and the encounter movement* (1974).

Kenneth J. Gergen is Professor of Psychology at Swarthmore College, Pennsylvania. As the author of *Toward Transformation in Social Knowledge* (1982) he is a central exponent of the social constructionist movement in modern psychology.

Gerry Ginsburg is Professor and Chair of Psychology at the University of Nevada, Reno. He is the editor of *Discovery Strategies in the Psychology of Action* (1985).

Rom Harré is a lecturer in the philosophy of science at Linacre College, Oxford. Since his seminal work with Paul Secord, *The Explanation of Social Behaviour* (1972), he has developed the social constructionist position further in numerous works including *Social Being* (1979) and *Personal Being* (1983).

David Holt is a practising Jungian analyst in Oxford and a central figure in the movement to explore the relation between theatre and psychotherapy. He is the author of *Theatre and Behaviour: Hawkwood papers* (1979–86).

Celia Kitzinger is the author of the first volume in this series, *The Social Construction of Lesbianism* (1987). She is currently teaching social psychology at North East London Polytechnic and is preparing a new book on feminist morality.

Kevin Murray is a lecturer in social psychology at the University of Melbourne. He has written extensively in recent years on the relations between narrative and selfhood.

Ian Parker teaches psychology at Manchester Polytechnic. His recent work is concerned with a critique of 'new paradigm' social psychology and discourse analysis. He is currently editing a volume, *Deconstructing Social Psychology*, with John Shotter.

Jonathan Potter is a lecturer in social psychology at Loughborough University. He is the author, with Margaret Wetherell, of *Discourse and Social Psychology* (1987).

Khachig Tölölyan is Associate Director of the Center for Humanities at Wesleyan University, Connecticut. He has written extensively on the problem of terrorism and is currently working on a set of essays on the politics and psychology of diasporas.

Nikolas Rose is a lecturer in the Department of Human Sciences at Brunel University. He is the author of *The Psychological Complex* (1985) and, with P. Miller, *The Power of Psychiatry* (1986).

Edward E. Sampson is Professor of Psychology at the California State University, Northridge. He is the author of *Justice and the Critique of Pure Psychology* (1983) and in recent years has written a number of influential articles analysing the relation of American psychology to American ideals.

John Shotter is Professor of Interdisciplinary Social Sciences at the State University of Utrecht. He is the author of *Social Accountability and Selfhood* (1984).

Ben Slugoski is Assistant Professor of Psychology at Simon Fraser University in British Columbia. He completed his DPhil at the University of Oxford in 1985 and is currently engaged in research on the interaction of linguistic usage and social psychological variables and processes.

Margaret Wetherell is a lecturer in social psychology at the Open University. She is co-author of *Discourse and Social Psychology* (1987) and, with Jonathan Potter and Peter Stringer, of *Social Texts and Contexts: literature and social psychology* (1984).

Katharine Young is a freelance folklorist living in Philadelphia. She is the author of *Taleworlds and Storyrealms: the phenomenology of narrative* (1987).

Preface and Introduction

The chapters of this volume are highly diverse in their particular foci; for example, the motivations of terrorists, the indignity of a medical examination, the mystery story, lesbianism, developmental theory; and the empiricist theory of science are all treated – and more. There is some diversity too in the writers' backgrounds. Yet there is a surprising degree of uniformity in their approach. For, all contributors share a concern with the issues of textuality, with the construction of identity and with cultural critique. They are concerned with the ways in which personal identities are formed, constrained and delimited within ongoing relationships. The major metaphor underlying these explorations is the text, both the finally produced text and the textually aware activities involved in its production. For, it is reasoned, the primary medium within which identities are created and have their currency is not just linguistic but textual: persons are largely ascribed identities according to the manner of their embedding within a discourse – in their own or in the discourses of others. In this way cultural texts furnish their 'inhabitants' with the resources for the formation of selves; they lay out an array of enabling potentials, while simultaneously establishing a set of constraining boundaries beyond which selves cannot be easily made. Because different cultural texts present differing sets of invitations and limitations, they also present themselves for critical comparison and assessment. And it is here that another point of agreement between the writers emerges. To be concerned with the comparison and assessment of texts of identity in the modern Western world is to be engaged in a struggle with a single dominant text: the centrality and sovereignty of the individual, and the problems to which it gives rise. And this is the central point of the volume: for in the process of critique, the boundaries of our current modes of being are softened, and intelligibilities for possible new forms of personhood are revealed.

The present series – *Inquiries in Social Construction* – is designed to furnish a forum for expression of what many find an intense and exciting dialogue taking place throughout the social sciences and humanities. In part, the dialogue results from the loss of confidence many feel in the classical foundations of knowledge – fixed rules, methods or philosophical assumptions which guide the acquisition and accumulation of knowledge in the various disciplines. In earlier decades an optimistic romance with the establishment of firm foundations was everywhere apparent; the means seemed available for generating objective truth, broad-scale social prediction, lucidity in interpretation, clarity in communication, and to do all while sidestepping murky problems of morality. But the means and ends are no longer clear. Self-reflexive critique of foundations has been steadily increasing since the 1900s. It has emerged, for example, in the history and philosophy of science, the sociology of knowledge, literary theory, hermeneutics, critical theory, the philosophy of history, ethnomethodology, feminist theory and even in mathematics. And as the critique has expanded, many have joined ranks in searching for new bases for understanding. Ethogenicists, humanists, semioticians, cyberneticians, rhetoricians, communications specialists and many others now take part in what many feel to be the dawning of a new age of scholarship, one marked by a far greater charity towards disparate voices, sharpened by a sensitivity to the processes by which knowledge claims are made and justified, with a heightened moral concern, and a keener appreciation of the communal character of understanding.

Central to the emerging dialogue is a recognition of the critical role played by linguistic constructions in social life. Instead of assuming that people's relations with nature and with society are unaffected by the language within which they are formulated, we find that these very relations are constituted by the ways of talk informing them, by the forms of accountability by which they are, so to speak, kept in good repair. Hence, rather than assuming, by the time we come to investigate the significance of the social world, or the nature of the identities of those who inhabit it, that both are already fixed, we find it more useful to assume that both are still in the making, and still open to further change and development. They are open first because their very origins are to be located within communal interchange, within the process of rendering everyday interaction intelligible. At the same time, these patterns may be reconstituted if formulated in a different idiom. Thus, if we now find ourselves experiencing ourselves as self-contained, self-controlled individuals, owing nothing to others for our nature as such, we need not presume that this is a fixed or 'natural' state of affairs. Rather, it is a form of historically dependent intelligibility requiring for its continued sustenance a set of shared understandings. It is a moment in a still ongoing historical process and may be reconstituted as understandings change.

For many, this broadly shared concern with the generation, sustenance and social ramifications of systems of intelligibility is nicely captured by the term 'social construction'. P. Berger and T. Luckmann's pioneering volume, *The Social Construction of Reality*, essentially established the term on the intellectual landscape. Nelson Goodman's *Ways of World Making* has also been a seminal contribution to this mode of thought. Since these early works, a host of related books and papers have been published across the intellectual spectrum. Attempts to synthesize these contributions into a more general framework can be found in Harré (1979, 1983), Gergen (1982), Gergen and Davis (1985) and Shotter (1984).

That the second volume of this series is called *Texts of Identity* is very apposite. For constructionism is a focus not simply upon the formative nature of social activity in general, but upon particular kinds of social practices and institutions. And, clearly, as any social practice entails the people involved in it treating both themselves and one another in particular kinds of ways, then, who they *are* to one another (and to themselves) is central to the nature of the practice. As Charles Taylor (1985) notes, a particular practice or social institution cannot be carried out without certain self-understandings; hence the identities of those conducting the practice are constitutive of its nature. In other words, the reality in question here is 'in' the character of the practices: it is informed by an image or vision or a prospect of how we might be – what we imagine plays a part in what we attempt to make. And this is what this book is about: the different ways in which discourse about the self is constitutive of social pattern.

References

Berger, P. and T. Luckmann (1966) *The Social Construction of Reality*. Garden City, New York: Doubleday.

Goodman, N. (1978) *Ways of Worldmaking*. New York: Hackett.

Harré, R. (1979) *Social Being*. Oxford: Blackwell.

Harré, R. (1983) *Personal Being*. Oxford: Blackwell.

Gergen, K.J. (1982) *Toward Transformation in Social Knowledge*. New York: Springer.

Gergen, K.J. and K. Davis (1985) (eds) *The Social Construction of the Person*. New York: Springer.

Shotter, J. (1984) *Social Accountability and Selfhood*. Oxford: Blackwell.

Taylor, C. (1985) *Human Agency and Language: Philosophical Papers I*. Cambridge: Cambridge University Press.

PART I

FOUNDATIONS FOR A TEXTUAL ANALYSIS OF SELFHOOD

1
The Deconstruction of the Self

Edward E. Sampson

It is almost a truism to suggest that a field of enquiry cannot proceed without general agreement and substantial clarity about its proper object of study. In spite of the many disagreements that continue to plague the field, the majority of psychologists appear to have reached a consensus that the individual person – what I term 'psychology's subject' – is the proper object for psychological enquiry. Whatever else it may do, psychology's task is to study the individual and to develop the laws of his or her functioning.

Psychology has implicitly assumed that this object of its enquiry is a natural entity with attributes that psychology can empirically study. My aim in this chapter is the critical analysis of that very familiar and taken-for-granted object of enquiry, the individual person that is psychology's subject. In this, I am carrying forward some of my previous work (e.g. Sampson, 1977), in which I described the special quality of the American ideal – that is, the North American version of psychology's subject – as a self-contained individualism. This refers to the firmly bounded, highly individuated conception of personhood, most aptly described by Geertz (1973, 1979) in the following passage:

> The Western conception of the person as a bounded, unique, more or less integrated motivational and cognitive universe, a dynamic center of awareness, emotion, judgment and action, organized into a distinctive whole and set contrastively against other such wholes and against a social and natural background is, however incorrigible it may seem to us, a rather peculiar idea within the context of the world's cultures. (Geertz, 1979, p. 229)

At least six discernible challenges to this commonly assumed subject of psychological inquiry have appeared. (1) Cross-cultural investigation has suggested the pecularity of the current North American view and has uncovered several significant, less individuated, alternatives (e.g. Geertz, 1973, 1979; Heelas and Lock, 1981; Shweder and Bourne, 1982; Miller 1984). (2) Feminist reconceptualizations of the patriarchical version of social, historical and psychological life have introduced some strikingly different views of personhood (e.g. Chodorow, 1978; Gilligan, 1982; Lykes, 1985). (3) Social constructionism has amplified the earlier ideas of Mead (1934), arguing that selves, persons, psychological traits and so forth, including the very idea of individual psychological traits, are social and historical constructions, not naturally occurring objects. Constructionism casts grave doubts about the inevitability of the currently dominant Western version (e.g. Gergen, 1985; Harré, 1984; Sampson, 1983). (4) Systems theory has presented an epistemological position in which ontological primacy is granted to relations rather than individual entities, once again raising serious questions about the inevitability and reasonableness of the entity-based North American ideal (e.g. Bateson, 1972; Dewey and Bentley, 1949; Maruyama, 1979, 1980). (5) Critical theory, originating in the Frankfurt School tradition, has located the current North American conception in the heartland of advanced capitalist ideology. These theorists not only question the inevitability of the North American ideal, but also force us to consider the possibility that psychology's subject is a character designed primarily to serve ideological purposes; that psychology, in studying that character and presenting so-called 'facts' about its qualities, helps contribute primarily to societal reproduction rather than truly to human betterment (e.g. Adorno, 1967, 1973, 1974; Habermas, 1971, 1973, 1975; Horkheimer, 1941, 1972; Horkheimer and Adorno, 1972; Marcuse, 1964, 1966, 1968). (6) Deconstructionism, a relatively recent perspective developed within post structuralist literary criticism and linguistic analysis, has challenged all notions that involve the primacy of the subject (or author). This perspective presents a very unsettling picture of the world and undoes the security which the current North American ideal presents (e.g. Coward and Ellis, 1977; Derrida, 1974, 1978, 1981).

The resistance of North American psychology to modify its assumptions in light of these devastating challenges is truly amazing. This stubborn refusal is testimony less to the validity of the current rendering of psychology's subject as some naturally occurring reality, than to the service which that view provides to current social structures. Needless to say, both the character of psychology's subject and its resistance to change are pieces of evidence that support the view propounded by the challengers. That is, if indeed psychology's subject is a sociohistorical, sociocultural product, as all the challengers in one way or another imply, then it must necessarily 'belong' to its particular time and place. In this sense, 'to belong' means to fit the ongoing structures and arrangements of current Western society. Changing conceptions of personhood, then, is somewhat equivalent to a Kuhnian paradigm shift: it is likely to occur only with a major shift in the shape of the underlying culture that has produced it and sustains it even as it reproduces that underlying culture.

In this chapter, I intend to examine in some detail only two of the preceding six challengers: critical theory, and deconstructionism. I believe that these two stand sufficiently outside the mainstream of common psychological writing, including writing that challenges the current ideal, to have been missed by readers who are familiar with the other challenges.

The Bourgeois Individual: Psychology's Subject as Ideology

Geertz's description of the Western concept of the person as a 'bounded ... universe ... a dynamic center of awareness, emotion, judgment, and action' provides us with a helpful summary of the concept of the bourgeois individual as developed more fully by several key theorists of the once flourishing Frankfurt Institute (e.g. Adorno, 1967, 1974; Habermas, 1973; Horkheimer, 1972; Horkheimer and Adorno, 1972; Marcuse, 1964, 1966, 1968). The concept of the person as a relatively autonomous self-contained and distinctive universe is said to reflect the sham and the illusion that is the bourgeois individual, not its reality.

The *concept* describes an entity who is the integrated centre of certain powers: one who is aware, who feels, who thinks, judges and acts. In concept, the individual is adopted as the primary reality, the ontological base from which issues the remainder, including society and social relations (also see Mayhew, 1981). The critical theorists argue, however, that the reality is quite different. The concept describes a fictitious character, the bourgeois individual, whose integrated wholeness, unique individuality and status as a subject with actual powers to shape events has become null and void. They greet this demise not with joy but with sorrow over the loss of someone who might have been, and with anger at the deceit that passes for normal everyday life.

The critical perspective adopts a view about the real nature of personhood in which such notions as 'integrated wholeness', 'dynamic universe' or 'self-contained centre' are invariably more false than true. Critical theorists argue that there is an essential *interpenetration* (see Jacoby, 1975; Meacham, 1977; Turkle, 1978) of society and the individual that warrants our approaching with scepticism any view that makes the individual a transcendent entity. We do not begin with two independent entities, individual and society, that are otherwise formed and defined apart from one another and that interact as though each were external to the other. Rather, society constitutes and inhabits the very core of whatever passes for personhood: each is interpenetrated by its other.

The Bourgeois Individual and Early Capitalism

Habermas (1975) provides a helpful account of the large-scale historical shifts in the underlying organizational principles of society that constituted different meanings and realities for personhood. He outlines four such principles: the primitive, the traditional, the liberal capitalist and the advanced capitalist.

Within the primitive social form, kinship played a dominant role in defining the nature and scope of personhood. People were not meaningfully defined apart from their family units. In the traditional social form, the bureaucratic apparatus replaced the family as the unit of social life. Fromm (1941) briefly describes this transition: the feudal household was shattered; private individuals emerged from their public, communal existence into the harsh glare of personal freedom of movement and choice. As Marcuse (1968) observed, the liberation that characterized this post medieval period empowered people as individuals to shape their own destiny. Life seemed then to be unmediated: individuals directly confronted the tasks of self-maintenance and survival without being the delegated representatives of some 'higher social bodies'. The individual 'arose as a dynamic cell of economic activity' (Horkheimer and Adorno, 1972, p. 203), interested in securing what economic benefits were possible.

From Liberal to Advanced Capitalism

The further development of the bourgeois individual awaited the liberal capitalist organizational principle. A group of corporate owners emerged, entrepreneurs with a generally wide latitude of autonomous functioning; and a class of workers emerged whose autonomy, while limited, was more substantial than in previous eras. A Civil Society developed with laws to protect the rights and freedoms of individuals.

Habermas suggests that the liberal form functioned according to the relatively anonymous market forces of supply and demand. There was a reasonableness to the concept that self-contained individual actors could function autonomously as little economic calculators guided by the unseen hand of the market-place. Success and failure were somewhat connected to the wisdom of choices made and the intensity of personal motivation.

This unseen hand of the market-place that characterized the liberal form was replaced in the advanced form by the longer arm of state intervention in market manipulation. Advanced capitalism developed along with the growing concentration of capital and the extension of corporations into international markets.

While the bourgeois ideas regarding freedom of individual choice and decision-making remain, they are increasingly disjunctive with the objective realities of systemic functioning under the advanced organizational principle. Autonomous entrepreneurs no longer compete on the open market seeking fair exchanges and following principles of supply and demand. Rather, state intervention creates and seeks to control conditions of supply and demand, scarcity and abundance. The state participates actively in establishing pricing policies and market options. The range of individual choice becomes restricted and narrowed; opportunities are channelled by national priorities and reflect the requirements of system maintenance, security and enlargement.

Decision processes form around alternatives dictated by such imperatives as corporate expansion and the control of international markets. Rationality of choice becomes limited to choosing between alternatives already predetermined by socioeconomic forces about which one is only vaguely aware or able to affect (see Adorno, 1967). And yet, the ideology of autonomy and of individuality remain carved deeply in the subjective consciousness of the culture.

The Bourgeois Individual and Societal Reproduction

Societies create both the types of character essential to societal reproduction and the ideologies necessary so that those characters will function to achieve this reproduction. The bourgeois individual is such a character. The ideologies concerning individuality, autonomy and freedom play an essential role in societal reproduction.

Caplan and Nelson's (1973) review of psychology's understanding of black Americans is illustrative of this point. Their review discovered that over 80 per cent of the psychological studies of black Americans attributed their problems to something about themselves rather than their circumstances. This tendency to interpret social ills as psychologically derived creates a psychological subject who is given the full burden of responsibility for correcting his or her troubles. In this manner, underlying structures that systematically thwart a group's opportunities (such as economic structures that breed racism and sexism) are reproduced in so far as we view the troubles of people to be a problem of their will power, motivation, intellect or personality dynamics.

In Conclusion

The message of the critical perspective for our understanding psychology's subject is complex. The reality of personhood cannot be grasped either at the extreme pole of individualism – in which the seemingly autonomous individual is the ontological reality and prime mover – or at the pole of mechanical collectivism – in which the individual is merely a mechanical copy of the underlying social order. There is an essentially dialectical interpenetration of subject and object in which neither has full primacy. We must refocus our understanding so that we can see what Giddens (1979) terms the 'quality of structuring' that describes the person–society relationship. The person is the mediated product of society and also, in acting, reproduces or potentially transforms that society. People can transform themselves by transforming the structures by which they are formed.

The unfolding of this process cannot occur in a structural vacuum even as it cannot occur under psychological conditions aversive to its achievement. While it would take us too far afield in this chapter to pursue the matter, some of Habermas' ideas on communication are important for interested readers to consider (e.g. Habermas, 1971, 1973; also see McCarthy, 1976, 1978).

Derrida's Deconstruction of Psychology's Subject

While there is no simple way to define either the structuralism of the 1950s and 1960s or the post structuralism of the 1970s and 1980s, the essence of each is its search for basic processes that lie beyond individuality and human awareness and out of which the individual-as-such is constituted (e.g. Kurzweil, 1980). This search has usually turned to the analysis of language and symbolic practices as the key to be deciphered. Each seriously challenges the Western understanding of the person–society relationship, in particular the centrality and the sovereignty of the individual:

> The lesson of ... structuralism was that man is to be understood as constructed by the symbol and not as the point of origin of symbolism. The individual, even prior to his or her birth, is always already subject-ed to the structure into which he or she is born. The structure is what sets

in place an experience for the subject which it includes. This demands a radical re-estimation of the position of the individual; it should no longer be possible to adhere to the notion of the individual as embodying some ideal pre-given essence. Being always subject-ed, the subject can never be the transcendental ... source. (Coward and Ellis, 1977, pp. 3–4)

Derrida's Deconstructive Analysis

Jacques Derrida's efforts to deconstruct Western metaphysics have helped inaugurate the post structuralist movement. Derrida's very term, 'deconstruct', sets his task and poses the dilemma. To deconstruct is to undo, not to destroy: to undo what Derrida sees to be a tradition that has dominated Western thought since early Greek philosophy and which lies at the very roots of our commonsense understanding. The dilemma is that the tools used to deconstruct this tradition come from that very tradition: 'Derrida thus finds himself in the uncomfortable position of attempting to account for an error by means of tools derived from that very error' (Johnson, 1981, p. x).

One of Derrida's central methodological devices to accomplish this feat hinges on the notion of placing a term under erasure (*sous rature*). To place something under erasure is, literally, first to write a word then cross it out, and then to print both the word and its deletion. For example, the word 'Being', under erasure, would appear thus: Being and B~~ein~~g. What this *sous rature* accomplishes is a strategy of telling us that we both need the term, in order to understand the points being made, and simultaneously should not employ the term: 'Since the word is inaccurate, it is crossed out. Since it is necessary, it remains legible' (Spivak, 1974, p. xiv).

The strategic device of the *sous rature* is necessary to Derrida's task of employing the familiar and commonly known in order to deconstruct the familiar and commonly known. Thus, we must use the terms that we believe to be inaccurate and inappropriate, under erasure, in order to reveal their status as useful, necessary and wrong. This brings a special subtlety and complexity to Derrida's works.

A further complication exists in that Derrida's deconstructive aim is not to undo the tradition of Western metaphysics in order to install in its place another tradition founded on the same frame. Indeed, his criticism of much of what heretofore has passed for a critique of that tradition, including the works of Nietzsche, Freud and Heidegger, is that they have undone the tradition, but only to restore what they have undone in another form. For example, hierarchies of binary oppositions founded on an identity logic dominate the Western tradition; it is not Derrida's aim to overthrow this frame only in order to install another of the same sort in its place. Rather, his deconstructive aim is to undo the very notions of identity and hierarchy in the first place.

In a manner reminiscent of Adorno (1973; see also Buck-Morss, 1977), Derrida challenges the core identity theory and logic on which opposition and hierarchy are based. Through his close readings of texts, he seeks to discover *within* the meaning of any single term its opposite member: e.g., to discover within A the meaning of its presumed opposite, Not-A. This challenges the notions of identity, opposition and entity because A is *both* A *and* not-A: each term contains both itself and its other. Derrida engages in considerable word play and word analysis, hoping to *catch* the author off guard: to undo the text by revealing its other sides in the way a word is used, in its diverse associations, in the metaphors it brings to mind, or even in the usages that it can have but which the author has failed to discuss.

We will find it helpful in examining Derrida's analysis to consider two themes. The first focuses on his challenge to what he terms the logocentrism and phonocentrism of all Western metaphysics. The second introduces some of the key concepts, especially his notion of *differance* (with an *a*) and its implication for deconstructing the familiar concept of the subject.

The Critique of Logo- and Phonocentrism

Derrida's works revolve around the fundamental structuralist thesis that all social practices, including the meaning of subject and subjectivity, are not simply mediated by language, but are constituted in and through language. Therefore, it becomes important to examine both the signifying system of language and the tradition by which language has thus far been understood. Derrida's aim is to deconstruct that tradition and so provide a better understanding of the manner by which persons are constituted in social and linguistic practice.

Derrida's review of the Western tradition since Plato reveals an emphasis on the union of mind, thought and consciousness with voice or speech. The presumption has been that speech provides a privileged access to the mind; that speaking and thinking are co-present; that speaking is in immediate rather than mediated presence with consciousness and being.

This logo- and phonocentric perspective locates writing as secondary (that is, derivative and mediated) to the full presence of speaking. Writing is what is non-present, a substitute for the immediacy (presence) of the voice. Derrida uses the term 'writing' in both its narrow and its familiar sense to refer to inscriptions on a page and, more broadly, to anything involving traces, basically, the absence of what is presumed to be fully present (namely, speaking and the voice). The aim of deconstructing this hierarchy is *not* to reverse its ordering (speech primary, writing derivative), but, more pointedly, to reveal the roots of writing and the trace within the very core of speech. In other words, Derrida's aim is to reveal how the presumption that speech occupies a privileged place *vis-à-vis* mind and consciousness is in error because speech is *always already* inhabited by writing and hence is mediated and derivative. Needless to say, if presence is always already inhabited by absence, then even the apparent 'presence' of the subject to itself becomes suspect.

There are several historical entry points that stress this privileging of speech over writing that Derrida seeks to undo. Derrida observes how in Aristotle's view, for example, 'spoken words ... are the symbols of mental experience ... and written words are the symbols of spoken words' (Derrida, 1974, p. 11). In the Aristotelian view, speech occupies a privileged status with respect to mental experience, while writing, being mediated and derivative, merely represents what is spoken: 'the voice, producer of *the first symbols*, has a relationship of essential and immediate proximity with the mind ... It signifies "mental experiences"' (Derrida, 1974, p. 11). Derrida argues that phonocentrism grants a special status not only to speech over writing but therefore also to presence over absence: that is, a privileging of what appears to be immediate and present, as for example the privileged ontological status that empiricism grants to whatever has here-and-now, observable, qualities (see also, e.g., Adorno, 1973; Keat and Urry, 1975).

The privileging of presence is based on the notion that, because speakers both speak and hear themselves speak *at the same time*, they must be constituted as subjects with subjectivity (mind and consciousness) on the basis of speech. Derrida notes that when a person speaks the voice seems spontaneously to carry forth the operations of subjectivity and of mental experience. What appears is 'the unique experience of the signified producing itself spontaneously from within the self' (Derrida, 1974, p. 20). Derrida sees this to be the master illusion of all Western thought. He likens this privileging of speech to the quest for an absolute centre, an origin, a beginning, a transcendental signified: that is, a source which itself has no source other than its pure being, pure spontaneity, pure presence; a source that serves as the ground for truth itself.

It will not serve our purposes to review or develop in detail Derrida's arguments on behalf of the Western domination of presence over absence, of the immediate over the mediated, of speech over writing. It is sufficient to observe that this lays the cornerstone to his whole analysis. His deconstructive task introduces writing and the trace – that is, what is absent, not present – as the key elements to turn around our whole manner of thinking.

Writing, the Trace and Differance

Derrida argues that what we presume to be present (speech and the voice) is constituted through something that is a non-present difference. There is a parallel here between Derrida and Bateson (1972), who similarly argues that within the world of communication and information (i.e. language) there are only *differences*, not things, events, forces or impacts: 'In the world of mind, nothing – that which is *not* – can be a cause' (Bateson, 1972, p. 452).

To unfold the meaning of what I have just outlined, let me employ the case that Derrida uses to illustrate his own model: Freud's analysis of the psychic apparatus as a process of writing (Derrida, 1978: Ch. 7). As befits his methodology, Derrida provides a close and detailed reading of Freud's works over a thirty-year period (from 1895 to 1925) as he moved towards the metaphor of writing to describe the psychical apparatus.

According to Freud (1925), the toy slate known as the Mystic Writing Pad provides an apt metaphor for the psychical apparatus itself. The problem with which Freud wrestled and which led him to this formulation involves the dual requirements of the psychic apparatus: there must be an element that receives messages from the external world while remaining relatively open and fresh to new materials and there must be an element that records permanent traces and thus is relatively resistant to the pure receipt of incoming materials. The Mystic Writing Pad solves this need by means of its several layers.

The surface layer is open and permeable to the reception of incoming materials; it remains forever fresh however, only by virtue of the erasure that occurs each time the surface is lifted from its wax underbase. Derrida sees it to be significant that the virgin status of the first layer is assured only through its being erased so that a fresh surface can remain exposed: the erasure of presence is thus essential to the continuing awareness of presence. The inner surface of the pad consists of the underlying wax layer. While it does not receive fresh imprints, it records imprints as permanent traces inscribed in its surface.

The fresh surface layer is present to our awareness; it comprises the system both of perception and of consciousness itself. Yet, it makes no lasting record. The second layer, within which are inscribed permanent traces, involves the system of the unconscious. What Derrida finds so especially informative about this Freudian metaphor is the notion that writing, that is the permanent trace, exists *always already* (a term Derrida frequently employs) before perception is aware or conscious of itself. To phrase this differently, the trace, which is absent from consciousness, forms the basis of consciousness itself: 'Writing supplements perception before perception even appears to itself ... "Memory" or writing is the opening of that process of appearance itself. The "perceived" may be read only in the past, beneath perception and after it' (Derrida, 1978, p. 224).

We have now encountered Derrida's deconstruction of the Western metaphysics of presence. The trace (writing in general) serves as the foundation of presence; and yet, the trace that informs presence is never itself present in awareness. Derrida deconstructs the thesis that speech provides an immediacy between what is spoken and what is meant. His contention is that, as the Freudian metaphor suggests, the apparent presence of speech is a mediated derivative of a non-present trace. Whatever is said to be immediately present is the result of a process that has always already taken place. 'To mean, in other words, is automatically *not* to be' (Johnson, 1981, p. ix).

Differance
Derrida's master concept, differance, captures this complex decon-structive process in a single word that stands for two other words: 'difference' and 'deferral'. 'Difference' refers to the Saussurian (or Batesonian) notion that all language and communication exists as a system of differences. As de Saussure (1959) argued, the distinction between the sound forms (i.e. signifiers) of a language is discerned only by their differences from other forms within the language system and not by anything intrinsic or essential to their nature as such. Differences describe relations, not entities; and relations are not locatable as specific presences. When Derrida speaks of 'differance' as involving differences, therefore, he is simply noting that the meanings that emerge in linguistic practice do so on the basis of differences and distinctions, not on the basis of essences or substances that are fully present as such.

The sense of deferral which the term 'differance' also rec-ommends derives rather directly from the Freudian metaphor we have just examined. 'Deferral' describes the inherent time lag (distance) between presence and what constitutes that presence, namely absence, writing, the trace. Recall that the model describes a delaying mechanism; whatever is consciously perceived 'may be read only in the past' (Derrida, 1978, p. 224). To say that differance inhabits presence and constitutes what is present, therefore, is to suggest that what we adopt as an immediate presence of being is the outcome of a complex, never-ending process of difference and deferral: '*differance* inhabits the very core of what appears to be immediate and present ... The illusion of the self-presence of meaning or of consciousness is thus produced by the repression of the differential structures from which they spring' (Johnson, 1981, p. ix).

The paradoxical quality of differance is that it is a non-presence: an interval, a space, a gap, a trace. Furthermore, differance defies the logic of identity, of either/or, through its emphasis on the logic of the supplement, of both/and.

Logic of Identity versus Derrida's Logic of the Supplement
The binarism that characterized structuralism is deconstructed by the opposing logic of the supplement as revealed in the concept of differance. As we have seen, Derrida argues that in whatever we take to be immediate and present there is always already absence, difference and deferral. If presence always contains absence, there cannot be a neatly drawn line of opposition between these two notions. It is not that presence and absence are opposites, not that there is *either* presence *or* absence, but rather that there is an inevitable defining of the one through the other: there is *both* presence *and* absence; absence inhabits and interpenetrates with presence. This appears clearly in the Freudian view in which what is conscious (present) is always already inhabited by what is unconscious (absent).

Derrida's logic of the supplement challenges the logic of identity. A supplement both substitutes for and adds to something else. Writing, for example, supplements speech. In supplementing speech, writing both substitutes for it and adds absence to its seeming presence. It is both different from speech and yet also inhabits speech. Thus, writing is both speech and its other, that is, what speech is not.

In mounting this challenge to identity logic, Derrida accomplishes what Adorno (1973) likewise sought to do in his complex and richly illustrative major work, *Negative Dialectics*. Adorno sought to undo the identity thesis that seemed to threaten civilization even as it formed the basis of certainty for civilization. In the hopes of deconstructing identity, Adorno recommended a negative dialectics, a *process* that never came to rest, as Hegel's dialectics did, with some final or originary identity: a process forever in motion, hence negative rather than affirmative, positive or self-present. Derrida's deconstructive attack on presence and identity likewise envisions a never-ending process, without beginning or end. This describes the undoing of the centre and the certainty that marks so many of our Western mastery-designed enterprises.

Derrida's versus Psychology's Subject

Once again, it will be helpful to turn to Geertz's fine description of the Western concept of personhood in order to sharpen the comparison with Derrida's analysis. Geertz appropriately describes the concept of person that one would expect to emerge from the very Western metaphysics which Derrida deconstructs. Rather than requoting Geertz's description, let me simply paraphrase and highlight three key elements to which Derrida's analysis is counterposed: (1) the person is a *centre of awareness*; (2) the person is an *integrated* universe and distinctive *whole*; (3) the person is a bounded entity *set contrastively against* other such entities.

A Centre of Awareness?
As previously noted, Derrida builds on the anti-phenomenologies of Marx, Nietzsche and Freud and the similar themes of French structuralism to question the notion of the person as a fully aware, self-present being. His critique of the concepts of mind, consciousness and subjectivity as immediately self-available presences leads us to question any psychology of the self and of subjectivity that fails to adopt a mediated perspective. There are several points to recall.

First, the Derridian psychic apparatus operates in such a manner that its workings are not entirely available to itself. Although the metaphor is not entirely apt, this idea is akin to a camera that can film everything but itself filming everything (see Wilden, 1980).

In addition, recall that Derrida's thesis is that presence is always already mediated by the absent trace; thus, self-consciousness is not a direct and unmediated experience but rather is an indirect and always already mediated experience. This way of understanding personhood and consciousness permits a key role for social and historical traces to enter and structure the very experience of consciousness and of self, even as those traces are unavailable to presence and awareness.

As Coward and Ellis (1977) observe, this perspective leads us to see ideology – specific sociohistorical traces contained within the language system – permeating the very core of personhood. Ideology is not a garment that one puts on and removes at will: ideology constitutes the person as a subject in the first place. What precedes consciousness, including the consciousness of the self as subject, as cogito, is thereby a process that constitutes that presence, mediates it and sets the subject in place. The process, however, remains beyond the grasp of any status as a present-in-itself:

> ideology is not a slogan under which political and economic interest of a class presents itself. It is the way in which the individual actively lives his or her role within the social totality: it therefore participates in the construction of that individual so that he or she can act. Ideology is a practice of representation; a practice to produce a specific articulation, that is, producing certain meanings and necessitating certain subjects as their supports. (Coward and Ellis, 1977, p. 67)

The point summarized in this passage, derivative from Derrida as well as from Lacan, among others (see Coward and Ellis, 1977; Lemaire, 1977; Turkle, 1978; Wilden 1980) argues that persons as subjects are constructed in and through a symbolic system that fixes the subject in place while remaining beyond the subject's full mastery. In other words, persons are not at the centre, fully aware and self-present masters, but have been *decentred* by these relations to the symbolic order. The very indeterminancy of the symbolic order, governed by the endless process of differance, always already inhabited by a non-presence that founds presence, introduces a picture of a subject who is open-ended and indeterminate except as fixed in place by the culturally constituted symbolic order.

The Western subject as one who is at the centre of awareness is thereby seen as the work of an ideological practice that represses the fluidity and indeterminacy of the process in the name of a fixed point of origin. Ideology is understood as an aspect of the symbolic universe that accomplishes this fixing in the service of certain cultural and institutional practices and requirements. In this view, the intervention required to produce a new subject, decentred and open to other fixings, demands a depth process akin to psychoanalysis joined with a structural change to support this new subject.

An Integrated Whole?
The Western conception of personhood, which has clearly permeated psychology's understanding of its subject, emphasizes the notion of persons as more or less integrated universes and distinctive wholes. The emphasis is placed on wholeness and integration, at least as an ideal state of personhood to be attained. Read through almost any developmental thesis, Erikson's (1959) for example, to discover the high value that is placed on the integration of opposing or contradictory resolutions to identity-crises. Or examine Loevinger's (1976) highly sophisticated conception of ego development to observe the value that is placed on what she calls the highest stage: Integrated. While Loevinger admits both the rarity of finding people at this high point of development and (hence) the

difficulty of its simple description or assessment, she tells us that it is like the previous stage of autonomy, where oppositions are united and integrated, but involves an even greater consolidation into a coherent, integrated whole, an identity-as-such.

The conception, then, is of a person who integrates all the contradictions of previous stages of ego development into one dominant hierarchy. Basically, it is the ego that strives towards this integrative high point. Derrida's conception, however, gives us a fully non-centred and non-centrable representation of personhood. His deconstruction of the metaphysics that requires 'centres' and 'points of origin or conclusion' creates the picture of a process without beginning or end, without a centre in charge:

> The 'subject' of writing does not exist if we mean by that some sovereign solitude of the author. The subject of writing is a *system* of relations between strata: the Mystic Pad, the psyche, society, the world. Within that scene, on that stage, the punctual simplicity of the classical subject is not to be found. (Derrida, 1978, p. 226–7)

Ogilvy (1979) pursued the consequences of this Derridian view of personhood in writing about a new ideal, the multi dimensional, decentred self rather than the integrated, hierarchically arranged Western conception. The concept of the self as integrated, and the valuing of that concept, flow from and participate in the reproduction of the Western worldview. The ego as master in its own household, seeking to integrate the competing demands it faces and being successful to the extent that it achieves a unified wholeness, has its parallels in theories of governance and of authority within the Western world. The alternative, more Derridian, view would give us a subject who is multi-dimensional and without centre or hierarchical integration. It would give us a process and a paradox, but never a beginning or an end.

Opposed Entities?
The Western logic of identity is a logic of either/or. By contrast, Derrida's logic of the supplement (of differance, rather than of identity) is a logic of both/and. The third theme culled from Geertz's description of the Western concept of personhood builds upon the logic of identity and either/or and speaks of one entity being set 'contrastively against', that is, opposed to, other entities. Contrast and opposition go hand in glove with the sense of an autonomous entity, one whose potential for unity and wholeness (i.e. for one identity above all) permits us to define this creature and to set it against others. In the Derridian logic of the supplement, what something is is thoroughly inhabited by what that something also is

not. Thus, entities are both what they are and also what they are not. Under these conditions, it is impossible meaningfully to understand the oppositional relationship between entities. This theme has been proposed as well by Wilden (1980) and Bateson (1972).

Bateson observes that the unit of natural survival is neither the individual nor the society, but that, in fact, there is no homogeneous unit of survival as such, only a system, termed the 'ecosystem'. This system comprises *both* organism *and* environment. Bateson observes that any organism that destroys its environment manages to destroy itself. It is apparent that, by thinking in terms of either/or, one creates the very conditions that oppose entities that are in fact members of the same system. In other words, only by thinking in terms of a logic of both/and can one see that the matter is not one of opposition but only of differences: and as we know, differences do not inhere in the entity, but rather describe the relations among the parts of a system.

Wilden sees the very concept of personhood that exists in the Western world, based on the requirement for either/or identity, to be one that threatens the very persons in whose name it is offered. This Western concept forces contrastive opposition where the mutual recognition of the other-in-self and the self-in-other is essential. The Derridian subject can never be set apart from the multiple others who are its very essence. Thus, the Derridian subject who would seek to oppose and enslave others can only suffer in kind, for those others are elements of the subject's own personhood.

Towards a Conclusion

This chapter began by suggesting that the subject of psychology's enquiry has occupied so familiar and unquestionable a status that it has rarely received the kind of careful scrutiny that such an important notion warrants. It has been my intent to enter into the critical dialogue by reviewing two distinct perspectives that challenge our present understanding.

Several of the authors who have contributed to this deconstructive challenge to psychology's subject have done so for reasons beyond the mere introduction of a new way of thinking about the universe and about human life. Many participate in the development of a new epistemology based on the belief that the old ways of understanding affirm Western civilization's material substrata and lie near the deep roots of the human dilemma of survival and wellbeing.

In a strikingly similar manner, the two perspectives we have examined plus the four we have not, locate the root psychological problem within the epistemological framework that has dominated the Western worldview. In so far as differences between people and between organism and environment have been understood to be non-reciprocal and hierarchical (with certain kinds of people on top), there has evolved a domination of group over group, individual over individual, humanity over humanity's environment, including both the natural ecology and its varieties of cultural representatives (e.g. see Leiss, 1975). As long as we persist in this individuated manner of viewing the world and its inhabitants, there will continue to be incursions that destroy in the name of momentary peace. Only when the alternative points of view can be sustained by underlying structural modifications will it be possible to grant non-hierarchical significance to the unification that differences provide.

Where will psychology be in this unfolding drama of human survival? As I see it, the challenge for psychology is to renovate its own formulations. This renovation must begin at its very base, the understanding of the subject that psychology examines and the methodologies appropriate to this new venture. In this way, psychology's subject may become a new and different character, and psychology will have helped contribute to the creation of a new subject instead of continuing to affirm the old.

References

Adorno, T.W. (1967) 'Sociology and Psychology', *New Left Review*, 46: 63-80.

Adorno, T.W. (1973) *Negative Dialectics*. New York: Seabury Press.

Adorno, T.W. (1974) *Minima Moralia*. London: NLB.

Bateson, G. (1972) *Steps to an Ecology of Mind*. New York: Chandler.

Buck-Morss, S. (1977) *The Origin of Negative Dialectics*. New York: Free Press.

Caplan, N. and S.D. Nelson (1973) 'On Being Useful: The Nature and Consequences of Psychological Research on Social Problems', *American Psychologist*, 28: 199–211.

Chodorow, N. (1978) *The Reproduction of Mothering*. Berkeley: University of California Press.

Coward, R. and J. Ellis (1977) *Language and Materialism*. London: Routledge & Kegan Paul.

Derrida, J. (1974) *Of Grammatology*. Baltimore: Johns Hopkins University Press.

Derrida, J. (1978) *Writing and Difference*. Chicago: University of Chicago Press.

Derrida, J. (1981) *Dissemination*. Chicago: University of Chicago Press.

de Saussure, F. (1959) *Course in General Linguistics*. New York: McGraw-Hill.

Dewey, J. and A.F. Bentley (1949) *Knowing and the Known*. Boston: Beacon Press.

Erikson, E.H. (1959) *Identity and the Life Cycle: Psychological Issues*. New York: International Universities Press.

Freud, S. (1925) 'A Note upon the "Mystic Writing-pad"', *Collected Papers*, Vol. 5 (J. Strachey, ed.). London: Hogarth Press, 1950.

Fromm, E. (1941) *Escape from Freedom*. New York: Holt, Rinehart & Winston.

Geertz, C. (1973) *The Interpretation of Cultures*. New York: Basic Books.

Geertz, C. (1979) 'From the Native's Point of View: On the Nature of Anthropological Understanding', pp. 225–41 in P. Rabinow and W.M. Sullivan (eds), *Interpretive Social Science*. Berkeley: University of California Press.

Gergen, K.J. (1985) 'The Social Constructionist Movement in Modern Psychology', *American Psychologist*, 40: 266–73.

Giddens, A. (1979) *Central Problems in Social Theory*. Berkeley: University of California Press.

Gilligan, C. (1982) *In a Different Voice: Psychological Theory and Women's Development*. Cambridge, MA: Harvard University Press.

Habermas, J. (1971) *Knowledge and Human Interests*. Boston: Beacon Press.

Habermas, J. (1973) *Theory and Practice*. Boston: Beacon Press.

Habermas, J. (1975) *Legitimation Crisis*. Boston: Beacon Press.

Harré, R. (1984) *Personal Being*. Cambridge, MA: Harvard University Press.

Heelas, P. and A. Lock (1981) *Indigenous Psychologies: The Anthropology of the Self*. London: Academic Press.

Horkheimer, M. (1941) 'Notes on Institute Activities', *Studies in Philosophy and Social Science*, 9: 121–3.

Horkheimer, M. (1972) *Critical Theory*. New York: Seabury Press.

Horkheimer, M. and T.W. Adorno (1972) *Dialectic of Enlightenment*. New York: Seabury Press.

Jacoby, R. (1975) *Social Amnesia*. Boston: Beacon Press.

Johnson, B. (1981) Translator's introduction to J. Derrida, *Dissemination*, pp. vii–xxxiii. Chicago: University of Chicago Press.

Keat, R. and J. Urry (1975) *Social Theory as Science*. London: Routledge & Kegan Paul.

Kurzweil, E. (1980) *The Age of Structuralism*. New York: Columbia University Press.

Leiss, W. (1975) 'The Problem of Man and Nature in the Work of the Frankfurt School', *Journal of Philosophy and Social Science*, 4: 163–72.

Lemaire, A. (1977), *Jacques Lacan*. London: Routledge & Kegan Paul.

Loevinger, J. (1976) *Ego Development*. San Francisco: Jossey-Bass.

Lykes, M.B. (1985) 'Gender and Individualistic vs. Collectivist Bases for Notions about the Self', *Journal of Personality*, 53: 356–83.

Marcuse, H. (1964) *One-dimensional Man*. Boston: Beacon Press.

Marcuse, H. (1966) *Eros and Civilization*. Boston: Beacon Press.

Marcuse, H. (1968) *Negations*. Boston: Beacon Press.

Maruyama, M. (1979) 'Transepistemological Understanding: Wisdom beyond Theories', pp. 373–89 in R. Hinshaw (ed.), *Currents in Anthropology*. The Hague: Mouton.

Maruyama, M. (1980) 'Mindscapes and Science Theories', *Current Anthropology*, 21: 589–600.

Mayhew, B.H. (1981) 'Structuralism versus Individualism, Part II. Ideological and Other Obfuscations', *Social Forces*, 59: 627–48.

McCarthy, T.A. (1976) 'A Theory of Communicative Competence', pp. 470–97 in P. Connerton (ed.), *Critical Sociology*. Harmondsworth, Middlesex: Penguin.

McCarthy, T.A. (1978) *The Critical Theory of Jurgen Habermas*. Cambridge, MA: MIT Press.

Meacham, J.A. (1977) 'Soviet Investigations of Memory Development', in R.V. Kail, Jr and J.W. Hagen (eds), *Perspectives on the Development of Memory and Cognition*. Hillsdale, NJ: Erlbaum.

Mead, G.H. (1934) *The Social Psychology of George Herbert Mead* (A. Strauss, ed.). Chicago: University of Chicago Press.

Miller J.G. (1984) 'Culture and the Development of Everyday Social Explanation', *Journal of Personality and Social Psychology*, 46: 961–78.

Ogilvy, J. (1979) *Many-dimensional Man*. New York: Harper & Row.

Sampson, E.E. (1977) 'Psychology and the American Ideal', *Journal of Personality and Social Psychology*, 35: 767–82.

Sampson, E.E. (1983) *Justice and the Critique of Pure Psychology*. New York: Plenum.

Shweder, R.A. and E. Bourne (1982) 'Does the Concept of the Person Vary Cross-culturally?', pp. 97–137 in A.J. Marsella and G. White (eds), *Cultural Concepts of Mental Health and Therapy*. Boston: Reidel.

Spivak, G.C. (1974) Translator's preface to J. Derrida, *Of Grammatology*, pp. ix–lxxxvii. Baltimore: Johns Hopkins University Press.

Turkle, S. (1978) *Psychoanalytic Politics*. Cambridge, MA: MIT Press.

Wilden, A. (1980) *System and Structure*. New York: Tavistock.

2

Language Games and Texts of Identity

Rom Harré

In my paper 'Enlarging the Paradigm' (Harré, 1987), I drew attention to the need to supplement experimental psychology with linguistic analysis. This followed from the fact that experiments make sense only when the scope of the phenomenon under study has been mapped out by careful attention to the rules for the use of the relevant vocabulary. Now this of course entails that the ultimate entity to which psychologists should be directing their attention is a text. I worked this out in terms of two sketches: that of an investigation of remembering, and of a study of the emotions. The latter sketch was filled out in *The Social Constructions of Emotion* (Harré, 1986).

The principle involved was that the phenomena to be investigated in a psychological study *are* what the relevant vocabulary picks out and its use creates.

At this point we must pause briefly to brush aside the ideas of some recent well-intentioned but chuckle-headed materialists – Searle, who ought to know better, and the Churchlands. All have argued that a neurophysiological vocabulary could take over the role of the myriad ordinary human languages in regulating our behaviour, demarcating our emotions and structuring our patterns of thought.

This involves three errors.

1. The first is the failure to appreciate that if the substitution could be achieved it would be a *new* family of language games, leaving the old ones still unexplicated, and thus a new form of life. For example, the moral dimensions that are crucial to the old form of life would not – indeed, could not – in general be reproduced in the new vocabulary and its uses. Having adopted the new linguistic practices we would no longer be us, nor would the behaviour of such beings be our behaviour.

2. This point of view, 'eliminative materialism', encapsulates an uncritical individualism. There is a failure, on the part of Searle et al. to grasp that our psychology is built around concepts that

are embedded in both an individual *and* a collective matrix. For example, the concept of rationality applies both to individual persons and to the collective conversations in which they engage. The new language games, since they are physiologically determinate, would be strictly individualistic. So the change would not be politically neutral, either.

3. There has also been a failure to consider how a neuro-physiological language would or could be taught. What the physiological language games that linked neurophysiology to public manifestations would be like has not been addressed. If these were concepts overlapping in identical ways with ours, for example 'pain' and 'discharges in the c-fibres', could we seriously teach an infant c-fibre talk? What would that possibility presuppose? Well, at least a prior scientific education and skill with a microscope. If that is not presumed, we have just translated the word 'pain' or given a synonym for it. So there is a dilemma: if a new language, of the sort envisaged by the Churchlands, did come into existence, it would be unteachable, and if it were teachable it could not be new, at least not in the fashion they envisage.

I want to take the programme of the enlarged paradigm further. The problem of how we might tackle the development of a psychology of human individuality has been the theme of much recent work (Yardley and Honess, 1987). Though that work has been methodologically comprehensive, there is much to update in the treatment, particularly that which is built around the concept of self. Second, there is a need to sketch a resolution to the metaphysical or ontological problems, given the current vogue for cognitive science, that arise for such basic matters as self-consciousness, agency and the like.

After a good start, cognitive science, at least in the confessions of some of its former enthusiasts (Winograd and Flores, 1985), seems to be flagging. It can be revivified, I believe, by relocating what it is about. In a confused kind of way it has been about two domains, physiology and language. But its theoreticians and practitioners have taken it to be about a third domain, the mind. It is abundantly clear that they have inadvertently reinvented Cartesianism. Cognitive science, as it has usually been practised, involves a further muddle about the nature of language: namely, that it is essentially a calculus, an error exposed by Wittgenstein, although the lesson has not been learned. It has been instructive to read reviews of Baker and Hacker's (1984) *Language: Sense and Nonsense*, some of which have shown an almost total incomprehension of the issues to which that book is addressed. We now can be, I think, as certain as one can be that the idea that language has a logical essence is quite fundamentally mistaken.

My current project, then, is to suggest how we can begin to conceive of selfhood without the threat of solipsism and the myth of 'self', as a diaphanous homunculus hidden within. By the same token, we should be able to formulate a concept of agency without the myth of the will. These will turn out to be matters involving the same core of grammar.

One useful, but, as always, potentially misleading, way of putting the basic insight of new paradigm psychology, is the aphorism

'People are what they believe they are'

(and what they believe they are is what the best authorities tell them they are). But the aphorism is misleading because beliefs are also implicitly claimed in certain practices. Certain ways of proceeding, for example rule-following, come to seem 'natural'; another is the practice of paying close attention to phenomenological states, in hypochondriacal cultures. For instance, someone may try to solve the problem posed in 'Am I really in love?' by examining a special feeling. In other cultures, however, people are trained not to pay attention to bodily feelings, to ignore symptoms, as was common amongst the nineteenth-century upper-class English, particularly those educated at boarding schools.

Taking this aphorism seriously for a moment leads to the following thoughts.

First, maturation and development can be looked on as the progressive acquisition of various systems of belief and or clusters of skills. But cultures may determine in what order various systems are acquired, and, of course, the relative prestige of having mastered this or that skill or capacity may vary with local ideas of human worth. There are serious problems to be investigated concerning the ways in which sets or groups of skills can be managed together. For instance, the acquisition of a new skill may render one already acquired inoperable. I do not propose to discuss at all the relationship between skill and belief in this paper; I will just leave these standing as autonomous but related concepts.

Second, we should expect cultural and historical heterogeneity and should be puzzled by and look deeply into apparent similarities. Yet the tradition has been to assume, in what has usually been a highly ethnocentric way, the universality of what has been found by European and American investigators, and to be puzzled by and to investigate apparent divergences from it. Apparent universality of certain 'main' emotions, for example those produced by the necessity to translate into our own language and our local system of concepts, is brought about by the fact that our way of life is continuous with our language. We could look into the problem engendered by the translational difficulties of rendering languages without pronouns into English, a language whose non-inflected verb system depends on pronouns to distinguish persons and makes do with an impoverished repertoire of them. Such a project is of the greatest interest and is currently being undertaken by a group of researchers in Oxford.

Continuing in the vein of belief, we can ask what we English-speaking heirs of Judaeo-Christian civilization and the schism between Protestants and Catholics believe about ourselves. Here we must keep in mind that there may be people, heirs to other histories, who do not believe these things, severally or together.

1. We believe that we are autonomous individuals.
2. We also believe that we are, in despite of being trapped in a web of conventions and an apparently inexorable natural order, agents.
3. We also seem to believe that we have both individually and collectively a past and a future, and so have histories.

The holding of these beliefs makes possible certain kinds of lives; our forms of life would be closed to people who believed otherwise, and, *pari pasu*, their form of life would not be open to us. For instance, contrast the romantic American attitude towards marriage with the unromantic practices of Hindus, or consider how we deal with people who take magic as a practical art.

The social constructionist line on all this, which I hope seems boringly obvious when set out as above, is that what I call 'beliefs' are carried by the learning of grammar. Or to put the matter clearly, we could express in the rhetoric of belief part of the grammar of certain kinds of discourses. That is, certain rules of grammar could be stated, were we so minded, as beliefs, for instance for expository purposes, as in this discourse. But we have to be extremely cautious in using this rhetoric, because we may be tempted to insert these beliefs into explanatory patterns borrowed from the natural sciences, in those places where hypothetical causally potent entities are usually located. We have to immunize ourselves against the reification of beliefs once again, for example as propositional contents and so on. What is remarkable is that the disease of Cartesianism keeps breaking out again and again.

In a certain sense, the ubiquity of language renders it invisible, even now. Because it is our medium for being as persons, there has been a tendency to take as metaphysical and/or empirical matters that are in a broad sense grammatical – for instance the self, agency, intention and so on. The studies inaugurated by Wittgenstein, which, as he himself predicted, are only now coming to be fully understood, have outflanked many apparent scientific endeavours in psychology. So let us not think that the hitherto neglected topics of individuality and agency call for a new scientific programme, until we have seen what a study of grammars can do.

The Grammars of Self-ascription and Self-command

Since self-ascriptions, for example of bodily feelings, intentions and the like, are not based upon criteria, they cannot be interpreted as the attribution of properties to or processes going on in a substance. This insight of Wittgenstein's has such profound consequences that it must be spelt out in some detail.

Three features of the way we use our psychological vocabulary are caught up in this. Wittgenstein realized there was an asymmetry between the grammar of psychological self-ascription and other ascription of first- and third-person uses. While epistemic claims like 'know', 'think' and 'doubt', and qualifications of epistemic claims like 'sure', 'certain' and 'perhaps', were proper in commentary upon the ascription of psychological states to other people, they were misapplied in the first-person case if interpreted epistemically. Thus, 'I know I'm feeling sick' is an emphatic way of saying 'I'm feeling sick', not a commentary on the reliability of my claim. When these words are being used in the contexts in which they acquire their meanings, neither doubt nor certainty are appropriate with respect to these uses. If epistemic uses of this vocabulary made sense, it would be proper to say such things as 'I did feel sick, but I didn't know it', and this is obvious nonsense. Sometimes these avowals are warnings. For instance, 'I think I am going to be sick' is not an expression of uncertainty, but a muted or qualified warning.

But if the psychological vocabulary is not used to state facts about oneself, what is its use? We *do* use it to discuss how we feel. Hintikka and Hintikka (1986) have introduced a helpful idea of a physiognomic language game. Physiognomic behaviour is that naturally expressive of certain bodily states experienced as feelings – 'green and sweating' when feeling nauseous, 'writhing and rubbing' when feeling pain. In a physiognomic language game words are used instead of, or as extensions to, the natural accompaniments to bodily states. Wittgenstein's insight was to realize that strict attention to the uses of psychological terms of Europeans revealed that they were generally used as part of physiognomic language games.

The final step in this analysis is to see that it is in such language games that our vocabulary for expressing how it is with us – for instance our intentions, our private feelings and so on – is acquired and gets its meaning. There could be no process by which our words for how we felt could get meaning by an inner attention to our own states, like a kind of pointing. Psychological words cannot get their meaning in the same way as, say, zoological terms like 'rhinoceros' get theirs. Unless there were public criteria for their correct use by others, they could never be talked to or learnt by themselves. The meanings of these words, that is their public conditions of use, do not coincide with that to which they refer, what they can be used to talk about.

All this is summed up in Wittgenstein's famous distinction between avowals, first-person uses of psychological terms which must be criterionless, and ascriptions, second- and third-person uses based on inductive evidence. Learning the vocabulary later put to first-person use must be achieved in contexts where the learner (I) is the second person (you) to you, the instructor. (See Shotter, this volume).

Dissimulation, lying and even self-deception are secondary linguistic activities, since the words dishonestly employed must have their proper meanings. From the fact that you can be deceived about what I think, feel or intend, it does not follow that only I am sure or know these things about myself. In my cries, you have criteria for ascription of feelings to me, but these criteria reflect the conditions for the determination of meaning and not the truth and falsity of judgements of feelings. The judgements are inductive. There is no room for knowledge or certainty where there is no place for doubt. This insight, one must remember, is grammatical, not empirical.

In avowing or expressing my thoughts and feelings, I am not describing how I feel but am showing it; that is, I am not judging in accordance with or on the basis of evidence. The model for analysing 'I want some more ice-cream', 'I have just thought of the answer' or 'I'm feeling rather down' cannot be 'This object x has a certain property y.' Again, the 'cannot' here is grammatical. The confusion between grammar and experience accounts for the daft idea, proposed by Darryl Bem, that I know how I am feeling in the same way as you know it, that is by observing my own behaviour. But grammar does not permit the form of words 'I know how I am feeling' to have epistemic sense.

It has only been by slipping into using this as one's grammatical model that the Cartesian ego has so repeatedly been reincarnated. The spell of this model leads to two complementary errors: that those aspects of a person we call 'mental', and which seem to be the subject matter of psychology (for example, the causes of behaviour), are states or processes occurring in some substance, and that this substance is the referent of 'I'. Plainly, the referent of 'he'/'she' is the person before us. What is the role of 'I'? It can't be to enable us to know who is speaking. Others simply look; I don't have to identify, among a number of mouths, the one that I speak from. Yet I, though not the Cartesian ego, 'is' the speaker. Looking still more closely at our conversation shows the enquirer that I, and in other languages the relevant first-person inflection, is used to perform a moral act, an act of commitment to the content of the utterance in the appropriate moral universe. From this it follows that the psychology of self-consciousness has the grammar of the first person, and indeed, its scientific study must be pursued as the study of ethnographies of systems of commitment. There is a science of the ego, but it is not to be found in the phenomenology of the structure of consciousness. It is part of the anthropology and history of morals, and in that way part of the grammar of performative utterances. The human individual is, above all, in those societies that recognize autonomy, a moral phenomenon.

Even among peoples whose cultures and forms of life admit no place for autonomy of action, nevertheless, the grammatical first person exists. The residual role seems always to be perceptual: how the world is from the point of view in space and time occupied by the speaker. Sincerity of he/she who sees or hears, rather than the integrity of he/she who promises, is the moral status at issue here. Of course, if I go to where you were standing, I can also look, and although I might not see the same things as does the mighty hunter with an eye of an eagle, I still generally can rate your observation for quality.

This is all a far cry from the 'cognitive science' preoccupations expressed by Dennett and Hofstadter as the concerns of 'mind's eye'. Dennett's more promising solo effort to find the ego among the black boxes of the cognitive computer (*Brainstorms*, 1978, and other places) raises after difficulties. But that is because he is looking for the wrong thing in the wrong place. 'I' is a word having a role in conversation, a role that is not referential, nor is the conversation in which it dominates typically descriptive fact-stating. It is a form of life, a moral community that has been presupposed by the uses of the first person, not a kind of hidden inner cognitive engine. So the question, Which part of that engine is picked out by 'I'?, is a trebly misconceived query, first that there is such an engine, second that the mind behind it is a substance with properties, and third that 'I' is used to refer to it.

All of this clarification of the conceptual basis of the behavioural studies has methodological consequences, just as had the corresponding clarification in physics and chemistry that occurred in the seventeenth and nineteenth centuries, respectively.

It makes sense to conduct experiments if you believe that there is a mechanism behind what happens. In much of human conduct there are no mechanisms, only practices. What may sometimes look like an experiment is the preparation per chance of at least the most notable conditions in which people engage in this or that practice. The source of a practice must be looked for in the customs and forms of life of a culture; that of a mechanism in the microstructure and internal processes of an active agent.

Contemporary academic psychology is shot through with confusion between mechanisms and practices. A mechanism is activated; one is trained in, inducted into (etc.), practices. Cognitive science is an expression of a confusion between these concepts. Rules are treated as the component parts of individual mental mechanisms. But the rules do not use us; we use them. Rule-bound necessities are the result not of the inexorability of those rules, but of our inexorability in using them. We must learn how to apply rules. So rule-following is an inculcated practice, not a rigidly constructed mechanism. Individualism is in part responsible for the persistence of the confusion. The computational model, for language closely allied with the myth of logical essence, seems to be the other major source of confusion.

To many of its adherents, cognitive science has proved a disappointment. No adequately mental working mechanisms have been constructed. But none will be, because none could be. If there is nothing but conversation, whose normativity is expressed in grammar, and material processes, whose necessity is represented by neurophysiological theories, the constructions of cognitive science must be assigned to one or other of these categories; that is, they must be interpreted as abstract models of physiological process, or as formally expressed fragments of grammar. Individuals are tied into the community of speakers through the acquisitions of skills and competences.

Nature presents the scientifically unsophisticated with innumerable examples of apparently spontaneous actions. 'Energetic' means 'capable of initiating change'. It is not as if we lack paradigms of agency. One could say that such paradigms hedged about our thought concerning our own human capacities for acting. The concept of agency has proved intractable, as if the problems of understanding it were metaphysical (for example, where and what is free will?), or as if somewhere hidden in the flux of causes and reasons was a source of true continuity, if only we could pin it down. Kant was wise enough to see that if there is agency in this sense, it is not part of the phenomenal world. Nevertheless, he thought 'it' existed, although nouminally, since people did lead lives in which choosing, feeling guilty, acting recklessly, blinding ahead and so on played a very large part. To put the matter in the rhetoric of Wittgenstein, Kant surely seems to have seen that the shedding of these concepts from our account of our lives would lead not to a revelation of what human life really was all along, but to a way of being that was not recognizably human at all. It seems to me that the problem of presenting human agency to ourselves has continued to be influenced by the assumption that at bottom the issue, and so the puzzlement, is metaphysical and empirical. So, for instance, we get the kind of treatment made popular by the philosopher Davidson, in which he purports to show that reasons can be likened to causes. If psychologists anxious to get the study of agency back on the agenda get too impressed by this kind of treatment, they will surely set off on another of their pursuits of *fata morgana*. I think the way forward is like the case of the self and self-consciousness to turn first of all to the grammar of the leading concepts; once this is clearly laid out, problems like, 'How can there be free self-determined actions, in a world of determinate causality (pace quantum effect)?' no longer seem to require an answer from metaphysicians or psychologists.

Much that is orderly in daily life seems to involve the following of rules and customs; Wittgenstein, and in his own way Sartre, have drawn our attention to the pitfalls involved in thinking about rule governance, in particular our tendency to think of rules as enforcing our conformity, rather than of our uses of them to maintain or create regularities. Rule-following, remember too, is possible only because there are natural regularities and trainable human capacities. The idea of a mental mechanism as invisible cranks and gears of rules is hard to shed.

Again, this is not an empirical point; I am not suggesting that, as a matter of fact, looking more closely at what people do will reveal the presence of rules and customs just as looking more closely at people's fevers reveals the presence of viruses and bacteria. The point is grammatical and depends on observations about the conditions under which the concept clusters of action, conduct, doing, easily led, strong minded and so on are properly applied. Remember that, were we mesmerized by the power and beauty of neurophysiology and/or computer science to try to adopt another way of living through our daily lives, a form of life would have changed and the problem of understanding human action would have been not solved, but shelved. Rather, to be taken as conduct, what people do is thereby embedded in a normative matrix.

There is a popular conception of the problem of understanding human agency which invokes the picture of mental machinery. The solution is sought through the proposals for adding special features to the machinery to account for the apparent distinction between human ways of acting and events produced by mechanistic determinism. There have been randomizers proposed, for instance quantum mechanical level switch-gear, and there have been various devices taken from control theory, such as multiple feedback loops and so on.

But, if choosing for oneself, sticking to a decision, being ornery and cussed, holding out against temptation and taking up a regime are things people can do, we had best look more closely at what these things are, that is, the conditions under which someone is properly said to have kept to a diet or to have made up his or her own mind. At the same time, the dispositions and powers that people exercise in doing these things should be displayed. Two salient features of such conditions stand out in the lives of people whose ways of being have been influenced by Judaism and Christianity: one is the extent to which the discourses that anticipate and justify our actions display open hierarchies of rules; the other is the ubiquitous rhetoric of self-command and self-exhortation, the grammar of which is patterned like those forms of speech, language games, in which we persuade, condemn, exhort and order about others. I believe that when these grammatical matters have been clarified, the conditions for their use delineated, the problem of human agency will have already been dealt with, and the temptation to propose mysterious emendations to the hypothetical explanatory mechanism will have lost its power to attract.

I owe to John Greenwood a useful scheme for structuring the discussion. He thinks that, in our analysis of the grammar of action, two root concepts are needed: intentions to act, and reasons for acting. His main point is that the logics (grammars) of these concepts are quite different. Intentions are normally related to actions and to the acts they may be used to accomplish. This is a conceptual rather than an empirical relation, so is not disturbed by such observations as 'The road to hell is paved with good intentions.' The answers, both to what would you have done and to what did you do, are given by reiterating your intention. It is thus a conceptual point that intention is ineliminable from any account of action, that is, from any account that is connected with a human form of life. Put in terms of a current controversy which is about as muddle-headed as it could be, this point requires that at least some aspects of folk psychology are fundamental.

Reasons, by contrast, are often externally related to actions and the acts they accomplish. It is often not a conceptual, but an empirical matter that the reason for an action is so and so. Two cases emerge: 'Having such a reason I do so and so'; and 'Having done or being about to do, so and so, I give such and such a reason.' The first case at least mimics the structure of causality, while the second has the form of a narrative. The traditional distinction in English between *a* reason for and *the* reason for partially maps the distinction that I am after. In these cases there is a gap between reason and action which could be filled by causal laws in the one case and narrative conventions in the other. I am by no means persuaded of the necessity to insert causality anywhere in this analysis, and I will shelve that issue for the remainder of this paper. The causal aspects will give us enough material to build a picture of human agency and thus to partially determine the texts of identity. To adopt a rhetorical device used by both Ryle and Wittgenstein, we should refuse to use the causal/non-causal, deterministic/indeterministic distinctions. To structure our discussion with them is the source of the mystery. We feel that, if the production of action is not deterministic, it must be indeterministic. The way forward is to refuse to be tempted into applying these distinctions at all.

You ask me *what* I propose to do. I tell you my intentions and in so doing I define the act. My efforts may fail, but that tells us nothing about the conceptual necessity that 'links' action and intention. (And the metaphor of linking must not lead us astray.)

You then ask, *why* I am bent on doing that. I tell you my reasons. I might cite a rule, refer to a custom or adumbrate a plan. Is this the 'why' of explanation? If we think it is, we are back in the causal framework again, the very framework we have reason to suspect is the source of our difficulties. An alternative framework comes with the 'why' of authorization. Responses to that 'why' show how what I intend to do is *right*. It has the inexorability of moral necessity, not the inevitability of causal necessity.

Further challenges to my responses may take our conversation further up the hierarchy of authorization. Trapped within the causal framework, a psychologist might try to reinterpret the regress with the model of the hierarchies of levels of mechanisms, the familiar pattern of explanation in physics and chemistry. I am falling back on morally impressive defences, not delving into universal causes or sub-strata; but I do provide a hierarchy of answers to my questioner.

The meaning of the notion of authorization cannot be accounted for solipsistically, that is, just with respect to attributes of notionally isolated individuals. I am authorized to undertake something when the judge, the committee, the king, the medical profession or all socially defined entities so decree. The structure of my account of taking up body-building should on this analysis be the same as that of my account of my going through your closets; namely, that some authority or other has pronounced on the rightness of what I am up to. Examples above show me as drawing authorization in my actions from extrinsic sources. Once I have grasped the technique of doing so, surely I can begin to authorize myself. In this way, I believe we get the reproduction in each individual brought up in the Judaeo-Christian tradition of the public-social-pattern-of-action validation. Clearly, not every action I perform is embedded in an authorizing soliloquy. When I do deliberate I suggest that the patter of my sotto voce discourse is made up of fragments that take the form of trial authorizations. But this is an empirical issue about how the conceptual structure, as I have sketched it, is applied.

Getting closer to the right question, we can now ask the conceptual question about the concept cluster that we can roughly pick out as 'agency'. Instead of asking, What must something be to be called an agent?, we should from now on ask, What sorts of things must people do to merit that characterization? The question has been answered already. The criterial doing, if I may put it that way, must be the ability to give a certain kind of account, one in which every action is displayed as intended, which is justified by reference to self-authorization. It seems to me that the defensive discourse against the accusations of either caprice or a wimpish capitulation to extrinsic influences is most important in continuing the display of oneself as an agent. This can be presented as a principled hierarchy of choices – 'I used to eat white bread, but now I prefer whole wheat, because *pan integral* is healthier'; 'I used not to be interested in healthy eating, but now I am because I want to be physically in better shape' – and so on up the hierarchy in which the principle or rule cited as authorizing the first choice is presented as itself something chosen at next level and so authorizable, in its turn.

But isn't this pattern of discourse self-defeating? Haven't I now displayed myself as a rule zombie, a mere captive of, say, the health fad? That would be to misunderstand the role of rules, customs, principles and so on in the control of action, a misunderstanding already exposed in Wittgenstein's treatment of which *Philosophical Investigations* 201[1] is the culminating *reductio ad absurdum* of the idea that rules cause acts and actions (Wittgenstein, 1953).

In his middle period, Wittgenstein was at pains to show that the appearance of intractability presented by certain ancient philosophical problems came about because the matter of the focus of attention had been embedded in distinctive *satzsysteme*. These are sentence systems with different grammars, patterns from one being projected on to another in the attempt, usually by philosophers, to explain or analyse the meaning of the fragmented discourse in the second system by the order provided by the first. This idea developed in his later period into the more sophisticated, but complex idea of multiple clusters of language games. In this context, 'being authorized to do something' and 'being caused to do something' are ideas belonging in distinctive *satzsysteme*. Intractable problems such as: How is agency possible? are engendered by using models of discourse drawn from patterns of causal explanation in trying to account for the grammar of authorization explanations. This is no news to philosophers, but grasping this idea should make a great difference to the way psychologists approach the newly revived problem of conation and the research programmes they set up to pursue it. In particular, the search for a mechanism, for choosing and then implementing choice, be it in the quantum mechanics of neurotransmissions or in the system properties of a cognitive model of the mind, is to hunt the snark, and of course individuality is tightly bound up with our sense of what it is to be an agent.

Islamic moral psychology emphasizes rather different aspects of the moral life from the Judaeo-Christian obsession with choosing. Interest has centred on how one brings oneself to do what in a sense has already been chosen, say by the decree of the Koran or the fatal sentences in Allah's book. The 'will', in sense of the power to act, to realize intentions, fulfil plans and so on, has to be accounted for. Muslim moral psychology emphasizes psychological training, particularly as it is carried on in the practice of fasting, and it is aimed at augmenting that power. We too recognize this matter as a gap between choosing and doing. It opens up when such phenomena as weakness of character are analysed. The will neatly fills the conceptual lacuna between, for instance, the having of an intention and its realization in action. Socrates seems to have thought that there was a conceptual or, as I now would say, in Wittgensteinian style, a grammatical relation between what one did and what one thought was good or right. Nevertheless, there were occasions when, so it seemed, despite my having a clear idea of what was good or right for me to do, nevertheless I actually did something that even I acknowledge was less good. All this can tempt one into thinking that there is a kind of parallelogram of forces of which, in less 'mechanistic' versions of this picture, the personal will is one vector component in the preparatory mental state of intending, proposing (etc.) and the resultant engendered action. More mental physics! I think it was just this picture that captured the scientific imagination of Kurt Lewin and, more recently, that of the American school of psychologists that followed Newcombe.

Can the methodological principle that human life is exhaustively distributed among the two realms of physiology and conversation be fruitfully invoked here too? Along with the idea of authorization which I have exploited above, there is the complementary idea of dictation, of the command that one may have over another. There are characteristic and very complex grammars of the language games in the course of the playing of which the actions of subordinates are conversationally prescribed by the dominant partner. What if there are no *forces* of character, of temptation, of attraction and repulsion, of acts, but only reflexive versions of the language games of persuasion and command? The theoretician's contribution will be to look closely at what is meant by such phrases as 'the struggle against temptation', 'wrestling with conscience', 'wimpish', 'sticking to one's decision' and so; that is, it will be to describe the grammars, their rules and conditions of use. One thing is abundantly clear, from even a cursory survey: that is the dominant role played by the metaphor of contending between opposing parties. The forces of Lewin and Newcombe look remarkably like abstractions from the picture of powerful beings contending for the human soul. The grip of the picture of the vector parallelogram could be accounted for by the diffusion of grammatical models of interpersonal discourse into the way we talk about our personal successes and failings, strengths and weaknesses. Comte pointed out the primitiveness of this step, although his solution, the construction of a positivistic science, was perhaps worse than the intellectual disease it was meant to cure.

But these metaphors are how we talk about our actions. So they contribute to the overall grammar of the concepts of action and agency. They are the texts of identity, for they create the illusion of the transcendental ego. It is not as if we can brush them aside, to reveal the true nature of conation. The project of a psychology of action needs to include the disentangling of the pictures that have captured the minds of psychologists, which are a legacy of the failure to examine the discourses of self-command, self-exhortation (etc.) and so to be subject to their influence. Only by analysing the texts of identity can we extract ourselves from their web. The folk who use the metaphors are not captured by the pictures: they use them for whatever needs to be said or done. Notice the nature of the critical project. It is not that of a programme of empirical research through which Lewin's 'field theory' or Newcombe's 'ABX system' would be refuted. The moves are conceptual. Once again, there are plenty of parallels in physics. The downfall of the Newtonian absolutes was not the result of any empirical study. As Lorentz demonstrated, the result of the Micheson–Morely experiment could be quite naturally incorporated into an aether explanation. The Newtonian scheme involved conceptual difficulties which were simply left high and dry by Einstein's rethinking the basic kinematic concepts.

The 'structure of illusion', so to say, has been the same in each of the cases I have examined. The investigation of a topic seems to be fraught with a tantalizing difficulty. Some critical part or sub-process in the working of the mechanism eludes us. But there are no such things. The illusion of their existence has come from a 'crossing' of grammars, between apparently similar, but very different, language games. The grammars of 'he/she' and 'John and Janet' cast shadows over the uses of 'I' obscuring our understanding. The grammar of causal explanation obfuscates our grasp of the grammar of justification and authorization.

The illusions so engendered can be dispelled and their effects neutralized, but why have they been so attractive? Why have psychologists immersed themselves again and again in this sea of confusions? Two unexamined presuppositions have been influential, I believe; individualism and scientism. Everything relevant to the actions of a person, must, it seems, have been assumed (for instance in the writings of Searle and Davidson) to have been found a place 'within' (and for both these authors that means literally inside the envelope of the individual). The idea of what is 'within' is dominated by a certain model of explanation. So instead of describing human customs and practices, psychologists have looked for (or imagined) mechanisms, abstract or concrete; and so comes the attraction for the shadows of grammar as the stuff of such mechanisms. Instead of ascribing to people the skills necessary for performing correctly, they have attributed hidden states.

The difficulties of taking the final step to a new and fruitful paradigm of psychological research are not just institutional, the kind of difficulties sociologists of science diagnose everywhere in the scientific community. They are also bound up with the persistence of religious and political traditions. Until the old psychology is seen clearly as a cultural phenomenon, akin to rain dances and the like, the spell of the illusion I have diagnosed will not be broken.

The task of psychology is to lay bare our system of norms of representation and to compare and contrast the enormous variety of systems; the rest is physiology. As for skills, dispositions, practices, powers and so on, there can be no a priori guarantee that there are universal kinds of groundings matched, one to one, with kinds of skills. This was Armstrong's mistake. This is because skill kinds are criterially determined by public manifestations, what they are directed towards, their tasks. Of course, it may turn out that skill kinds and physiological kinds match, but current evidence turns the other way.

Note

1. In no. 201, Wittgenstein (1953) is concerned to make it clear that obeying a rule is a *custom*, or a *practice* that involves a judgment by others as to whether the action is being done rightly or not. It is not a way of acting, by individuals, by reference to something which can be said to be 'standing behind', or (in the jargon of cognitive science) 'underlying' the person's actions, and thus to be the cause of their structure. Wittgenstein does this, first, by showing how every course of action can be 'made out' to accord with a rule; and then, if that is so, how it can also be 'made out' to conflict with it. But he then goes on to say:

> It can be seen that there is a misunderstanding here from the mere fact that in the course of our argument we give one interpretation after another; as if each contented us at least for a moment, until we thought of yet another standing behind it. What this shows is that there is a way of grasping a rule which is *not* an *interpretation*, but which is exhibited in what we call 'obeying the rule' and 'going against it' in actual cases.

In other words, in Wittgenstein's deep and ultimate sense of the term, following a rule is a matter of doing what is *right*. Thus to repeat, a rule is not to do with the inevitability of causal necessity, but with the inexorability of moral necessity.

References

Baker, G.B. and P.M.S. Hacker (1984) *Language, Sense and Nonsense*. Oxford: Basil Blackwell.

Dennett, D.C. (1978) *Brainstorms*. Hassocks, Sussex: Harvester.

Harré, R. (ed.) (1986) *The Social Construction of Emotions*. Oxford: Basil Blackwell.

Harré, R. (1987) 'Enlarging the Paradigm', *New Ideas in Psychology*, 5: 3–12.

Hintikka, J. and M. Hintikka (1986) *Investigating Wittgenstein*. Oxford: Basil Blackwell.

Winograd, T. and G. Flores (1985) *Understanding Computers and Cognition: a New Foundation for Design*. New York: Ablex.

Wittengstein, L. (1953) *Philosophical Investigation*. Oxford: Basil Blackwell.

Yardley, K. and T. Honess (1987) *Self and Identity*. Chichester: John Wiley.

3
Ego Identity and Explanatory Speech

B.R. Slugoski and G.P. Ginsburg

The paradox of personal identity – that at any moment we are the same as, yet different from, the persons we once were or ever will be – has inspired many attempts at resolution. Philosophers such as Descartes, Locke, Hume, Kant and Sartre, to name but the most prominent, have addressed themselves to the issue of what must logically be postulated to explain the unity, continuity and self-sameness in man. However, psychologists since William James have recognized that the problem has a distinctly psychological aspect. Here the question is one of accounting for the *experience* of continuity over time and the *sense* of unity despite diversity in conceptions of oneself.

The most ambitious contemporary psychological account of identity formation must be attributed to Erikson (1956, 1959, 1968), who located the genesis of one's 'ego identity' (as distinct from the fortuitously appropriated network of childhood identifications which precedes it) in his fifth (adolescent) stage of psychosocial development. In achieving an ego identity, there are said to be certain subjective concomitants to the structural alterations that have taken place. In this regard, Erikson (1956, p. 74) speaks of 'a sense of psychosocial well-being', 'a feeling of being at home in one's body' and 'an inner assuredness of anticipated recognition from those who count'. At the process level, in achieving an ego identity the individual makes 'choices and decisions which will ... lead to a more final self-definition, to irreversible role patterns, and thus to commitments "for life"'. The necessity of making 'choices' and 'decisions' reflects, for Erikson, the fact that the individual must go through a 'crisis' in achieving an ego identity. That the person emerges from this with a sense of 'commitment' to some of the alternatives considered is supposed to represent the crystallized product of this experience.

In this chapter we challenge some central assumptions of Erikson's theory of identity formation. We argue that it is predicated upon an impoverished and highly delimited conception of society, and we demonstrate that its ultimate reliance on internal, ego-integrative processes results in a normative model of identity that is class-, race- and sex-bound. Because of its fidelity to Erikson's theoretical formulations, we draw on previous research which has used Marcia's (1966, 1980) Identity Status Interview (ISI) to measure ego identity development. This will allow us both to make transparent some of the shortcomings of the theory and to argue that 'crisis' and 'commitment' be conceived not as concomitants of a private, underlying process, but as culturally appropriated modes of discourse by which individuals imbue their actions with rationality and warrantability. We also attempt to show that reconstruing Erikson's criteria for identity as ways of talking that have identity implications and social consequences makes possible the resolution of several recurrent anomalies within the identity status literature.

Critique of Eriksonian Ego Identity Theory

Conceptual Issues
Erikson's theory of identity formation has proved particularly attractive to students of the 'self' in psychology because it has been seen to acknowledge a social dimension to personality development that had been lacking in orthodox psychoanalytic theory. For Erikson, the choices and decisions that people make in the course of jettisoning infantile superego introjects and integrating significant identifications into a coherent identity are possible only with respect to the occupational and ideological role alternatives provided by society. For identity formation to occur, there must, in the end, be a meshing of the individual's needs and capabilities with society's demands and rewards.

Such an account, however, incorporates an impoverished view of society and its relation to the individual. As Holland (1977, p. 34ff.) points out in his assessment of Erikson's theory, societies are seldom so benign as to provide even a sizeable proportion of their youth with niches in the social order which are consonant with their potentials, much less a range of alternatives from among which to 'choose' and 'decide'. Furthermore, by predicating the formation of an identity on the notion of a 'moratorium' (i.e. a period of 'free role experimentation' which is provided by society to the growing adolescent), Erikson neglects the objective conditions of a large segment of humankind for whom the envisaging of alternative possible futures would be a futile, self-delusory exercise. For a great many people, then, the notion of a normative 'crisis' and hence identity achievement may simply not apply; for such individuals 'there is no *problem* of identity. The question, "Who am I?" is unlikely to arise in consciousness, since the socially predefined answer is massively real subjectively ... ' (Berger and Luckmann, 1967, p. 184).

Not only may Erikson's scheme be inappropriate for marginal and economically underprivileged groups, but there is little place for women's identity within the scheme he has proposed. Because it most clearly exemplifies the deficiencies in the ego psychoanalytic treatment of identity achievement, we will have much to say about the problems the theory has in coping with female identity formation. For the moment it is sufficient merely to note Erikson's assessment of women's proper role in society. He says in one place that 'she creates in each child the somatic ... basis for his [sic] physical, cultural and individual identity. This mission, once a child is conceived, must be completed. It is woman's unique job' (Erikson, 1968, p. 289). Clearly, this prescription leaves little leeway for women to contemplate alternative roles and occupations, the purported processual prerequisites to identity formation. We will take it as one of our tasks to show that Kroger's observation (quoted in Marcia, 1987) that 'it may not be until well past the thirties that vocational, political and religious issues can be resolved [for women]' is less 'support ... for the psychoanalytic view that identity formation for women is a lengthy and complex process' than that this view is both reflective and supportive of the dominant institutional order that gave rise to the phenomenon.

Taken together, the above observations suggest that the prerogative of achieving an identity – of 'self realization and mutual recognition' – during adolescence may be a privilege extended only to Western males living in a surplus economy. However, several other important implications follow directly from Erikson's overly harmonistic view of society.

First, as a normative goal, identity achievement is in the final analysis an *individual* achievement. Accordingly, variance in identity formation is ascribed to *intra*-psychic processes, in particular to the integrative properties of the ego: 'No other inner agency could accomplish the selective accentuation of significant identifications throughout childhood and the gradual integration of self-images which culminates in a sense of identity' (Erikson, 1968, p. 209). Second, as an individual achievement, ego identity implies both that the individual has *control* over the process and that anything less than identity achievement is a *deficit*. By 'control' we do not mean that the person consciously opts to achieve or not to achieve an identity, but rather that, in the absence of parameters specifying antagonistic social forces, the determining factors can only remain internal to, and thus can be susceptible to influence by, the individual. There are two senses in which not achieving an ego identity represents a 'deficit' in Erikson's scheme. First, and more obviously, a failure to achieve an ego identity represents a *psychological* deficit on the individual's part, since identity achievement anchors a continuum of psychological adjustment (or 'ego strength') which is characterized by such positive attributes as increased psychosocial effectiveness, lesser reliance on defence mechanisms and a greater sense of personal continuity and well-being.

Second, though less transparently, failure to achieve an identity implies a *moral* deficit. By assuming a benign social structure coupled with an implied internal locus of control, responsibility for any failure to mesh with society's demands and thereby reap its rewards is seen to lie not in the social order but rather within the individual.[1]

Before proceeding to sketch how these implications might be avoided by reconstruing Erikson's criteria of 'crisis' and 'commitment', it will prove worth while briefly to examine some empirical research which has employed Marcia's (1966) operationalization of the ego identity concept. In the following section we hope to show that Marcia's Identity Status approach is faithful enough to Erikson's theory to incorporate its strengths and make transparent certain of its weaknesses.

Marcia's Typology and Related Research
Taking as his point of departure the most observable concomitants of identity formation, the twin criteria of crisis and commitment in the areas of occupation and ideology, Marcia (1966) has developed a semi-structured interview measure which discriminates adolescents and youths with respect to four ego identity 'statuses'. These statuses, or 'styles of coping with the identity crisis', are delineated as follows.

— *Identity Achievement* individuals have experienced a period of crisis and have made commitments in the areas of occupation and ideology.
— *Moratorium* individuals are currently in an identity crisis and hold only vague commitments.
— *Foreclosure* individuals are committed to occupational and ideological positions but show little or no evidence of having gone through a crisis. Their positions usually have been parentally rather than self-determined.
— *Identity Diffusion* individuals may or may not have undergone a crisis, but in either case they have no set occupational or ideological positions.

This is an essentially 'filled-in' version of Erikson's dichotomy between Identity Achievement and Identity Diffusion, and, as with

Erikson's dichotomy, the ordering of the identity statuses is held to reflect an underlying dimension of ego strength. The measure has, over the past two decades, accrued considerable construct validity (see Bourne, 1978a, 1978b; Waterman, 1982, for reviews), some of the more interesting findings of which are as follows. High-identity status individuals (Identity Achievements and Moratoriums) are less susceptible to self-esteem manipulation (Marcia, 1968), have a more internal locus of control (Waterman and Waterman, 1974), and are more cognitively flexible (Bob, 1967, 1968) and complex (Slugoski, Marcia and Koopman, 1984) than are low-identity status individuals. In an investigation of the social–interactional styles of the four identity statuses, the latter researchers found the high-identity statuses to exhibit more interpersonal solidarity, less tension and less antagonism than the low-identity statuses. Further, Identity Achievement individuals appeared the most open of the statuses to others' differing opinions and beliefs in their interactions. These results are all in line with what one would expect from the psychological deficit hypothesis of ego psychoanalytic theory.

On the other hand, Marcia's scheme applies with differential success to males and females. If, as we show more rigorously later, identity achievement is an essentially *bourgeois* concept, then one might expect the identity status paradigm to apply only within that population identified earlier as white, college-educated males living in Western societies, and in fact, almost all of the studies that have employed the Identity Status Interview have confined their samples to males, the bulk of which were drawn from North American colleges and universities. The studies cited above, the results of which are readily interpretable within an ego psychoanalytic framework, are representative of this trend.

The results of the few studies that have employed females as subjects (e.g. Marcia and Friedman, 1970; Toder and Marcia, 1973; Schenkel and Marcia, 1972) have presented an entirely different picture. In general, Foreclosure females score as well or better on cognitive structural and psychosocial effectiveness variables as do Identity Achievement females. Moratorium females, by contrast, form a homogeneous subset with Identity Diffusions on these variables, scoring lower than the two committed statuses (see Marcia, 1976b, 1980, for reviews). It also has been found that Identity Achievement females have the lowest self-esteem scores of all the statuses, with Foreclosure females scoring the highest (Marcia and Friedman, 1970). These results are clearly inconsistent with the 'psychological deficit' hypothesis of ego psychoanalytic theory. Discussing such anomalies, Marcia (1976b) has rightly appealed to social factors such as the lack of social support for Identity

Achievement females and the adaptive potential of the Foreclosure status for women. However, ego psychoanalytic theory, which fails to make differential predictions for males and females, has yet to be called into question on the basis of these data.

Some attempts to make the ego identity statuses valid across the sexes have incorporated into the Identity Status Interview content areas presumably more germane to female identity than the traditional ones of occupation and ideology. Those include attitudes towards premarital sexual intercourse (Marcia and Friedman, 1970; Schenkel and Marcia, 1972) and sex role attitudes (Schiedel and Marcia, 1985). However, if there is a masculine ethos associated with Eriksonian identity achievement, this might well transcend particular content areas, and these modifications should make little difference. One indication that this might be the case comes from a study conducted by Rogow et al. (1983), who found, using males as subjects, that these supposedly 'feminine' content areas are, if anything, even more predictive, both of overall identity development and of cognitive sophistication, than are the traditional 'masculine' content areas of occupation and ideology.

Additionally, three studies have shown high identity to be contingent on high masculinity, as assessed by Bem's (1974) Sex Role Inventory (Prager, 1977; Orlofsky, 1977; Schiedel and Marcia, 1985), a set of findings that has been interpreted to mean that 'traditional masculine socialization expedites identity development', with the implication that child-rearing practices for females be altered accordingly (Schiedel and Marcia, 1985). The latter authors do not call for a change in the dominant social order with its masculine values of self-assertion, dispassionate rationality, field-independence and frontier expansion; nor do they consider that women's projected identity might be perfectly appropriate to its context within a male-dominated social order. (Recall here that female Foreclosures score relatively well on dependent measures.) We can imagine analogous prescriptions for other oppressed groups within North American society (for example, for inner-city blacks, '*A stint in the suburbs expedites* ...'), and even for other societies, whose members' disadvantaged status in part has provided the Western world with the economic means to participate in moratoria. In general, there has been a continuing commitment to the ego psychoanalytic underpinning of Erikson's theory.

On the other hand, Erikson's conception of identity as a competence formed in social interactions is a genuinely social notion. In the following section we show that this social theme can be retained while rejecting the implications that follow from Erikson's highly circumscribed view of society and the integrative properties of the ego. We accomplish this by reconstruing his criteria of 'crisis' and 'commitment' in terms of a competence for explanatory speech which is normative in its implications and largely justificatory in its functions.

A Reconceptualization of Erikson's Criteria for Identity

In *The Idea of a Social Science*, Winch (1958, Chapter 2) discusses what makes behaviour meaningful as opposed to an ad hoc collection of movements in time and space. He concludes, following Wittgenstein (1953), that meaningful behaviour consists of an act that is governed by the application of a rule. Latterly, two criteria are involved: (1) the actor must be able to give a reason for an action; and (2) the actor must be bound by what she does now to doing something else in the future. Only if these criteria are met, says Winch, can the actor's behaviour be said to have a *sense*. With certain qualifications to these criteria for intelligibility, we will argue that there is a conceptual isomorphism between them and Erikson's criteria for identity.

Regarding the first criterion, an actor can perform an action without attending to it as an action and without having formulated an account in advance. However, the actor must have the capacity to offer an account of it, and the behaviour must be susceptible to reason descriptions. Moreover, a proffered reason need not be an 'accurate' one, but need only be recognizable as a reason and not incompatible with other evidence. Winch's second criterion can be said to apply to most behaviour by a wide range of species, if the phrase 'must be bound' is taken in a weak sense. But when taken in conjunction with the first criterion, the requirement than an actor be bound by his or her current behaviour to something else in the future implies accountability. That is, if the actor can be held accountable for future actions which are not compatible with the current activity, the current activity is an action; and, in conjunction with the first criterion, the current activity can be said to be intelligible.

Given these qualifications of Winch's criteria for intelligibility, let us consider Erikson's criteria for identity. We will start with the requirement that an individual experience a 'crisis' before he or she can be said to have achieved an identity. 'Crisis', it will be recalled, refers to a cluster of experiential attributes including 'choices and decisions' (Erikson, 1968), 'exploration of alternatives' (Marcia, 1976b) and 'a period of decision-making' (Marcia, 1980). So conceived, the lynchpin connecting achieved identity with the rationalization of action consists simply of what it means to be a *human agent*. Analytic to the notion of 'agency' is the idea of choice through self-intervention – that an individual *could have done otherwise*. This is seen quite clearly in Taylor's (1977) conception of the 'strong evaluator', and the individual who is able to reflect upon and choose according to the qualitative worth of different desires. The behaviour of the strong evaluator is not predetermined by the ongoing stream of events; he or she is able to intervene in them by exercising choice according to higher-order principles. To experience and resolve identity crises is to engage in active choice and is part and parcel of being a strong evaluator: 'In order to speak of choice we cannot just find ourselves in one of the alternatives. We have in some sense to experience the pull of each and give our assent to one' (Taylor, 1977, p. 121). The ability to give a reason (account) for a particular course of action hence implies a crisis inasmuch as it also implies a plurality of competing visions from among which *that* course was chosen. Moreover, if the course of action and the related account pertain to occupational and ideological choices, then the crisis and its resolution reflect the achievement of identity as conceptualized by Erikson.

The relation between Winch's second criterion and Erikson's 'commitment' criterion is more straightforward, since for current behaviour (for example, the expression of an occupational preference or an ideological stance) to regulate one's future behaviour *is* to be committed to that course of action. But, unlike the requirement that one be able to provide grounds for one's behaviour, it is not at all obvious why commitment should be a *sine qua non* of intelligibility. On the other hand, the concept of commitment implies strongly that a person hold an evaluative *attitude* towards some object or end, and we can apply Smith's (1982) structuralist interpretation of the Fishbeinian equation relating attitudes to behavioural intentions. (We won't complicate matters by including the subjective norm component.) Suppose that, in response to the question, 'Do you have any political preferences?' in the Identity Status Interview, the interviewee replies, 'Yes, I'm a Democratic Party supporter', and then, in response to a follow-up question, 'Will you be working for the Democrats in the coming election?', says, 'Probably won't be bothered – I'm not all that interested.' There is clearly something amiss here. Either the respondent doesn't know what it *means* to be a 'Democratic Party supporter' (i.e., she doesn't know the rules of the language), or she is crazy (i.e., her intended behaviour contradicts her expressed interests). These are just the sorts of inferences made by Smith's subjects when they were asked to evaluate transgressions of the intelligibility rules represented by the Fishbeinian equation.

'Commitment', then, is an essentially communicational concept. It demonstrates a consistency between reasons for action and linguistically expressed intentions and thereby constitutes a precondition to the very possibility of successful interpersonal communication. It functions in much the same way as the various 'sincerity' assumptions in the communication system requirements of Searle (1969), Grice (1975) and Habermas (1979).

Readers familiar with hermeneutic interpretations of Freudian theory (cf. Fingarette, 1969; Ricoeur, 1970; Habermas, 1971) will not be surprised by the fact that, stripped of its own mechanistic and energic terminology, Erikson's theory of identity formation might yield a comparable hermeneutic reading. Our task, however, is to go beyond a hermeneutic interpretation of Erikson, because hermeneutic analysis persists in taking discourse about behaviour as a pointer to underlying psychological structures and processes; therefore, it allows for inferences of the type we criticized in the previous section. To avoid this consequence, we will follow Foucault (1972) in treating discourse as relatively autonomous with respect to both conscious and unconscious psychological processes. The aim is thence to locate the source, or 'conditions of emergence' (Foucault, 1972, p. 127), of the normative propensity to articulate one's biography in terms of decision points and commitments 'for life' in particular social practices and institutions. First, however, we need to develop the idea that identity-relevant explanatory speech makes action not only intelligible, but also warrantable. That is, identity-relevant explanatory speech serves justificatory functions. Such a position is contained in more recent ethogenic writings.

Ethogeny takes an extreme *inter*personal position with respect to the consequences of people's explanatory speech, emphasizing the quasi-independence of their internal states and their accounts.[2] It is worth quoting Harré at some length on this point:

> in accounting we are very much inclined to represent that which we experienced as mere randomness, as if it were principled choice. We may even go so far as to represent our actions as the ultimate product of reasoned choice with which to make principled choice. To publicly represent one's actions as being generated in the linear, random mode is indeed to claim a kind of freedom, but it is the morally empty freedom of a mere patient. But to represent one's actions as issuing from the workings of a complex cognitive machinery is to claim agency ... it is to claim that one's actions were 'principled'. (Harré, 1979, p. 256)

Identity Achievement individuals have the ability to articulate a 'crisis' in arriving at their present positions and are able to demonstrate a consistency of cognitive (intentions) and motivational (reasons) structures; therefore, they claim the status of 'agents' by the very mode in which they talk about themselves and their choices. Identity Diffusion individuals, on the other hand, can make no such claim, since they can classify their behaviour only in terms of the 'random mode' of efficient causality. To this extent, the latter's behaviour is not only seen to lack meaning, it is seen to lack 'justification'. This does not mean that an Identity Diffusion person's claim is devoid of value or potential social advantage. On the contrary, it relieves the person of responsibility for occupational choice and ideological positions, and even of the obligation to *have* consistent positions, and it implies that the person is more open to attractive opportunities, more flexible interpersonally, and less demanding of other persons. Nevertheless, within the ethogenic framework, the behaviours of such a person are neither intelligible nor warrantable, as defined above, with respect to occupational or ideological commitments.

Central to the ethogenic account, then, is the idea that there exists a normative social demand that one be able to make one's actions appear intelligible and justifiable. The question of what 'really' exists inside the person's head is set aside in favour of asking how the task of meeting this demand is achieved. By contrast, Marcia's Identity Status Interview assumes a veridical observer over time. In Erikson's scheme, a sense of identity is experienced preconsciously, the expression of 'crisis' and 'commitment' being the mere outward manifestations of this internal, subjective state. There is thus held to be a one-to-one correspondence between level of identity formation and the explanatory speech from which it is inferred.[3] Rather than regarding language as an expression of thought, account and discourse analysts tend to view it as a social instrument, as a means of achieving interpersonal goals. Perhaps the most important of these is the establishment and maintenance of a socially desirable identity (cf. Alexander and Knight, 1971; Backman, in press; Goffman, 1959; Harré, 1977; Schlenker, 1980; Scott and Lyman, 1968). The existence of a norm for intelligibility, combined with the advantages of projecting a positive self-image, makes the discourse of identity achievement a valued commodity (given, as we shall see, certain limiting conditions). One happy consequence of this analysis is that we need not appeal to a biologically innate 'epigenetic principle' to account for the immanence of an identity crisis and its resolution in commitment. Instead, identity talk ordinarily is justificatory, and comes into play under justificatory conditions (present or anticipated). The occupational and ideological content of such talk during the adolescent and youth periods can be presumed to reflect anticipatory socialization of a pre-adult stage in Western society (Hareven, 1986), anticipatory of the adult stage when such positions are generally expected to have been established.

It would thus be naive to assume that people explaining their behaviour generally, and subjects participating in the Identity Status Interview in particular, are immune from the self-presentational consequences of their public espousals. One of us (BRS), while administering the Identity Status Interview to male subjects, was confronted several times with low-identity individuals who had become visibly flustered by the way the interview had gone. They were clearly aware at some level that they had been giving socially undesirable responses to the explanation-seeking questions, and at the end of the interview they occasionally engaged in post hoc attempts to salvage the intelligibility of their accounts. For example, after demonstrating a lack of commitment to an expressed position, they might appeal to meta-rules, such as failure to satisfy enabling conditions or negative gating (cf. Abelson, 1973), as means of exonerating themselves.

The Identity Status Interview assumes not only a veridical observer, but also that the interview situation represents a neutral context where the individual's fundamental identity structure can be measured. This idea has been seriously challenged as it has been applied to the elicitation and measurement of attitudes (cf. Lalljee et al., 1984), and there is no reason to suppose that the identity interview is an exception. In fact, there is some evidence that 'crisis' and 'commitment', as ascertained in the Identity Status Interview, bear little relation to subjects' 'actual' conscious or preconscious experiences.[4] In a follow-up study, Marcia (1976a) found that over 40 per cent of subjects who had been classified as Identity Achievement individuals in his original study conducted six years earlier had made a theoretically 'impossible' regression to the Foreclosure status (that is, where they had formerly expressed that they had gone through a period of questioning and decision-making before settling on occupational and ideological positions, they no longer did). This anomalous finding was interpreted by Slugoski et al. (1984) in terms of a corresponding regression in conceptual structure attendant on entering a milieu not supportive of cognitively sophisticated functioning. However, it now seems to us that the finding may be interpreted more parsimoniously as reflecting the normative demand to *report* a crisis period in a college milieu which was no longer acute in the individual's current milieu. Note that this explanation for the retrospective disappearance of adolescent identity crises also differs fundamentally from that of Baumeister et al. (1985), who view the phenomenon as a distortion of memory of pre-adolescent activities. In our view, the individual's later account need be no less veridical than the earlier one; it is the justificatory context within which the individual is required to produce an account that has changed. By this account, the observation that 'The adolescent becomes, of necessity, a philosopher for the first time and must, like all humans, find a way of silencing a too keen perception of man's (and his own) fate' (Becker, 1973; quoted in Josselson, 1980) is at least as *prescriptive* as it is descriptive.

A related implication is that speech that renders action intelligible and warrantable need not necessarily be positively evaluated by others. Harré admits of this possibility when he says that 'there could be societies in which public presentation of consistency or the logical framing of complexes of speech and action might not be valued or admired' (1979, p. 286). An example of this can be found in Japan, where cross-situational consistency in action – presumed in North America and Western Europe to reflect attitude behaviour consistency, and consequently personal integrity – is construed as immature, naive and inconsiderate of one's interaction partner; proper conduct entails sensitivity and accommodation to the requirements of the situation and the needs of the interaction partner (Iwao, 1986). This raises the general issue of boundary conditions under which being seen to meet Erikson's criteria for identity will eventuate in a positive or negative evaluation. We address this issue in the next section, and by doing so we hope to resolve some of the anomalies in the empirical literature noted in the first section.

The 'Average Expectable Environment' of the Bourgeoisie

The *Oxford English Dictionary* dates the noun 'self' from about 1595, and in the same year Montaigne's *Essais* problematizing the *moi* were published. Although it is impossible to date the transition from feudalism to capitalism precisely, Hunt (1978) suggests that the sixteenth century represented a 'watershed' in this regard. About fifty years later, Descartes' *Discourse on Method* was published, laying the epistemological foundation for the coming Newtonian cosmology. The use of the word 'identity' to refer to personality and individuality also emerged about them (1638, per the *Shorter OED*). We take it that these events are not unrelated, and we follow Anthony Wilden (1980) in tracing their mutual implications.

Specifically, Wilden shows that by equating self with substance (*cogito ergo sum*) Descartes' epistemology resulted in an ethos of personal freedom, equality, individual autonomy and the assumption of separable and individual responsibility (see also Rorty, 1979, for a related analysis). The emergent free market economy was justified because its forces, like those in a Newtonian universe, operate on atomic units (selves, souls, egos) which are dependent upon nothing outside themselves for their existence. Each being endowed with an equal portion of reason, these atoms were then free to compete – to sell their labour power for the best price – within the closed, homeostatic (and therefore benevolent) system of the market-place. This ethos of individual freedom, equality and responsibility, along with its corollaries, private property and a har-monistic society, is deeply embedded in Western culture; indeed, its principles are enshrined in the constitution of the United States.

It is becoming increasingly evident that social/personality psy-chology frequently finds itself complicit in reinforcing the dominant social order by, *inter alia*, reifying concepts that emerged only as a matter of historical contingency (cf. Moscovici, 1972; Gergen, 1973, 1982; Sampson, 1977; Billig, 1983). Identity achievement, as a normative ideal, is a particularly clear example of such reification and reflects the discipline's unwitting complicity in serving the interests of the dominant group. Like the Cartesian treatment of 'self', we have seen the concept of identity achievement to entail the notions of individual freedom, self-efficacy and personal responsibility, notions which, when the material conditions of actual working men and women are taken into account, hardly seem to reflect their situation. The dominant discourse positing identity achievement as psychologically normative is especially pernicious because it can lead to a state of false consciousness. That is, the dominant set of personally descriptive discourse devices within a culture, such as those just described, will be shared by all members of the culture, and will be presumed by each to be shared by all. Furthermore, the devices will be embedded in the institutions of the society as expressions of its values (e.g., means tests as a basis for who deserves welfare). As shared discourse devices, all members of the culture will use them to construe actions, accomplishments and failures – including those with*out* resources among which to choose, as well as those *with* such resources. As Wilden points out, '"Do your own thing" is a useful metaphor to play with when the things are doing you' (1980, p. 92).

As an example of the socioeconomic constraint on identity-relevant explanatory speech, consider a recent study in which the relative importance of different content areas of the Identity Status Interview (i.e., occupation, religion, politics, sex role orientation, and attitudes to premarital sexual intercourse) were assessed (Rogow et al., 1983). It was found, contrary to impressions based on data collected in the 1960s and early 1970s, that the expression of crisis and commitment in the area of *occupation* had the least predictive utility with respect to both a dependent variable (cognitive complexity) and overall identity status. The authors observed that, owing to the economic recession in Canada at the time the data were collected, 'means of resolving occupational decisions may be more determined by bureaucratic and/or economic necessity than by personal exploration'. It appears that the construct validity of the identity status paradigm becomes less determinate as socioeconomic conditions depart from the bourgeois ideal. We would therefore agree with Berger and Luckmann's contention that 'The "individualist" ['Identity Achievement' in the present vernacular] emerges as a specific social type who has at least the potential to migrate between a number of different worlds' (Berger and Luckmann, 1967, p. 91).

In the first section we showed that the identity status paradigm was similarly deficient with respect to predictions it makes for females. Of those denied equal opportunity in the market-place, women represent the greatest single proportion. Given their primarily integrative social roles as supporters of men and reproducers of labour power, females may be expected to produce a different pattern of identity-relevant explanatory speech from that of men, and historically this seems to have been the case. Whereas males are expected to project as deliberative, rational agents, Harré (1979) observes that some of Dickens' female characters went to quite extraordinary lengths to create the impression that their behaviour was capriciously motivated, irrationally grounded and practically incompetent.[5] Matters actually appear not to have changed a great deal in the intervening century. The plight of a group of women calling themselves the Greenham Common Women for Peace is a potent recent example of the risks females run by engaging in role-inconsistent behaviour and explanatory speech. These women expressed a common desire, and acted under frequently adverse conditions, to rid the British Isles of nuclear weapons, particularly the American-owned and -controlled cruise missiles that had recently arrived there. Those who were interviewed by news media came across as being articulate, and as having given a great deal of thought to what they were doing in *choosing* their course of action in lieu of conventional commitments and life-styles. By any standards of 'crisis' and 'commitment', the women are Identity Achievers (at least as regards this issue). Yet it is precisely on the basis of these *process* variables (rather than on *what* they were doing) that segments of the British popular press appeared to us to mount a campaign discrediting them (the logic running something like, '*Real* women to do not *decide* to leave their husbands and children to fight together for a political cause; ergo ... ').[6] On the other hand, had it been males engaged in the same action, the process variables would have been normative and hence the press might well have had to address the issues raised.

It is important to note that, although the different identity statuses (Identity Achievement, Moratorium, Foreclosure, Identity Diffusion) apply differentially to males and females in Western societies, differential evaluation of the sexes is likely to be consensually shared within the societies. Thus, women as well as men should think highly of Identity Achievement men, but less so of Identity Achievement women. However, some qualification of the basic point probably is in order; specifically, the appearance of a differential evaluation of an identity status for men in contrast to women is likely to be tied to types of social roles. For example, an Identity Achievement female physicist might be as highly evaluated as an Identity Achievement male physicist, but the same might not be true for potential boyfriends and girlfriends. We would expect an Identity Achievement young male to be widely attractive as a potential boyfriend, but an Identity Achievement young female to be much less attractive as a potential girlfriend.

Conclusion
Meeting and failing to meet Erikson's criteria for identity formation, then, may have radically different implications for females' *situated* identities than it does for males. Given the present distribution of power between the sexes, it would appear generally not to be in females' self-interest to articulate their biographies in high-identity terms. Nor, given our broader analysis, would we expect individuals belonging to other social groups which do not share in the resources and advantages of the dominant group to share in the rights and privileges otherwise accruing through its discourse. Consequently, we advise a shift in attention, from treating Eriksonian 'Identity' as a deep-seated psychological universal, the absence of which implies a psychological and moral deficit, to focusing more on the cultural and social structural parameters which produce different criteria for socially desirable patterns of explanatory speech. Studies examining relationships with cognitive structural and psychosocial effectiveness variables would then have to focus upon people's semiotic resources for co-ordinating the identities which they project by way of their explanatory speech with the normative expectations of the particular societies and sub-cultures within which they must survive. That Marcia's identity status paradigm appears to apply well to young white males of middle class and decent education can thus be viewed, at least in part, as an artefact, since the criteria for a socially desirable 'situated identity' and for an 'ego identity' are of necessity one and the same, given

a theory that itself incorporates the dominant values of the society whose members it is describing. This does not mean that Erikson's theory, or Marcia's elaboration of it, is viewed by us as being totally invalid. Rather, Erikson's theory of ego identity formation is seen by us as a model of culturally sanctioned ways of talking about oneself and others during a certain stage of life in Western societies. As such, the model is best understood as a rationalized description of self-narratives (Gergen and Gergen, 1988). This reconstrual of the theory brings it into the general class of argument in which putatively intrapsychic processes are seen to have their sources and even their loci in the social world of institutions and mundane interactions (e.g., Swanson, 1985). One's sense of personal continuity is grounded in the continuity created in the self-narratives one generates, reinforced by the stability of one's social network and one's society and its institutions (Sampson, 1976 and this volume). These features of one's life are repeatedly instantiated in the justificatory identity- talk in which one mundanely engages, and it carries with it acknowledgements of obligations and responsibilities and claims of privileges. The sense of continuity, of unity over time, is not to be explained by such intrapsychic concepts as ego identity. They, instead, are a reflection of the dominant values and the presuppositions of the society which contains both the theorist and his or her objects of analysis.

Notes

This chapter is based on a paper presented at the International Conference on Self and Identity, Cardiff, Wales, 9–13 July, 1984. B.R. Slugoski is indebted to James E. Marcia, under whose mentorship the ideas expressed in this chapter were germinated. Naturally, this is not to imply his endorsement of our conclusions. Preparation of this chapter was assisted by the Social Sciences and Humanities Research Council of Canada, by the Committee of Vice-Chancellors and Principals of the Universities of the United Kingdom, and by the sabbatical fund of the University of Nevada, Reno.

1. Marcia (1987) took issue with this contention, allowing that 'there is room within [Erikson's] scheme of ego developmental stages for societal as well as individual adaptation'. Indeed there is, but only on the assumption, to be challenged later, that the genesis and developmental trajectory of people's needs, capabilities and aspirations can sensibly be talked about independently of particular institutional frameworks. In any case, it remains that a positive relationship between ego identity development and moral development (in Kohlberg's, 1958, sense) is one of the most robust findings in the empirical literature on ego identity (see Marcia, 1980).

2. Actually, Harré's position on this has changed considerably since publication of the original ethogenic manifesto (Harré and Secord, 1972). The primacy of 'personal powers' and the 'open souls' doctrine developed there are quite inconsistent with the present analysis. Harré's radical constructionist thesis is most fully developed in

his recent *Personal Being* (1983), but its flavour can be discerned in his earlier essay, 'The Self in Monodrama' (1977).

3. Marcia (1976b) quotes George Kelly's dictum, '*If you want to know something about someone, ask him – he just may tell you.*'

4. It should be stressed that our concern here is not with citicizing Marcia's interview technique in the sense that we think that a *better* technique for exposing people's underlying levels of identity formation could be found: on the contrary, we are convinced that the demonstrated research generativity of the Identity Status approach can be attributed precisely to the interpersonal – indeed, conversational – nature of its technique. Where Marcia and we clearly differ is in the reasons for its successes, as well as its failures.

5. A more complex illustration of this point as it applies to racial stereotypes can be found in Harré (1983, pp. 66–7). Here he observes that, in the old *Lone Ranger* television series, Tonto was denied use of the double-functional *I*, and hence the complex psychic life that its use implies.

6. Not all of the Greenham women (as they are colloquially called) were tarred with this particular brush, however. Those who impulsively followed their feelings or their friends, for example, were allowed to retain their status as females, and were described as merely silly or misguided in their sympathies.

References

Abelson, R.P. (1973) 'The Structure of Belief Systems', in R.C. Schank and K.M. Colby (eds), *Computer Models of Thought and Language*. San Francisco: W.H. Freeman.

Alexander, C.M. and G. Knight (1971) 'Situated Identities and Social Psychological Experimentation', *Sociometry*, 34: 65–82.

Backman, C.W. (in press) 'The Self: A Dialectical Approach', in L. Berkowitz (ed.) *Advances in Experimental Social Psychology*. New York: Academic Press.

Baumeister, R.F., J.P. Shapiro and D.M. Tice (1985) 'Two Kinds of Identity Crisis', *Journal of Personality*, 53: 407–24.

Becker, E. (1973) *The Denial of Death*. New York: Free Press.

Bem, S.L. (1974) 'The Measurement of Psychological Androgeny', *Journal of Consulting and Clinical Psychology*, 42: 155–62.

Berger, P. and T. Luckmann (1967) *The Social Construction of Reality*. Harmondsworth: Penguin.

Billig, M. (1983) *Ideology and Social Psychology*. Oxford: Basil Blackwell.

Bob, S. (1967) 'Ego Identity and Two Cognitive Styles', unpublished master's thesis, State University of New York at Buffalo.

Bob, S. (1968) 'An Investigation of the Relationship between Identity Status, Cognitive Style, and Stress', unpublished doctoral dissertation, State University of New York at Buffalo.

Bourne, E. (1978a) 'The State of Research on Ego Identity: A Review and Appraisal', Part 1, *Journal of Youth and Adolescence*, 7: 223–51.

Bourne, E. (1978b) 'The State of Research on Ego Identity: A Review and Appraisal', Part II, *Journal of Youth and Adolescence*, 7: 371–92.

Erikson, E.H. (1956) 'The Problem of Ego Identity', *Journal of the American Psychoanalytic Association*, 4: 56–121.

Erikson, E.H. (1959) 'Identity and the Life-cycle', *Psychological Issues*, 1 (whole monograph no. 1).

Erikson, E.II. (1968) *Identity: Youth and Crisis*. New York: W.W. Norton.
Fingarette, H. (1969) *Self-deception*. London: Routledge & Kegan Paul.
Foucault, M. (1972) *The Archeology of Knowledge* (trans. A.M. Sheridan Smith). New York: Harper Colophon.
Gergen, K.J. (1973) 'Social Psychology as History', *Journal of Personality and Social Psychology*, 26: 309–20.
Gergen, K.J. (1982) *Toward Transformation in Social Knowledge*. New York: Springer-Verlag.
Gergen, K.J. and M.M. Gergen (1988) 'Narrative Form and the Construction of Psychological Theory', in T.R. Sarbin (ed.), *The Narrative Perspective in Psychology*. New York: Praeger.
Goffman, E. (1959) *The Presentation of Self in Everyday Life*. Garden City, NY: Doubleday Anchor.
Grice, H.P. (1975) 'Logic and Conversation', in P. Cole and J.L. Morgan (eds), *Syntax and Semantics*, Vol. 3. *Speech Acts*. New York: Academic Press.
Habermas, J. (1971) *Knowledge and Human Interests* (trans. J. Shapiro: originally published 1968). Boston: Beacon Press.
Habermas, J. (1979) *Communication and the Evolution of Society* (trans. T. McCarthy; originally published 1976). Boston: Beacon Press.
Hareven, T. (1986) 'Historical Change in the Family and the Life Course: Implications for Child Development', pp. 8–23 in A.B. Smuts and J.W. Hagen (eds), *History and Research in Child Development* (*Monographs of the Society for Research in Child Development*), 50 (4–5; ser. no. 211)).
Harré, R. (1979) *Social Being*. Oxford: Basil Blackwell
Harré, R. (1983) *Personal Being*. Oxford: Basil Blackwell.
Harré, R. and P. Secord (1972) *The Explanation of Social Behaviour*. Oxford: Basil Blackwell.
Holland, R. (1977) *Self and Social Context*. London: Macmillan.
Hunt, E.K. (1978) 'The Transition from Feudalism to Capitalism', in R.C. Edwards, M. Reich and T.E. Weisskopf (eds), *The Capitalist System: A Radical Analysis of American Society* (2nd edn). Englewood Cliffs, NJ: Prentice-Hall.
Iwao, S. (1986) 'The Pitfalls of Cross-cultural Attitude Survey', paper delivered at the International Congress of Applied Psychology, Jerusalem, Israel, 13–18 July.
Josselson, R. (1980) 'Ego Development in Adolescence', in J. Adelson (ed.). *Handbook of Adolescent Psychology*. New York: John Wiley.
Kohlberg, L. (1958) 'The Development of Modes of Moral Thinking in the Years Ten to Sixteen', unpublished doctoral dissertation, University of Chicago.
Lalljee, M., L. Brown and G.P. Ginsburg (1984) 'Attitudes: Dispositions, Behaviour or Evaluation?' *British Journal of Social Psychology*, 23: 233–44.
Marcia, J.E. (1966) 'Development and Validation of Ego Identity Statuses', *Journal of Personality and Social Psychology*, 3: 119–33.
Marcia, J.E. (1976a) 'Identity Six Years After: A Follow-up Study', *Journal of Youth and Adolescence*, 5: 145–60.
Marcia, J.E. (1976b) 'Studies in Ego Identity', unpublished research monograph, Simon Fraser University.
Marcia, J.E. (1980) 'Identity in Adolescence, in J. Adelson (ed.), *Handbook of Adolescent Psychology*. New York: John Wiley.
Marcia, J.E. (1987) 'The Identity Status Approach to the Study of Ego Identity Development', in K. Kardley and T. Honess (eds), *Self and Identity: Psychosocial*

Perspectives. London: Wiley.

Marcia, J.E. and M.J. Friedman (1970) 'Ego Identity Status in College Women', *Journal of Personality*, 38: 249–63.

Moscovici, S. (1972) 'Society and Theory in Social Psychology', in J. Israel and H. Tajfel (eds), *The Context of Social Psychology: A Critical Assessment*, New York: Acadamic Press.

Orlofsky, J.L.(1977) 'Sex-role Orientation, Identity Formation, and Self-esteem in College Men and Women', *Sex Roles*, 3: 561–75.

Prager, K. (1977) 'The Relationship between Identity Status, Intimacy Status, Self-esteem and Psychological Androgeny in College Women', *Dissertation Abstracts International*, 38: 2343–8b.

Ricoeur, P. (1970) *Freud and Philosophy; An Essay in Interpretation*. New Haven and London: Yale University Press.

Rogow, A.M., J.E. Marcia and B.R. Slugoski (1983) 'The Relative Importance of Identity Status Interview Components', *Journal of Youth and Adolescence*, 12, 387–400.

Rorty, R. (1979) *Philosophy and the Mirror of Nature*. Princeton, NJ: Princeton University Press.

Sampson, E.E. (1976) *Social Psychology in Contemporary Society* (2nd edn). New York: John Wiley.

Sampson, E.E. (1977) 'Psychology and the American Ideal', *Journal of Personality and Social Psychology*, 35: 767–82.

Schenkel, S. (1975) 'Relationship among Ego Identity Status, Field Independence and Traditional Feminity', *Journal of Youth and Adolescence*, 4: 73–82.

Schenkel, S. and J.E. Marcia (1972) 'Attitudes toward Premarital Intercourse in Determining Ego Identity Status in College Women', *Journal of Personality*, 3: 472–82.

Schiedel, D.G. and J.E. Marcia (1985) 'Ego Identity, Intimacy, Sex-role Orientation, and Gender', *Developmental Psychology*, 21: 149–60.

Schlenker, B.R. (1980) *Impression Management: The Self Concept, Social Identity, and Interpersonal Relations*. Monterey: Brooks-Cole.

Scott, M.B. and S.M. Lyman (1968) 'Accounts', *American Sociological Review*, 33: 46–62.

Searle, J.R. (1969) *Speech Acts: An Essay in the Philosophy of Language*. Cambridge: Cambridge University Press.

Slugoski, B.R., J.E. Marcia and R.F. Koopman (1984) 'Cognitive and Social Interactional Characteristics of Ego Identity Statuses in College Males', *Journal of Personality and Social Psychology*, 47: 646–61.

Smith, J.L. (1982) 'A Structuralist Interpretation of the Fishbeinian Model of Intention', *Journal for the Theory of Social Behaviour*, 12: 29–46.

Swanson, G.E. (1985) 'The Powers and the Capabilities of Selves: Social and Collective Approaches', *Journal for the Theory of Social Behaviour*, 15: 331–54.

Taylor, C. (1977) 'What is Human Agency?' in T. Mischel (ed.), *The Self: Psychological and Philosophical Issues*. Oxford: Basil Blackwell.

Toder, N. and J.E. Marcia (1973) 'Ego Identity Status and Response to Conformity Pressure in College Women, *Journal of Personality and Social Psychology*, 26: 287–94.

Waterman, A.S. (1982) 'Identity Development from Adolescence to Adulthood: An Extension of Theory and a Review of Research', *Developmental Psychology*, 18: 341–58.

Waterman, C.K. and A.S. Waterman (1974) 'Ego Identity Status and Decision Styles', *Journal of Youth and Adolescence*, 3: 1-6.
Wilden, A. (1980) *System and Structure: Essays in Communication and Exchange* (2nd edn). London: Tavistock.
Winch, P. (1958) *The Idea of a Social Science and its Relation to Philosophy*. London: Routledge & Kegan Paul.
Wittgenstein, L. (1953) *Philosophical Investigations*. Oxford: Basil Blackwell.

4
Discourse and Power

Ian Parker

In this chapter I want to take up two issues addressed in this volume. The first is to do with how our current texts of identity emerged in the Western world. I will describe Foucault's analysis of the crucial links that have been forged in modern culture between self-understanding and power. The second issue concerns the possibility of full and unfettered communication. Foucault's contribution to the history of identity would suggest that a desire for such 'free speech' is one that could never be fulfilled. I will speak, following Foucault, of 'discourse' rather than texts. I see 'texts' as delimited areas (such as thrillers, terrorism or ego psychology) of the many wider-ranging discourses in a culture, which constitute an object of interest. In this case the object is 'the self'. The self is constructed in discourses and then re-experienced within all the texts of everyday life.

Among such texts are those that are elaborated in academic social psychology. I will relate my account of Foucault's work to what was optimistically called, more than a decade ago, the 'new paradigm'. The 'new paradigm' championed people's accounts against laboratory-experimental social psychology, and it insisted on the primacy of human agency (Harré and Secord, 1972; Shotter, 1975). A complementary argument was that social psychology should become a variety of history (Gergen, 1973). This collection emerges from those debates, and it is, then, useful to discuss how and why the 'new paradigm' did not account for power. To that extent, it was not as 'new' as it claimed; its discourse was embedded in wider culturally bounded discourses.

Foucault's History

What self-definitions does the organization of language allow us? How do labelling and stigmatizing work to channel possible accounts of the self into the forms acceptable to society? How are oppressive self-images governed by the parameters of available discourse?

Some of these questions have been tackled by social psychology, but an explication of the critical links between self-understanding and power has always been overlooked. In contrast, Foucault's work can show us what these links are. Foucault dealt with the phenomenon of what social psychologists call 'identity' or 'the self'. He highlighted problems of self-understanding, of the way that a kind of 'double-bind' works in contemporary culture which makes us individually responsible for social processes, and which also implicates us in the reproduction of relations of domination.

The project announced by Foucault in an overview of the direction of his work should immediately be of interest to social psychologists. His aim, he said, was 'to create a history of the different modes by which, in our culture, human beings are made subjects' (1982, p. 777). This is a theme that runs through much of his work. Although he claimed to have realized it quite late on, this type of study can be pursued only in the context of an analysis of power relations. Many theorists inside and outside social psychology have been concerned with the social organization of language and subjectivity, but it is in Foucault's writings that the phenomenon of power is brought to the fore.

There have been shifts of emphasis over the years in Foucault's various books and articles. In his earlier writings he talked of the organization of discourse into 'epistemes' lasting roughly 150 years each; at this stage his work was heavily influenced by structuralism, an approach he later rejected. However, this early work is still crucial to an historical sense of the relationship between cultural changes and social-scientific theory. Foucault later came to recognize the importance of connecting this discursive level of social life with physical constraints – the 'violent, bloody and lethal character of conflict' (Foucault, 1980a, p. 115). At the same time, the rather crude 'anti-humanism' of the early works was replaced by a more subtle description of the historical foundations of subjectivity. It is useful, though, to trace a path through his work as a whole, and I will deal, in turn, with his analyses of the 'epistemes', 'confession' and 'discipline' before relating his history to developments in social psychology.

Epistemologies

Foucault (1970) claimed that the organization of knowledge has mutated in the past centuries to create new objects of human understanding. It is in the last of these major shifts that the human being itself came under scrutiny, and the 'self' was formed as a new object. He described the epistemological configurations, or 'epistemes', as overarching discursive regimes that effectively determined what it was appropriate to discuss (and think).

Writings in the history of science have helped throw social psychologists into a state of doubt as to the 'truth' of their models of the person and the 'facts' they have discovered. However, while Kuhn's (1970) talk of a 'disciplinary matrix' within a science strikes a chord with the analysis of power described in this chapter, Foucault's work on 'epistemes' is more ambitious than descriptions of mere scientific 'paradigms'. (This is a point that has more than a little bearing on the attempt to construct 'new paradigms' in social psychology.) In Foucault's work, the knowledge is described as circulating in practices throughout the body of society. The knowledge manifests itself in literature and art, for example, and, as Foucault came to realize, in everyday discourse (Foucault, 1978, 1980b). In addition for Kuhn, 'Science' is still a highly cumulative enterprise. Of course, there are differences of interpretation and many meanings in Kuhn's work of the term 'paradigm' (Masterman, 1970). The overall impression that is given, however, is that facts are collected and reviewed as nature demands, periodically, through the presentation of inconsistencies, a different account within a new paradigm.

In contrast, the knowledge that Foucault describes is riven by contradictions, differences of interpretation and conflicts of interest. It is not conceptualized as a type of 'Gestalt' whose change is prompted by the discovery of anomalies. Notions of 'progress' are thus viewed with a great deal of suspicion in his work. Scepticism and pessimism are therefore more thoroughgoing than in the tradition of thought that his historical work parallels, that of the Frankfurt School and German Critical Theory on 'modernity' (Foucault, 1984).

The 'epistemes' are the historical frames that have successively governed Western thought. A simplified outline of their terms of reference (and the 'referents' that their organizations of terms construct) is as follows.

The Renaissance
This period, which lasted from about 1500 to the middle of the seventeenth century, was a world held together by the theme of resemblance. God's law was reflected in Nature and in texts. Because God had created the world and language at one and the same time, it was possible, it was thought, to interpret even the languages that resulted from the fragmentation of Babel to discover His signature. Symbolism reigned. Hermeneutics was directed to the biblical texts to discover the true word of God.

The Classical Age

The next period transformed Renaissance conceptions and lasted until the end of the eighteenth century. Mere resemblance did not suffice and was thought to lead to confusion. Analysis then turned to the representation of signs patterned on rationalistic mechanistic models. The 'Idéologues', for example, attempted to produce a linguistic uniformity which could represent thought. The social and physical world, covered by Natural Science, was understood by means of taxonomy: if the ordering of the world was rigorous enough, it would represent the real world. Although language did not immediately reflect the world, the pattern it could be brought to form could reflect the pattern of the world.

Modernity

The end of the eighteenth century engendered a mutation in the organization of language that saw the human being emerge as the locus of knowledge. While the Classical Age was concerned with representation, the Modern Age turned its attention to that being who was taken to be responsible for the representation. From a mere clarifier, as in the Classical Age, the human being came to be seen as the producer. This meant that within the scheme of representation an account had to be given of that which had produced it. The 'Ideologist' fell from grace, and 'ideology', as a term, gathered its prejorative connotations. It was no longer seen as a 'science of ideas' but as mystification, and to it was counterposed the new, ostenibly progressive, Romanticism.

'Epistemes' and Paradigms

Turning to social psychology for a moment, it would be tempting to draw a parallel between the Classical Age and the positivist study of behaviour that was long dominant in our discipline. The interest in the human being's autonomous creative activity in modern times could be hailed as a positive move. Does not the 'new paradigm' value human agency against attempts to view it in a mechanistic fashion? Does not hermeneutics value the meanings a person divines from her actions? In addition, did not Wittgenstein, whose later philosophy of language was an important resource for new social psychology, rebel against his earlier positivist claims that a logical, scientific language could picture reality?

Foucault's work would signal caution. Instead, interpretations that rest on the individual's ability to manufacture and control meaning are shown to emerge more as traps than as solutions. The beginning of the Modern Age saw humans far from being elevated to the status of creator (or a god on Earth, as the humanists would wish), fall subject to a new system of explanation and investigation. In the Modern Age, the truths of life are thought to reside in the depths of the human being: the standard puzzle over the person, who could be at once the subject and the object of her own understanding, became inscribed in discourse with the arrival of this historical period. This puzzle is a trap, as will be seen when we consider the ways in which the person became an individual 'subject' glued in place from within by the phenomenon of responsible agency (confession) and from without by the apparatus of surveillance (discipline).

Confession

The consequences of the shift in knowledge were not confined to philosophy but also made sense of changes in social organization. The early historical work of Foucault must now be connected to his later analyses of power. Foucault (1977) turned his attention to the way in which the break at the end of the eighteenth century was accompanied by an intensification of social practices connecting knowledge with individuality. A meticulous description of the activities and characteristics of the population was then, he points out, beginning to be built up. The organic metaphors of a social 'body' suffused with 'pathologies' mirrored the popular psychologies that were constructed by administrators. Within institutions, instruments to regulate the behaviour of individuals became finely articulated. Outside the institutions, the identification of abnormalities, of which every person was a potential bearer, became a pressing concern.

Individuality
Other historical work on the emergence of individuality has identified earlier expressions of the phenomenon. The twelfth century, for example, has been described as the period when autobiographies first started being produced and when the concept of an 'I' was appreciated. Foucault is concerned with the particular twist that was given to individuality and self-responsibility in the nineteenth century.

Sexuality
Foucault (1981) argues that it was in sexuality that the deepest truths were thought to be found. Sexuality itself, in Foucault's account, is socially produced. Social and sexual practices were, and are, suffused with accounts. These accounts both warrant practices

and reproduce them. They are organized in a discourse that is predicated on the assumption that a truth exists within the individual and that, through confession (the religious and the psychoanalytic are the paradigmatic examples), it may be released. Foucault was concerned, as a result of this analysis, to dispel a myth regarding sexual repression and liberation. According to the myth, the Victorian age was marked by the suppression of sexuality. Some taboos on self-expression were being broken, but it was not until later in the present century that the full liberation of sexuality became possible. There emerged wide-ranging discourse relating to sex, and we now imagine it to be possible to express and fulfil long-repressed desires. This myth, Foucault argued, is dangerous: for the very discourse that appears to give liberation is itself the condition of a more insidious oppression. For example, the proliferation of discourses relating sexuality to personal self-definitions has produced an arsenal of categories and labels with which sexual 'minorities' are typified against a norm. Foucault should be seen, then, as describing the 'conceptual infrastructure' for varieties of sexual 'stigma'.

The notion of confession is organized into modern discourse in such a way that it becomes impossible for an individual to believe that she has developed a 'healthy' identity without acknowledging troubling hidden secrets about the self. It thus becomes a condition of liberation that deep-felt needs are produced, and are actually experienced as 'real' – needs that conform to the prevailing cultural norms. A paradoxical consequence and twist to this process is that an individual seeking 'awareness' and 'liberation' risks becoming bound all the more tightly in the meshes of modern culture. Should we experience difficulty in showing, to others or to ourselves, this personal and repressed truth, we are incited to believe all the more in the power of the constraints that hold it down. As Foucault puts it, 'it is in the confession that truth and sex are joined, through the obligatory and exhaustive expression of an individual secret' (1981, p. 61).

Discipline

Foucault argues that what counts as true knowledge is ostensibly defined by the individual, but what is permitted to count is defined by discourse. What is spoken, and who may speak, are issues of power. As well as organizing and excluding forms of knowledge, discourse relates and helps organize social relations as power relations. Power is usually thought of as the exercise of the will of one social actor over others. This model of power is most appropriate, according to Foucault, to the period up to the end of the eighteenth century. After that date the growth in population, and the concentration of economic production, had reached the point where 'disciplinary' power became dominant. This is a type of power that operates independently of the intentions of individuals. The first model of power can be thought of as 'sovereign' power. The second is relational – 'disciplinary' – and is best understood through the historical illustration Foucault offers in his description of the Panopticon. The character of disciplinary power is masked by the invitation that modern discourse makes to us to assume full responsibility for our acts and intentions.

Sovereignty and Modernity

It is doubtful whether the 'sovereign' power model was ever fully operative. The paradigm case, in which the will of the king was exacted against the body of the criminal, could not be thought of as completely free of a relational power, which enmeshes the putative power-holder as well as the power-subject, in the way Foucault describes. Studies of recent feudal regimes do demonstrate a complex interplay between a Machiavellian sovereign and the intrigues of the court circles (cf. Kapuściński, 1983). So grim is the picture Foucault paints of 'modernity', though, that his story sometimes implies that times past, when the crowd could revolt and save a popular felon from the executioner, were preferable.

The point that can be emphasized for present purposes is that the transformation in penal style and the emergence of a particular form of rationality that Foucault described allow us to see that the concern with the wellbeing of the prisoner is accompanied by a more subtle regime of power than that based purely on physical violence. It is a regime in which individuals take responsibility for exercising control over themselves. Foucault's studies describe the emergence of a form of power that traditional social psychology neglects. This is because that power embraces and forms social psychology as a discipline, and 'new paradigm' alternatives which emphasize the agency of the person do not escape that embrace. I will return to this point below.

The Panopticon

The transition to self-control was closely linked with the change in the apparatus of the prison system. The procedures and practices that comprised this change were stimulated by the emergency measures needed to curb the plague. In turn, these spilled out into the rest of society. For Foucault (1977), the apparatus is symbolized by the architecture of surveillance proposed by Bentham in the plan for the Panopticon. In the Panopticon a central guard tower is encircled by cells which are backlit so as to render visible the activities of the inhabitants. The prisoners do not see the observer. As Bentham (1791) points out, what is important is that the prisoners should believe themselves to be seen.

The Panopticon taken as a model of power illustrates the placing of power-subjects in relation to authority in such a way that the power is not reducible to any intentions to exert power. It is not necessary that anyone should actually occupy the guard tower. This does not mean that the deliberate manipulation of others within already discursively established power relations does not occur. Foucault's history, though, highlights the way in which knowledge, constructed through a system of surveillance, is intimately linked with power.

Power and Truth

The knowledge that circulates in discourse is employed in everyday interaction in relations of submission and domination. For example, delinquency is an essential correlate of law; it is nonsense to speak of a judicial system without some conception of the types of behaviours that count as infractions of that system. In addition, the discovery of a 'truth' about the nature of the normal individual, and an apparatus to elicit that 'truth', necessitates conceptions of deviance. The question that social psychology should ask about the exercise of power is then transformed. We can move from a concern with the 'will' or 'intention' of a power-holder to an analysis of the positions from which power is exercised. We gain an understanding of how the 'normal' person and the 'deviant' each reproduce power relations in their everyday interaction. It is in this sense that the modern construction of deviance works to 'hierarchize individuals in relation to one another' (Foucault, 1977, p. 223). Abnormalities are categorized, and identified, and must be recognized as 'true' by the bearer. In this way a hierarchy is set up which becomes a model for, and pervades, all social relationships.

Foucault's work, then, opens up a way of making sense of studies in social psychology that demonstrate the routine oppression that occurs in 'normal' interaction. Henley's (1977) work, for example, has shown the place of 'ordinary' non-verbal behaviour in sexual subordination.

Interpretation and Understanding

To summarize and draw together these three aspects of Foucault's work, Foucault argues that the 'self' is constructed as the subject and object of discourse at a particular historical conjuncture. The price of being seen as a 'reasonable' agent meant that the individual was expected to account for errors in personal terms. At the same time, the discourse pertaining to normality and deviance intensified the models of confession that were already present in the religious apparatus. In order to achieve enlightenment, the individual would have to produce hitherto repressed truths. The role that an interpretative, or hermeneutic, social science would play within a discourse that incited and judged the validity of this truth would be to increase the subjection of the person. It is possible, then, to take the double-play on the meaning of 'subjection' in this context quite seriously: a *subjectivity* is produced in discourse as the self is *subjected* to discourse.

At the same time, this means, as Smart (1982) has pointed out, that the sociological attempts to account for agency within social structures becomes an impossible task. The 'human sciences', in their present form, are historically transient enterprises. Smart shows that the very problem of reconciling 'structure' and 'agency' is conditioned by the preoccupation with individuality that Foucault describes. The dichotomy, and the discourse that holds it, is not susceptible to resolution.

Binding
Foucault's account also means that confession ('a ritual of discourse in which the speaking subject is also the subject of the statement': 1981, p. 61) functions to 'bind' subjects into discourse. It is useful here to refer briefly to a theoretical framework from which another but similar notion of 'binds' issues. Bateson's (1973) work, deriving from systems theory, focuses, like structuralism, on relations rather than on the peculiarities of individuals. His use of the term 'double-bind' to describe a tangle in communication patterns in families, and the resultant schizophrenia in the victims, employs the concept of 'an unconscious frame as an explanatory principle' (p. 159). (This device is, in turn, borrowed for the analysis of closed systems of meaning by Goffman, 1975.) The conflict between the message and the frame, which cannot be resolved, is said by Bateson to induce schizophrenia. Foucault's work would suggest that there should be an attempt to locate such a set of relations within the discourse of the surrounding culture. (The demand, for example, to 'be spontaneous' would seem to be as self-defeating outside as inside family life.) Sluzki and Verón (1971) have already attempted to extend the concept of 'binding'. Foucault effectively stretches the notion to the cultural frame.

Another aspect of Bateson's work, that on alcoholics, which follows from the systems theory framework he proposes, is relevant.

Bateson recommends that alcoholics should relinquish self-control, and should recognize, in order to follow the route to cure, that 'there is a power greater than the self' (p. 302). Foucault indicates that this power resides, in large part, in a discourse that deludes persons into supposing that power is located in them. Shifting from Bateson's concern with the 'system' to Foucault's use of the notion of 'discourse' introduces a fluidity into social life which enables an account of change. The logic of both perspectives is that the humanist search for self-knowledge and self-potential would be seen as a bind in modern discourse.

Social Psychology's Discourse

I now want to apply Foucault's work to the criticisms that have been made of the 'old' laboratory-experimental paradigm in social psychology. We may, as a result, be able to move beyond some of the alternative formulations that have been advanced as part of the 'new paradigm' in the discipline.

The 'Old Paradigm'

The efforts of experimental social psychology to break the mental processes of individuals into measurable and manipulable components can be seen as part of the power pattern of contemporary society. Foucault's work could only reinforce the opposition to positivism and individualism that characterizes the 'old paradigm'. At the same time, what is sometimes described as a shift within the discipline of psychology away from obsessive quantification has to be linked with intellectual, social and political changes outside, changes in the discourse of the social world.

History

The importance of situating social psychology is once again emphasized. Gergen (1973), arguing for history in social psychology, suggested that the sensitivity of the psychologist could be an aid to the historian in return for the loan of some perspective on our discipline. Foucault's work suggests that even assumptions that would motivate a location of (albeit transient) processes in the individual must be interrogated historically. For example, Foucault's analysis at once highlights and questions the ahistoricism of the Meadian account of self-construction taken up by 'new paradigm' social psychology. Mead, in the tradition of German Romanticism, was concerned with the predicament of a specifically 'modern' self. However, he did not give an historical account of why and how it emerged when it did. Mead's 'Other' acts as the source and guarantor for individual self-identity and for the formation of an 'I'. In contrast, Foucault's 'Other' is historically constituted. The 'I' recognizes itself, in relation to the 'Other', in modern society, for example in the mode of surveillance. (Marxist writers in the tradition of critical theory have described the experience as one of 'alienation'.)

True Selves
Symbolic Interactionism has shown the 'new paradigm' that, as Gergen (1977) points out, there is 'true self'. Although it is not 'true', or composed of universal properties and experiences, it is still thought to be potentially transparent. A statement of this position by Rock (1979), for example, should be re-read in the light of Foucault's writings as an historically specific statement. Rock argues that 'each man is his own panopticon, an external monitor of himself and others, and an interpreter of the hidden dialogues that prompt others to act' (1979, p. 110).

Foucault insists that such interpretations can only be in discourse, and do not refer to 'hidden dialogues'. Such interpretations of inner states simply draw upon other discourses. This also makes the bid of hermeneutics a dubious alternative, and a return to a Renaissance humanism, suggested by Shotter (1975) in an early text of the 'new paradigm' movement, may be oppressive and impossible. Impossible because experience is composed of a fantastic variety of contradictory impulses, no one of which is 'true'; oppressive because self-accounts vary depending on the situation, a factor glossed over by a researcher looking for a single account and keen to press 'subjects' into conforming to it.

Normality
Further, the drive towards an idealized 'authenticity' of any variety is seriously questioned. This serves to reinforce the last point, and bears on the particular cast that humanism is given in the hermeneutics of the 'new paradigm'. The touchstone for undistorted communication and authentic action is often thought to be exemplified by 'ordinary language' (Harré, 1979). The inspiration for this position is Wittgenstein's later philosophy of language. Authenticity then involves faithfully respecting and employing the 'language of the folk'. Because this ordinary language is reflective of the agency of persons, and the final responsibility for ensuring that it stays sound rests in that agency, deviations from it can all too easily be taken as evidence of delinquency on the part of the speaker. So, while it is the case that Harré is not uncritical of the language he describes, it is possible for those 'lacking' the ability to

account fully to be described charitably as suffering from a type of 'false consciousness' (Harré, 1977, p. 332). If the work of Foucault is taken seriously, it would be necessary to take more notice of Wittgenstein's cryptic comments, reported by Wright (1982) on the deep 'sickness' of language in West European culture. An obsession with technological progress is linked to the alienation people feel in everyday life. Now, following Foucault, we could see such phenomena as manifestations of the apparatuses of discipline and confession which suffuse modern life.

Power
Power becomes a central relational attribute of any inquiry directed to self-knowledge. Not only are social relations stressed, and social relations as they are embodied in discourse, but we may view these relations as power relations. This opens up an opportunity to rework instances of social interaction and self-definition in the politically judged patterns of racism, hetero-sexism, and other forms of domination at work in society. Instead of operating in discourse merely to constrain and disallow, however, power is treated as being productive of subjectivity. This links with the idea of what Shotter (1984) describes as a 'political economy of selfhood' (p. 174). In Foucault's view, the present 'political economy' would be one in which the characteristics of individuals' bodies and behaviour are prone to be labelled as pathologies within discourse and in which, in Goffmanesque terms, every culturally appropriate identity is 'spoiled' and requires management. The operation of power relations in this manner makes it impossible to attain resolution and consensuality, in Meadian fashion, by simply 'taking the place of the other'.

Difference
When the notion of a unitary self is put into question, the construction of fragments of subjectivity in different, contradictory, discourses can be studied. A crucial contribution of new social psychology has been, in Harré's (1979) work, the resurrection of the notion of a multiplicity of social selves clustered around any single biological individual. Goffman's (1971) dramaturgy is often accused of promoting the image of the person as a cynical manipulator of others through the self-conscious adoption of social roles. However, Foucault's description of the self in discourse(s) would aid a reading of Goffman which would rebut such criticisms. For Foucault (1972), 'we are difference … our selves the difference of masks' (p. 131). Selves should be seen not as 'parts' selected at will, but as set in a variety of power-infused discourses. We do not rationally 'choose'

to display our-selves as willing participants, for example, in the rituals of close personal relationships or to experience our-selves as discerning readers in the presence of an academic text.

Conclusion

Now the critical voices in social psychology that spoke for a 'new paradigm' in the 1970s are turning to the role of texts and discourse. The movement needs to be accelerated (Parker, 1989), and we also need to take the opportunity to draw up an assessment of the values and problems that attend a simple faith in human agency. This faith, a touchstone of humanism, informed their own texts at that time of academic crisis and uncertainty. What the work of Foucault shows us is that, if we really want to break out of the cultural assumptions that underpinned the 'old paradigm', we need to be even more uncertain about agency and the self. We need, in fact, to ask how the self is implicated moment by moment, through the medium of discourse, in power.

References

Bateson, G. (1973) *Steps to an Ecology of Mind*. London: Paladin.

Bentham, J. (1791) *Panopticism*. Reprinted in J. Bowring (ed.), *Works of Jeremy Bentham*, Vol. 4, Edinburgh, 1843.

Foucault, M. (1970) *The Order of Things*. London: Tavistock.

Foucault, M. (1972) *The Archaeology of Knowledge*. London: Tavistock.

Foucault, M. (1977) *Discipline and Punish*. London: Allen Lane.

Foucault, M. (ed.) (1978) *I, Pierre Riviere, having slaughtered my mother, my sister, and my brother ...* Harmondsworth: Penguin.

Foucault, M. (1980a) *Power/Knowledge: Selected Interviews and Other Writings, 1972-1977*. Brighton: Harvester Press.

Foucault, M. (ed.) (1980b) *Herculine Barbin: Being the Recently Discovered Memoirs of Nineteenth-century French Hermaphrodite*. Brighton: Harvester Press.

Foucault, M. (1981) *The History of Sexuality*, Vol. 1. *An Introduction*. Harmondsworth: Penguin.

Foucault, M. (1982) 'The Subject and Power', *Critical Inquiry*, 8: 777–95.

Foucault, M. (1984) 'Structuralism and Post-structuralism: An Interview with Michel Foucault', *Telos*, 55: 195–211.

Gergen, K.J. (1973) 'Social Psychology as History', *Journal of Personality and Social Psychology*. 26: 309–20.

Gergen, K.J. (1977) 'The Social Construction of Self-knowledge', in T. Mischel (ed.), *The Self: Psychological and Philosophical Issues*. Oxford: Basil Blackwell.

Goffman, E. (1971) *The Presentation of Self in Everyday Life*. Harmondsworth: Penguin.

Goffman, E. (1975) *Frame Analysis: An Essay on the Organisation of Experience*. Harmondsworth: Penguin.

Harré R. (1977) 'The Self in Monodrama', in T. Mischel (ed.), *The Self: Psychological and Philosophical Issues*. Oxford: Basic Blackwell.

Harré, R. (1979) *Social Being: A Theory for Social Psychology.* Oxford: Basil Blackwell.

Harré, R. and P.F. Secord (1972) *The Explanation of Social Behaviour.* Oxford: Basil Blackwell.

Henley, N.M. (1977) *Body Politics: Power, Sex, and Nonverbal Communication.* Englewood Cliffs, NJ: Prentice-Hall.

Kapuściński, R. (1983) *The Emperor.* London: Picador.

Kuhn, T.S. (1970) *The Structure of Scientific Revolutions.* Chicago: University of Chicago Press.

Masterman, M. (1970) 'The Nature of a Paradigm', in I. Lakatos and A. Musgrave (eds), *Criticism and the Growth of Knowledge.* Cambridge: Cambridge University Press.

Parker, I. (1989) *The Crisis in Modern Social Psychology, and How to End It.* London: Routledge.

Rock, P. (1979) *The Making of Symbolic Interactionism.* London: Macmillan.

Shotter, J. (1975) *Images of Man in Psychological Research.* London: Methuen.

Shotter, J. (1984) *Social Accountability and Selfhood.* Oxford: Basil Blackwell.

Sluzki, C.E. and E. Verón (1971) 'The Double Bind as a Universal Pathogenic Situation'. Reprinted in C.E. Sluzki and D.C. Ransom (eds), *Double Bind: The Foundation of the Communicational Approach to the Family.* New York: Grune and Stratton, 1976.

Smart, B. (1982) 'Foucault, Sociology, and the Problem of Human Agency', *Theory and Society.* 11 (2): 121–41.

Wright, G.H. von (1982) *Wittgenstein.* Oxford: Basil Blackwell.

5
Warranting Voice and the Elaboration of the Self

Kenneth J. Gergen

We have at our disposal an immense vocabulary for speaking of the psychological interior – that secret domain of which the structure and process of self are traditionally held to be constituents. We speak with ease and confidence of our thoughts, beliefs, memories, emotions and the like. We also possess an extended discourse through which we render accounts of the relationships among aspects of the mental world. We speak of ideas, for example, as they are shaped by sense data, bent by our motives, dropped into memory, recruited for the process of planning and so on. And we describe how our emotions are fired by our ideas, suppressed by our conscience, modified by our memories and seek expression in our dreams. In effect, we have at our disposal a full and extended ontology of the inner region. When asked for accounts of self, participants in contemporary Western culture unflinchingly agree that emotions, ideas, plans, memories and the like are all significant. Such accounts of the mind are critical to who we are, what we stand for and how we conduct ourselves in the world.

The Problematic Origins of Self-discourse

How are we to understand the origins of our vocabulary of self-understanding and the elaborated discourse into which it is woven? It is tempting to suggest that such discourse is wedded to observation, logical inference, or phenomenological givens. That is, such discourse is built up from, or inductively derived from, experience. Certainly this has been a founding supposition within the discipline of psychology – virtually since its birth in the Wundtian laboratories. Yet, doubt in this position begins to germinate when we step outside our contemporary cultural milieu. In times past it would have been equally as plausible to explicate the self in terms of Apollonian inspirations, demon possession and endemic humours.

And if we scan the contemporary cultural horizon we find numerous differences in the ontology of mind. As only one of many possible examples, Rosaldo's (1980) research on the Ilongot tribe in the Philippines reveals a mental state termed 'liget'. This state is said to resemble the Western concept of anger. Yet, the possession of liget is often treated as admirable and desirable; it points to a readiness to be socially unique or to have conviction; it suggests that one is young, quick-moving and strong. Babies are also the product of liget; without liget to move one's heart, it is said, there would be no human life. Instances such as these begin to rouse us from the complacency of conceptual sedimentation. We begin to confront bothersome questions of justifying the Western ontology of mind.

Elsewhere I have attempted to demonstrate the impropriety of this, the inductive approach (Gergen, 1985). As I have tried to show, one enters conceptually perilous waters when the attempt is made to show how discourse on mind could be derived from observation – either direct or inferential. There are problems of separating the observer from the observed, identifying qualities of mental states, and accounting for differences between correct and incorrect inferences. These arguments are rather extended and cannot be recapitulated here. It is sufficient to point out that at this juncture we fail to possess an adequate means for understanding the development of our mental vocabulary and the extended propositional network in which it figures.

Although the present chapter will hardly rectify this state, it is my hope to present a fresh perspective of some further promise, and to develop its implications in a way that bears particular relevance both to our understanding of psychology and to the concept of self in contemporary society. At the outset I shall take seriously two major features of Wittgenstein's (1953) later writings. First, there seems good reason to view mental predicates as semantically free-floating. That is, the vocabulary of mind is not anchored in, defined by or ostensively grounded in real-world particulars in such a way that propositions about mental events are subject to correction though observation. (Readers wishing to pursue the rationale for this commitment may consult Gergen, 1982). Second, I take seriously the view that linguistic discourse is essentially part of a social process. The uses of and constraints over the language of mind are social derivatives. Or, to follow Austin (1962), mental talk is largely performative – that is, it does not mirror or map an independent reality but is a functioning element in social process itself. In the case of mental predicates, one is thus invited to look not for their referents but for their consequences in social life. This view is also shared by the Shotter, and the Wetherell-Potter chapters in this volume (Chapters 9 and 13).

In preceding work I have attempted to extend these assumptions in several ways. Queries have been raised, for example, regarding the origins of various rudimentary distinctions in the commonly shared ontology of mind (Gergen, 1985). In this case it was possible to demonstrate that the intentional character of mental language, along with the separation of the mental world into distinct units, is the result of employing a verbal language (as opposed to some other form of medium such as dance) in carrying out the reference function. In effect, to employ the linguistic medium in social interchange places certain unwitting constraints over the prevailing concept of mental life. Other work has attempted to demonstrate the circular character of propositions relating mental events to the external world, and to demonstrate that virtually all that can be known (which is to say 'intelligibly stated') about the mind already lies implicit in the definitional structures of the language (Gergen, 1984).

It is in yet another direction that I wish now to press. Earlier work has attempted to furnish a rationale for why concepts of mind are both presumed and essential. Although this account is far from complete, discussion must now be opened on what may be viewed as the elaboration of the inner region. Specifically, I wish to raise the question of why we assume what we do about the functioning of various mental entities or processes. To assume an inner region of self is one thing – to presume its thoroughfares, the shape of its structures, the colour of its interior surrounds and so on is quite another. Again, I cannot hope to offer anything like a complete analysis in the pages that follow. However, I shall propose that in important measure the mental world becomes elaborated as various interest groups within the culture seek to warrant or justify their accounts of the world. In effect, our vocabulary of self shifts as pragmatic exigencies dictate. After exploring several facets of this proposal we may consider the role of contemporary psychology. As will be proposed, the experimental wing of the discipline has largely elaborated the vocabulary of mind in such a way as to justify the favoured pursuits of the profession. Psychological discourse has too often been self-serving for the profession itself.

World Construction and Psychological Warrant

If a mother can convince her children that sharing is a virtue, she may enjoy hours of tranquillity. If a suitor can demonstrate that he is replete with fine qualities, he may win the love he so desires. If a lawyer can persuade the jury that his/her client intended to slay a bear rather than a business colleague, the client may go free. And if the scholar can make a clear and compelling case, he or she may enjoy position, and respect (ones dare not add 'fortune'). This is all by way of illustrating the vast importance in social life of hegemony in world construction. If one's linguistic construction of the world prevails, the outcomes may be substantial. Failing to achieve intelligibility in construction is to have little role in the co-ordinated set of daily activities from which life satisfactions are typically derived.

It is also clear that an indeterminate array of constructions may be applied to any given occasion. Whatever it is I am doing in these few pages may alternatively be viewed as propaganda, sharing important insights, seeking companionship or self-aggrandizement, living out the expression of humane ideals, mystifying foolishness and so on. Only the limits of our imagination could contain the range of possible and plausible constructions. To be sure, I would prefer that certain of these constructions were shared as opposed to others. My future relationships may indeed depend on which accounts prove most compelling. Likewise, for various reasons, others might prefer alternatives to those I would favour. (I will not consider the misguided reasons for the latter alternatives.) However, the general point should be abundantly clear: given a range of competing constructions, and sufficient stakes in the outcomes, there may be brisk competition over whose voice is honoured. Whose voice prevails in a sea of alternatives may be critical to the fate of the person, relationships, family life, community, and in a significant sense to the future of humankind.

I take these views to be relatively unproblematic. Indeed, much of history can be written in terms of how various individuals or groups have come to gain or lose voice. It is plausible to argue that, on the most basic level, might has made right. People have been simply forced by threat of punishment or death to accept certain constructions and their behavioural implications. Equally plausibly, one might view economic resources as the chief means of gaining voice. Whether advertising plastics or politicians, rest homes or religion, money will often enable one to gain advantages in voice – in terms of its availability, its beauty, its intensity, its reputation and son. However, the effects of both arms and economic resources must be viewed as derivative. In the final analysis, the effects of force and finance depend on a configuration of shared understandings. The threat of death is of little moment to one who does not place a premium on life; charismatic models fail to inspire action unless one holds the characteristic of the model in high esteem. And whether one values a range of particular characteristics depends on the understandings or intelligibilities hammered out on the forge of daily relationships. Present attention is drawn, then, to the means by which people achieve voice in the common situations of daily life. When I am speaking with colleagues, members of my family or my friends, how am I to achieve voice? On the level of government debate, judicial process, academic argumentation, labour negotiations and so on, how do people achieve power of world construction?

It is my view that one of the chief means by which voice is achieved in such wide-ranging situations is through *conventions of warrant*. That is, people furnish rationales as to why a certain voice (typically their own) is to be granted superiority by offering rationales or justifications. One claims a right to be taken seriously or to be granted superiority on the grounds of specified criteria. But how are such justifications to proceed? On what grounds are they to rest? It is at this point that the relevance of our analysis to contemporary conceptions of self becomes apparent, and we may begin to understand an important means by which mental discourse becomes elaborated.

One of the most compelling and essential means of achieving warrant is through reference to mental events. That is, one may claim superiority of voice by virtue of possessing particular characteristics of mind. One may denigrate others' claims to voice by elucidating their infirmities of the inner region. The selection of the mind as the domain of warrant is a particularly auspicious one. For, as proposed earlier, there is little save social convention that serves to curb or modify propositions about mental events. Thus, to the extent that one can master or extend these conventions, there is little means of demonstrating the shortcomings of any given warrant. By the same token, if an antagonist has succeeded in generating or sustaining warrant for his or her construction of the world, one may extend or elaborate once again the language of the inner region. The new language may be used to discredit the old. In effect, in the attempt to generate warrants for voice, the world of the self is extended and elaborated – its constituents are multiplied, their capacities made known, and their vagaries elucidated.

Let us first illustrate this warranting process at work in common discourse conventions. Shortly we may turn to more heady fare. On the everyday level, for example, one may justifiably make a claim to voice on the grounds of possessing privileged mental representation or experience. 'I know', it may be ventured, 'because I saw it with my own eyes'; 'I heard it'; 'I tasted it'; and so on. On the other hand,'You are ignorant because you have no experience.' Or alternatively, one may claim, 'My position is based on reason; I am logical while your position is irrational.' As a third alternative, 'He should be trusted because he has good intentions; I realize his opponents have good arguments but I don't trust the intentions behind them.' Fourth, 'True understanding comes only from a passionate engagement in life; the unfeeling, uncaring, cool and disengaged are somewhat less than human.' And finally, 'Our common sense of morality demands that we take action; failing to do so we are morally contemptible.' In each of these cases, then, justification for voice rests on the declaration of an allegiance to a different mental process, entity or characteristic: observation, rationality, intention, passion and moral value.

Yet, from the present perspective such warrants are not likely to remain unchallenged. For others to accept them would be to give up their pretensions for voice. Thus, counter-moves are made in the game of mental accounting. 'You may have seen it,' one might counter, 'but you had no real *comprehension* of what you were looking at.' Or, 'Your logic is only misleading sophistry.' Further, 'The road to hell is paved with good intentions', or, 'Calm your feelings, or we shall never be able to make a realistic evaluation.' And 'What makes your moral code better than mine?' With observation, rationality, intention, passion and moral value thus impugned, the stage is set for more extended elaboration. Further distinctions may be drawn in the mental vocabulary as a means of sustaining various forms of warrant. We may begin to discriminate between true observations and those that are biased, between circular and non-circular reasoning, between conscious and unconscious intentions, between the profound passions and the self-deceived, and between more and less well developed forms of moral principle. Further, we may locate ways in which these various mental capacities or processes may be improved. As it is argued, one may learn to think through education in Latin, learn about emotions from psychotherapy, develop a keener sense of moral value through religious participation and so on. In effect, as warrants are developed, disputed and elaborated in defence, the result is a rich and variegated language of the self along with sets of supporting institutions and practices. What we take to be the dimensions of self in the present era may be viewed, in part, as the accumulated armamentarium of centuries of debate. They are symbolic resources, as it were, for making claims in a sea of competing world constructions.

This is further to suggest that self-knowledge is not, as is commonly assumed, the product of in-depth probing of the inner recesses of the psyche. It is not the result of acute sensitivity to the nuances of emotion, motivation, intention and the like. Rather, it is a mastery of discourse – a 'knowing how' rather than a 'knowing that'. This is not at all to subtract from the importance of such discourse. Rather, without grasping the linguistic skills to make the inner world come to life, one ceases to become a full participant – with all the rights that may accrue – in social life. Thus it is not the person who professes a flagging self-esteem, a low level of morale or a guilty conscience who has an 'inadequate' conception of self: each of these forms of self-accounting can be vitally effective, and often enable one to achieve a certain form of power in social life. Rather, it is the inarticulate or linguistically undifferentiated individual who requires attention. Such an individual is simply bereft of the symbolic resources necessary for full social functioning.

Self-elaboration: Precedents and Functions

Although the unfolding of psychological discourse frequently takes place on the level of daily relationships, special power may reside in certain enclaves. Specifically, the culture and/or its various interest groups) may rely on those with well-honed language skills. If the language is to be forcibly reshaped or transformed, then those with a talent for games of language are required. Persons of letters – including poets, historians, journalists, essayists, philosophers, novelists and the like – are of special interest for the study of the diachronic development of self-understanding. It is such groups in particular that have most effectively pushed forward the dialogue of self-construction.

Consider the position of Plato, for example, who at approximately forty years of age founded the Academy at Athens, the first university of Western Europe. His major concern was with educating statesmen. At least one major hope was to see the establishment of a republic in which philosophers were to play a major role in decision-making. At the same time, the then prevailing Sophist philosophy had abnegated a right to warrant. Knowledge for the Sophist was evanescent or non-existent; the primary question was whether one had the skill to argue any side of a question. Thus, if Plato was to have an effective influence over Athenian political life, it was necessary to rescue the concept of knowledge from the shoals of relativism. This was accomplished by the doctrine of pure ideas.

Both pre-Socratic philosophers and Sophists had despaired of the possibility of basing knowledge on experience or appearances of the world. The world of experience was said to be in continuous flux with each observer occupying a different perspective. Plato countered, however, by adding to the compendium of the mind non-material realities – or pure ideas. The true object of knowledge is not, thus, the material order but the internal, eternal, order of the idea. For example, triangles of the material world are mere approximations to the pure idea of triangularity. Knowledge, then, was to be discovered by accessing the inner recesses of the self. Further, such access was to be furnished primarily through the method of dialectic discourse – a method in which only the Socratic philosophers – including Plato - were skilled. The method was one that thereby placed the Platonic philosopher in the position of discerning when knowledge had been achieved and when it was lacking. In effect, with the expansion of the concept of self to include pure ideas, Plato had achieved a powerful warranting device. His Academy had obtained a superior right to voice in Athenian affairs.

A further chapter could be written to demonstrate how Aristotle, in establishing his Lyceum, attempted to wrest warrant from his master by further populating the mind with three forms of soul: the vegetative, the sensitive and the rational. It is the rational soul, in particular, that has the capacity to build up true understanding through induction, deliberation and logic. Additional chapters in the search for warrant would have to include:

1. Thomas Aquinas' elaboration of the concept of the multiple powers of the incorruptible soul – a conception of human selves which lent justification to church authority;
2. Locke's distinction between simple and complex ideas, a distinction that enabled him (along with other Enlightenment thinkers) to argue for the dependence of the mind on sense data; in this contention, warrant was wrenched from the hands of the Church – whose cthno-psychological base rested on the primacy of the spiritual self;
3. Kant's detailing of the *a priori* idea – or the categorical imperatives of mind – a conception that enabled him both to stave off the empiricist threat to the metaphysical warranting of ideas, and to rescue the concept of morality and divinity from the relativism implicit in empiricist doctrines.

Many additional instances could be cited. In each case we would find the concept of self elaborated and extended in the service of achieving voice.

The Emergence of Professional Psychology

One of the most absorbing cases in the history of warranting devices is that of contemporary psychology. At the outset it should be clear that psychologists occupy a privileged, perhaps awesome, position in the process of warrant itself. They have essentially become the official guardians and progenitors of that range of discourse essential for warrant. They possess cultural sanction for ruling on the nature and significance of rationality, the emotions, motives, morals and the like. The critical question thus becomes, What kind of warrant has been privileged within the development of psychological theory? What interest groups or institutions are favoured by such theory and its concomitant warranting practices? Given the position of power, what conceptions have been constructed and why? Although psychologists have hardly spoken with univocal voice, it is interesting to consider the case of the more scientistic wing of the discipline – that which many consider the central core of the discipline. An examination of one of the domain gives reasons for significant pause.

It is the present contention that during the twentieth century most (but not all) major theories within the central core of the discipline have served to justify or reinstate the warranting rationale for scientific psychology itself. To illustrate, early psychophysical work was concerned primarily with charting the relationship between the physical and the psychological realms. One of its more general messages was that there are many more distinctions in the physical realm than sensory processes can detect (a proposition that is itself of indeterminate truth value). However, one is invited by such a contention to conclude that reality may well be misperceived unless the sensory processes are augmented in some way. In particular, laboratory instruments and especially crafted measures of the kind developed by psychologists are essential for proper knowledge to be generated. In the case of learning theories of the 1930s–1960s, the major problem was understanding how the organism adapted to a pre-established environment. Three of the most important conclusions to emerge from such work were that (1) powers of sensory discrimination are required to make proper adjustments to environmental shifts (and to prevent unwarranted generalization), (2) some form of logical calculus is required to develop proper expectancies, hypotheses, interpolations and the like, and (3) the emotions are likely to play a disruptive role in the process, as are values (which bias) and motives (if in a high register). Each conclusion favours the metatheoretical premises that ground the discipline. (For further elaboration, see Gergen and Benack, 1983).

Although Piagetian theory is not fully consistent with the warranting rationale of science, its major programme is one of empiricist justification. The endpoint of genetic epistemology is, after all, the stage of formal operations in which, on the one side, one's cognitive structures have accommodated themselves to the contours of the real world; on the other side, the cognitive process of assimilation is one in which, as Piaget (1952) put it, 'all the given data of experience [are incorporated] within its framework' (p. 6). Again, experience and cognition are united in their favourable or 'true' appraisals of the world. Finally, with respect to contemporary cognitive theory, there are inconsistencies, but we again locate a sub-text of self-justification. The cognitive category, schema or prototype is essentially a carry-over from the idealist concern with rational essence (Graumann and Sommer, 1983). Further, if such constructs are to be adaptive, they require the activation of attentional processes – the equivalent of accurate experience in the positivist tradition. As George Kelly (1955) realized many years ago, this image of human functioning (in which category systems increasingly match the contours of reality) is precisely the image of the good scientist.

Many additional lines of enquiry could be added in illustration – psychophysics from its inception to the present, perceptual learning, expectancy value formulations, traditional theories of memory and Kelly's attribution theory are all exemplary. In each case, the world is related systematically to psychological process and the organism's capacity for survival is thereby enhanced. There are exceptions to this tendency – psychoanalytic theory, dialectic theory and drama-turgical theory are among them. However, it is interesting to note that none of the latter plays a dominant role within the experimental tradition. This is largely so because the suppositions on which they are based would, if extended, undermine the warrant of psychology as a science.[1]

Much more could be said about these matters – in both extenu-ation and mitigation. However, we are now compelled to draw conclusions. One can scarcely fault the discipline of psychology for using its investigations to gird its own loins. Warrants for voice are required if one is to be heard, and the discipline's capacity to employ strong warrant to gain voice, and voice to fortify its warrant, must be viewed as an epitome of self-sustaining efficacy. Yet, one must raise the painful question of the social utility of the discipline if its major goal is that of sustaining itself. Of what value to the culture is an institution that is resistant to entering reciprocally benefiting relationships with others? There must be alternative possibilities for the discipline, and indeed there are. Psychological discourse is employed in multiple ways in social relationships. The range, complexity and flexibility of this discourse furnishes an essential basis for what may be accomplished in such relationships – whether they prosper or perish, enrich or exploit, bolster or belittle. Thus, if psychology is to fulfil its avowed role of benefiting humankind, the doors should be opened to multiplicity in perspective. Rather than singing the same old refrain decade after decade (albeit in different words), a premium should be placed on new songs.

I do not believe that the discipline will risk its status in departing from its grounding epistemology. Psychology's traditional warrants have undergone substantial deterioration in the intellectual world more generally. The dialogue has moved on, and it seems only a matter of time before 'experience' and 'reason' will be fossils of an earlier era. For the benefit of both the profession and the culture more generally, we should welcome innovative, invigorating and emancipatory alternatives in the construction of contemporary selves.

Note

1. The cognitive movement is an interesting case in this respect, for its present emphasis on 'top-down' processing also threatens the warrant of the sciences. If cognition operates to sustain itself, then so do psychologists. And if the latter is true, then on what grounds should the pronouncements of the profession be trusted?

References

Austin, J. (1962) *How to Do Things with Words*. Cambridge, MA: Harvard University Press.

Gergen, K.J. (1982) *Toward Transformation in Social Knowledge*. New York: Springer-Verlag.

Gergen, K.J. (1984) 'Aggression as Discourse', in A. Mummendey (ed.), *The Social Psychology of Aggression*. Heidelberg: Springer-Verlag.

Gergen, K.J. (1985) 'Social Pragmatics and the Origins of Psychological Discourse', in K.J. Gergen and K.E. Davis (eds), *The Social Construction of the Person*. New York: Springer-Verlag.

Gergen, K. (1986) Correspondence vs. Autonomy in the Language of Understanding Human Action', in D. Fiske and R. Shweder (eds), *Pluralism and Subjectivity in Social Science*. Chicago: University of Chicago Press.

Gergen, K.J. and S. Benack, (1983) Metatheoretical Influences on Conceptions of Human Development, in M. Lewin (ed.), *In the Shadow of the Past: Psychology Portrays the Sexes*. Heidelberg: Springer-Verlag.

Goldman, A.I. (1986) *Epistemology and Cognition*. Cambridge MA: Harvard University Press.

Graumann, K. and M. Sommer (1983) 'Schema and Inference: Models and Cognitive Social Psychology', in J. Royce and L. Mas (eds), *Annals of Theoretical Psychology*, Vol. 1. New York: Plenum Press.

Green, T.N. (1883) *Prolegomena to Ethics*. Oxford: Clarendon Press.

Hampden-Turner, C. (1970) *Radical Man: The Process of Psycho-social Development*. Cambridge, MA: Schenkman.

Hollis, M. (1977) *Models of Man*. London: Cambridge University Press.

Kelly, G. (1955) *The Psychology of Personal Constructs*. New York: W.W. Norton.

Koch, S. (1959) Epilogue, in S. Koch (ed.), *Psychology: A Study of a Science*, Vol. III. New York: McGraw-Hill.

Mandelbaum, M. (1971) *History, Man and Reason*. Baltimore: Johns Hopkins University Press.

Nisbett, R. and L. Ross (1980) *Human Inference: Strategies and Shortcomings of Social Judgment*. Englewood Cliffs, NJ: Prentice-Hall.

Piaget, J. (1952) *The Origins of Intelligence in Children*. New York: W.W. Norton.

Rosaldo, M. (1980) *Knowledge and Passion: Ilongot Notions of Self and Social Life*. Cambridge: Cambridge University Press.

Sampson, E.E. (1981) 'Cognitive Psychology', *American Psychologist*, 36: 730–43.

Shotter, J. (1975) *Images of Man in Psychological Research*. London: Methuen.

Wittgenstein, L. (1953) *Philosophical Investigations*, trans. G. Anscombe. New York: Macmillan.

PART II

THE DISCURSIVE CONSTRUCTION OF IDENTITIES

6
Liberal Humanism as an Ideology of Social Control: The Regulation of Lesbian Identities

Celia Kitzinger

'Identity', says the radical lesbian feminist Jill Johnston (1973), 'is what you can say you are according to what they say you can be.' In her analysis, identities are not the freely created products of introspection, or the unproblematic reflections of the private sanctum of the 'inner self', but are conceived within certain ideological frameworks constructed by the dominant (patriarchal) social order to maintain its own interests. Identities, in this analysis, are profoundly political, both in their origins and in their implications. Members of oppressed and socially marginalized groups have, for a long time, recognized the ways in which the accounts we give of ourselves can serve to reproduce and legitimate the very social order that oppresses us. Recent social psychological theory reiterates this same insight:

> Our ways of accounting for ourselves, our accounting practices, work both to create and maintain a certain pattern of social relations, a social order, *and* to constitute us as beings able to reproduce that order in all of our practical activities. (Shotter, 1985)

Departing from psychology's traditional interest in identity as a personal and 'subjective' account of the self (to be compared with the 'objective' account of the person's self as assessed by the psychologist), research interest within a social constructionist framework is focused not on the 'accuracy' of the identity account, but on the social and political functions it serves. Whereas traditional psychology has conceptualized the identity account as the exclusive property of the individual who provides it, as inextricably bound up with and produced in the context of that

person's private needs and personal problems, research within the
new theoretical framework proposed here suggests that the origins
of accounts might be more readily located in their sociocultural
and political contexts. This chapter illustrates the value of this
thesis in researching lesbian identities.

Lesbian identities first emerged, in the late nineteenth and
early twentieth centuries, in the social and political context of
the first wave of feminism. Before the turn of the century, with
the early sexological invention of the lesbian as a special 'type' of
person, defined by a specific, potentially describable 'essence', a
lesbian identity was not possible: women had, of course, enjoyed
passionate sexual and loving relationships with each other, but such
relationships had no particular implications for identity (Faderman,
1980). Historians (e.g. Faderman, 1980; Jeffreys, 1982) have argued
that the invention of lesbianism as an identity took place as a
reaction to women's developing analysis of sexuality as a major
site of political struggle. Many women of the time were advocating
the withdrawal of women from heterosexuality: 'there can be no
mating', said Christabel Pankhurst in 1913 (quoted in Jeffreys,
1982), 'between the spiritually developed women of this new day
and men who, in thought and conduct with regard to sex matters,
are their inferiors': the slogan, 'Votes for Women and Chastity for
Men' (Pankhurst, 1913; quoted in Weeks, 1981, p. 164) summarized
their message. Early sexology responded to this political attack on
two fronts: through the attempt to woo women back into heterosexuality through the orchestration of female sexual pleasure by
improved male sexual technique, and through the pathologization
of lesbianism. Overwhelmingly, these early sexological formulations
imputed pathology to the lesbian, and this remained the dominant
model in social scientific and medical texts until the mid-1970s.

The construction of lesbianism as pathology thus provided, until
recently, the major resource upon which lesbians could draw in
explaining their 'sexual orientation' to themselves and others. In
fact, with rare exceptions, this was the only explanation considered
acceptable, and lesbians offering alternative accounts were likely
to find them 'ironicized' (Pollner, 1975) – dismissed or faulted
in favour of a more prestigious social scientific interpretation of
the 'real' underlying causes and concomitants of lesbianism. One
researcher, for example, describes the homosexual's belief that she
or he is not sick as 'a face-saving rationalization' (Socarides, 1972),
and another writer comments on an interviewee, 'like many other
lesbians she keeps up a facade, but beneath it lurks the abyss of
self-destructive feelings' (Wolff, 1971, p. 113). The construction of
lesbianism as pathology thus possessed a 'morally coercive' (Shotter,

1985, p. 168) quality: it served to structure lesbians' experience of themselves such that lesbianism was removed from the political arena and relocated in the domain of personal pathology.

Since the mid-1970s, however, alternative modes of discourse have been developed within a liberal humanistic perspective which offer alternative texts of identity from which lesbians can fashion legitimating accounts. These liberal humanistic texts de-pathologize lesbianism, presenting it as a normal, natural and healthy sexual preference or choice of life-styles, and are widely applauded within the gay movement. However, in this chapter I argue that, while the selective application of aspects of the dominant liberal humanistic construction serves the purposes of the lesbian by assuring her a relative social acceptability, it also, by the same token, serves the purposes of the dominant order by reinforcing and validating its moral rhetoric. As I will show below, liberal humanistic accounts of lesbianism which appeal to widely accepted Western social norms and values (the centrality of romantic love, the importance of personal happiness) serve, ironically, to buttress those very ideologies and social structures undermined by lesbian reality. Such identities are actively encouraged and promoted by social science, while identities involving challenge and counter-definition (e.g. political lesbian–feminist) are discredited and suppressed.

Liberal Humanism: Denying our Differences

Contemporary liberal humanistic ideology provides an elaborate repertoire of self-descriptive discourse for, and rhetoric about, members of oppressed and socially marginalized groups. As it relates to lesbianism, this ideology finds expression, in its indigenous or folk form, in sentiments such as:

If two people really love each other, then it shouldn't matter whether they are a woman and a man, or two women.

People should not be pigeonholed just according to their sexual orientation.

If through lesbianism a woman becomes a truly happy and fulfilled human being, then obviously lesbianism is what's right for *her*.

What people do in bed is their own business.

Lesbians shouldn't hide away in ghettos, mixing only with their own kind and narrowly defining themselves as nothing but lesbian. Only by being *people* first and foremost can they explore all that life has to offer, and achieve their full potentials as human beings.

Together, notions such as these constitute a coherent ideological framework – characterized here as 'liberal humanistic' – which stresses the essential personhood of the lesbian and the relatively trivial nature of her sexual preference: the liberal–humanist rejects classifications that pigeonhole people into labelled boxes and emphasizes that the lesbian should not be segregated as an alien species, but accepted as part of humanity in all its rich variety.

Elaborated versions of this ideology are presented in much of the popularized literature dealing with homosexuality (especially in the context of protest against recent anti-gay legislation in the UK (Kitzinger, 1988)), and have been given detailed legitimation by the bulk of social science research over the last decade and a half. Ever since Kinsey's (1953) famous invention of the 'heterosexual–homosexual continuum', and corresponding recognition of people's alleged 'bisexual potential', an increasing number of major researchers have tended towards this same liberal humanistic approach of dissolving any specific differences between lesbian and heterosexual women. Gagnon and Simon (1973) de-emphasize specific sexual acts and draw attention to the basic normality and 'femininity' of the lesbian, suggesting that she possesses 'a conformity greater than deviance'. Bell and Weinberg (1978) argue that there are more differences among lesbians than between lesbian and heterosexual women, and coin the word 'homosexualities' (plural) to emphasize our heterogeneity. And Masters and Johnson's (1979) report argues that we are not even very different from heterosexuals in our sexual expression. As one cynical commentator puts it,

> It reports that homosexual men and women are basically just like heterosexual men and women: they have the same genital apparatus, the apparatus functions according to the same physiological rules, and the things they do to each other sexually are not really different from the things that nice people do; therefore, they are just folks, and one can be nice to them. (Cooper, 1980, p. 288)

It is, then, within the context of this pervasive liberal humanistic ideology, emanating from both academic and folk theorizing, that contemporary lesbian identities are constructed.

No longer seeing themselves exclusively as the 'miserable sinners' and 'hapless cripples' of the early decades of this century, and no longer dependent solely on novels like *The Well of Loneliness* ('God's cruel; He let us get flawed in the making': Hall, 1928, p. 204), or on psychoanalytic formulations like those of Bieber (1971), Caprio (1955) and Socarides (1965), who variously presented the lesbian as the product of a disturbed upbringing, suffering from unresolved castration anxiety or oedipal conflicts, pursuing other women in a futile attempt to substitute a clitoris for a nipple as a result of their unresolved weaning problems, many lesbians today are drawing on, adapting and embellishing liberal humanistic discourse in constructing a text for their own identities as lesbians. On the whole, this has been seen as a positive development, and liberal humanism is conceptualized – by both those who do and many of those who do not share its beliefs (cf. Kitzinger, 1987) – as a 'favourable' or 'unprejudiced' view of lesbianism.

The argument of this chapter, however, is to repeat it once again, that liberal humanistic identities are actively promoted because they reflect a socially sedimented ideology which functions as an instrument of social control, depoliticizing lesbianism, and nihilating its threat to the reified institutions of the dominant moral and social order. Such lesbian identities are actively encouraged and promoted by representatives of the dominant order because they reinforce and validate its moral rhetoric.

Promoting the Liberal Humanistic Text:
Homophobia and the Well Adjusted Lesbian

The suggestion that social science might function to legitimate and support status quo definitions of reality is hardly a new one. The use of the ideology of mental illness as an instrument of social control has been widely documented, and many researchers have pointed to the political utility of assigning a 'sick' identity to those who threaten to disrupt the established order (Szasz, 1970; Pearson, 1975). But researchers in the liberal humanistic mould continue to invoke concepts of 'sickness' and 'health' to support and justify their own version of lesbianism, resorting to the familiar technique (cf. Gergen, 1973) of arguing that one's mental health depends on sharing the (current) beliefs of the social scientist. The two main techniques through which this is accomplished in research on homosexuality are the invention of 'homophobia' – a 'severe disturbance' (Freedman, 1978, p. 320) characterized by 'an irrational, persistent fear or dread of homosexuals' (MacDonald, 1976) – and the invention of the 'well adjusted' lesbian.

'Homophobia' scales, dozens of which have been developed over the last decade or so – modelled on early 'anti-semitism' and 'racism' scales – are scored in such a way that the mentally healthy person must present herself or himself as conforming to the tenets of liberal humanistic psychology. She or he must believe that homosexuals are basically just the same as heterosexuals, that we should be permitted to participate fully in all the institutions of the dominant culture, and that we do not constitute any threat to that culture. The responses marked below are all penalized by a 'homophobia' point (or equivalent), and the 'homophobe' is discovered to be authoritarian (Smith, 1971; MacDonald and Games, 1974), guilt-ridden (Dunbar et al., 1973), dogmatic (Hood, 1973), status-conscious (Smith, 1971) and sexually rigid (Minnigerode, 1976).

	Yes/ Agree	No/ Disagree
Homosexuals are just like everyone else, they simply choose an alternative lifestyle (Hansen, 1982).		x
The basic difference between homosexuals and other people is only in their sexual behaviour (cf. Dannecker, 1981).		x
A person's sexual orientation is a totally neutral point upon which to judge his or her ability to function in any situation (Thompson and Fishburn, 1977).		x
A homosexual could make as good a president as a heterosexual (Lumby, 1976).		x
Homosexuals should not hold high government offices (Hansen, 1982).	x	
Homosexual 'marriages' should be officially recognized (Dunbar et al., 1973).		x
It would be beneficial to society to recognize homosexuality as normal (Larsen et al., 1980).		x
If laws against homosexuality were eliminated, the proportion of homosexuals in the population would probably remain about the same (Smith, 1971).		x
Homosexuality endangers the institution of the family (Larsen et al., 1980).	x	

The invention of the 'well adjusted' lesbian fulfils the same function of promoting liberal humanistic beliefs as the only 'mentally healthy' or 'developmentally mature' constituents of identity. Liberal humanistic psychologists have constructed a variety of models of gay and lesbian identity development (Cass, 1979; Coleman, 1982; Minton and McDonald, 1984), all of which share an operational definition of 'maturity' (as represented by the highest developmental stage in their hierarchical models) based on the tenets of liberal humanistic ideology. In such models, individuals following the proper developmental pattern work through the early stage of identification with the aggressor, through subsequent intermediary stages, to achieve the dizzy heights of liberal humanistic self-conception, in which the alleged deviance ceases to be of any great importance in the person's life and she or he becomes a creative, loving, self-actualizing human being, integrated into and contributing to the wider society generally.

Clearly, then, at least part of contemporary psychological writing on lesbianism is overtly engaged in promotional work on behalf of liberal humanistic ideology or narrative: people (whether heterosexual or not) who account for lesbianism in terms compatible with this ideology are rewarded by being described as 'well adjusted' or 'non-prejudiced' people who have attained the highest level of consciousness.

In examining *why* these accounts are so rewarded, I will present in some detail two particular liberal humanistic accounts of lesbianism – one relying on notions of romantic love, the other on concepts of self-actualization and personal happiness – both of which I have documented (in both lesbians and heterosexuals) through interview and Q-methodology (Kitzinger, 1987).

'True Love': A Liberal Humanistic Text for Lesbian Identity

One common lesbian identity, clearly conceived within this liberal humanistic framework, relies on the invocation of the culturally approved rhetoric of romantic love:

> 'I just fell in love with her, and it seemed that if I really loved someone that deeply and that passionately, then nothing we did together could really be wrong.' (From tape-recorded interview)

In the terms of the dominant order of Western culture, the rhetoric of romantic love offers a powerful source of justification and provides a legitimating context to sexual activity. If two people really love each other, then in an important sense their actions are beyond moral censure – at worst exonerated as 'crimes passionels'.

The extent to which the rhetoric of romantic love 'belongs' to the dominant culture is demonstrated in the frequency with which lesbianism is judged in these terms: 'true love' is depicted as a moral imperative, the overwhelming effects of which may excuse, but the incapacity for which must condemn, homosexuals and their relationships. Those professionals who present lesbianism as a sickness are at pains to deny the homosexual's ability to form loving relationships: lesbian liaisons are 'inherently self-limiting' (Moberly, 1983, p. 84); they 'do not contribute to the individual's need for stability and love' (Wilbur, 1965, p. 281); and, 'although basic sexual urges may be fulfilled to varying degrees, a feeling of complete attainment of romantic longings probably never occurs' (Bieber, 1971).

In contrast, liberal apologists draw on the *same* rhetoric of romantic love to argue the basic equality or isomorphism of heterosexual and homosexual relationships:

> The essence of a committed relationship is the same whether the union is between two men, two women, or a man and a woman ... Love and commitment transcend sexual orientation. (Mendola, 1980)

And Bell and Weinberg (1978) describe five 'types' of homosexual, but confer their scientific approval on those they label 'close-coupled', who approximate to the heterosexual ideal of a happy marriage: they have tastefully furnished homes, radiate warmth, provide the interviewer with freshly baked chocolate chip cookies, and are discovered to have 'superior adjustment', being the 'least depressed or lonely' and the 'happiest' of all homosexual types.

Many of the lesbian (but few of the heterosexual) accounts generated within the framework of this 'true love' ideology rely on the notion that one 'falls in love' with 'a person not a gender': a lesbian is a woman who is 'in love with a person who *happens* to be a women' – a variation on love's theme. This account has been well documented. Within lesbian feminist literature, Cartledge and Hemmings (1982) have described a process they call 'Cupid's Dart (the romantic conversion)', which largely parallels the pair-bonding theme presented here; and Johnston (1973, p. 92) describes 'the dark ages of our political consciousness', when 'the person you were involved with was first and foremost a person or special love object with no certain significance as to gender so that it if happened to be a woman it could as well be a man the next time if the right *person* came along.'

In a third twist, this same rhetoric of romantic love can, of course, also be used to assert the *superiority* of lesbianism by arguing, for example, that, because of social inequalities between men and women, 'the conditions for learning to love fully and without fear are at present met only in a homosexual setting' (Kelly, 1972).

However, whether one argues that lesbianism is *inferior* to heterosexuality because true love must for ever elude us, that it is *superior* to heterosexuality because only for us is 'true love' possible, or that lesbianism and heterosexuality are *equal* in so far as either can yield deeply loving and committed relationships, the debate is still conducted within the terms laid down by the dominant value system of Western culture. In applying the 'true love' rhetoric to lesbianism, a sort of 'romantic androgyny' is often postulated, which refuses to acknowledge differences between heterosexual and homosexual relationships; and 'falling in love' is presented as the product of inner drives, needs and passions, independent of a social control.

From the perspective of the dominant order, this account of lesbianism is useful in that it affirms the pervasive moral rhetoric of romantic love fundamental to the official morality, which serves to remove personal relationships from the political arena, and to legitimate the institution of marriage. The effect of this ideology is to privatize sexual–romantic love as a kind of opium of the masses.

> [T]he narrow enclave of the nuclear family serves as a macrosocially innocuous 'play area', in which the individual can safely exercise his [sic] world-building proclivities without upsetting any of the important social, economic and political applecarts ... The marital adventure can be relied upon to absorb a large amount of energy that might otherwise be expended more dangerously. The ideological themes of familism, romantic love, sexual expression, maturity and social adjustment ... function to legitimate this enterprise. (Berger and Kellner, 1964)

An account of lesbianism in terms of romantic love, then, serves the purposes of the lesbian in that it enables her to present her 'deviant' experience in conformity with the idiom of the dominant culture, relating her own experience to that presumed to be enjoyed by heterosexuals, and presenting her lesbianism in a morally unimpeachable light. The *irony* of this account of lesbianism (and its usefulness to the dominant order) is that the lesbian achieves (in some measure) assimilation into the dominant culture from which she deviates by articulating its morality and, paradoxically, providing evidence of its wide scope and applicability: the ideology of romantic love is seen to explain the experience even of those who are, in theory, least committed to upholding the official ideology of which it forms a part. In this way, lesbianism is converted from an embarrassment for to a vindication of the dominant morality, and the lesbian reinforces the very system that oppresses her.

'True Happiness': A Liberal Humanistic Text for Lesbian Identity

The second liberal humanistic lesbian identity I want to discuss can be characterized as a laywomen's version of Self Theory and the pursuit of positive psychological health (cf. Jahoda, 1958; Rogers, 1959; Maslow, 1962). In this account, lesbianism is presented as an arena for the flowering of womynhood, personal growth and self-actualization: through lesbianism, a woman can 'discover her true self', 'get in touch with her own feelings' and become a more fulfilled and joyous human being:

> 'To me it's been a flowering of my own autonomy and independence ...
> For me being a lesbian really is a positive experience – freedom, happiness, peace with myself, everything!' (From tape-recorded interview)

Other women have written of how, through lesbianism, 'I am reclaiming my true womynhood, learning to truly know and love myself and other wimmin'(Toll, 1980, p. 29); coming out as lesbian, 'I am whole, a rediscovered self' (Faye, 1980, p. 178).

The ideology of true happiness and self-fulfilment, which became socially sedimented during the decade 1965-75, and which is well represented in the wide selection of glossy American psychology textbooks of that era, with titles like *The Way to Fulfillment: Psychological Techniques* (Buhler, 1971) or *Growth of Personal Awareness: A Reader in Psychology* (Stricker and Merbaum, 1973) – showing loving couples running through fields of daisies, or silhouetted against a setting sun, or naked children playing on seashores – has acquired considerable socially persuasive power as a justification for otherwise questionable behaviour.

Social scientists in the traditional model emphasize that the lesbian 'leads a lonely, difficult and unhappy life' (Kenyon, 1978, p. 112) of 'frustration and tragedy' (West, 1968, p. 261), troubled by all the 'personal confusion, anguish, and fruitless search for love which may be the products of maldevelopment' (Pattison, 1974); 'agony, sorrow, tragedy, fear and guilt of both conscious and unconscious nature pervades the homosexual's life' (Socarides, 1972). One psychologist claims that, 'despite propaganda to the contrary, there is such thing as a well-adjusted, happy homosexual' (Kriegman, 1969).

Liberal apologists have increasingly argued the contrary, and a spate of psychological testing in the early 1970s revealed lesbians to be significantly less neurotic than heterosexual women (Wilson and Greene, 1971), possessing more 'inner direction' and 'spontaneity' (Freedman, 1971, p. 78), 'goal direction' and 'self-acceptance' (Siegelman, 1972). Just as some people have extended the 'true love' justification to argue that, in a patriarchal society, it is possible *only* between women, so others have extended the 'true happiness' position to claim, for similar reasons, that this can best be attained through lesbianism. One psychologist argues that 'homosexuals may be healthier than straights' because their sexual 'orientation' encourages them to 'centre' ('discover and live according to their own values'), and to enjoy a freer sexuality (Freedman, 1975).

However, whether one argues *for* lesbianism on the grounds that it can supply true happiness and inner peace, or *against* lesbianism on the grounds that *no* lesbian can be truly happy and fulfilled, the debate remains firmly within the framework of the liberal humanistic discourse prescribed by the dominant value system. The 'self-fulfilment and inner peace' account supports a fundamental aspect of the dominant ideology – the focus on personal change as a substitute for political change. Lesbianism, in this account, is a product sold on the basis of what it is supposed to offer the individual, and, like psychodrama, encounter groups, rebirthing therapy and the like, it is, in Cohen and Taylor's (1976, p. 103) words, 'deliberately directed towards accommodation rather than resistance to paramount reality'. As Schur puts it,

> [S]elf awareness is the new panacea. Across the country, Americans are frantically trying to 'get in touch' with themselves, to learn how to 'relate' better, and to stave off outer turmoil by achieving inner peace. ... While the movement provides middle-class consumers with an attractive new product, attention is diverted away from the more serious problems that plague our society – poverty, racism, environmental decay, crime, widespread corporate and governmental fraud. (Schur, 1976, pp. 1, 8)

Achieving inner peace surrounded by this society as it is is a conformist rather than a revolutionary goal. In representing lesbianism as a route to perfect bliss and inner harmony, lesbianism becomes a private solution to an individual malaise.

The 'true happiness' account, like the 'true love' account, simply reverses the traditional privatized definitions of the dominant order, while maintaining their validity as criteria of evaluation.

The Radical Feminist Challenge: A Politicized Text

What these liberal identities have in common – and this they share with the traditional version of lesbianism as a form of mental illness – is their evasion of the political implications of the deviant experience: where the traditional account translates lesbianism into personal pathology, liberal humanism translates it into a private sexual orientation, or a personal quest for 'true love' or 'true happiness'. In these accounts, lesbianism is depoliticized through the creation of a 'private' sphere, an atomized 'personal' zone supposedly unconnected to the public and political, in which 'individual difference' can be located and, thereby, made acceptable. And these liberal accounts accept and thereby reinforce the dominant culture's moral postulates.

> Society can rely on those who are the least accepted as normal members, the least rewarded by the pleasures of easy social intercourse with others, to provide a statement, clarification and tribute to the inward being of every man [sic]. The more a stigmatised individual deviates from the norm, the more wonderfully he [sic] may have to express possession of the standard subjective self if he is to convince others that he possesses it, and the more they may demand that he provide them with a model of what an ordinary person is supposed to feel about himself [sic]. (Goffman, 1963, p. 41)

In contrast to this apparent promotion of 'liberal' self-descriptive discourse, *radical* deviant versions of reality, such as the political lesbian–feminist account, are discredited or suppressed. The political lesbian–feminist account is generally unpalatable because it removes lesbianism from the personal zone to which it has been assigned and thrusts it back into the political arena.

In this account, the socially constructed nature of sexuality is emphasized, and it is argued that, in a patriarchal society, heterosexuality is instituted for the benefit of those who 'at every level' control it, namely men:

> The heterosexual couple is the basic unit of male supremacy. In it each individual woman comes under the control of an individual man. It is more efficient by far than keeping women in ghettos, camps or even sheds at the bottom of the garden. In the couple, love and sex are used to obscure the realities of oppression, to prevent women identifying with each other in order to revolt, and from identifying 'their' man as part of the enemy. Any woman who takes part in a heterosexual couple helps to shore up male supremacy by making its foundations stronger. (Leeds Revolutionary Feminist Group, 1981, p. 6)

On this basis, it is claimed that 'serious feminists have no choice but to abandon heterosexuality' (Leeds Revolutionary Feminist Group, 1981, p. 5). In this account, then, lesbianism is a blow against the patriarchy and is justifiable (indeed, necessary) in these terms: the commonsense, taken-for-granted (patriarchally defined), notions on which the liberal accounts base their defence of lesbianism are undermined. Instead of accepting the concepts of 'natural' and 'unnatural' and seeking only to change their scope and applicability, the political lesbian–feminist challenges the very validity of these concepts; and, rather than acknowledging the centrality of personal happiness and romantic love as guiding principles for action, she questions the moral and political implications of giving priority to such individualistic goals. Where a liberal account might describe lesbianism as a *sexual orientation*, this account discusses the *socially constructed* nature of sexuality. Where a liberal account might offer lesbianism as a source of true love, this account examines the role of romantic love, coupledom and monogamy in the oppression of women. Where a liberal account might promise personal fulfilment through lesbianism, this account places the goal of individual happiness secondary to the political goals of women's liberation.

The various feminist critiques of romantic love, for example – developed by, among others, Greer (1970), Firestone (1971), Johnston (1973) and Lewis (1982) – have often presented romantic love as individualistic, objectifying and 'tied firmly at the far end to the great institution of marriage which helps to keep the cogs of society ticking over' (Goodison, 1983, p. 48): 'Love, perhaps even more than childbearing, is the pivot of women's oppression today', asserts Firestone (1971), adding that 'the panic felt at any threat to love is a good clue to its political significance.' And the political lesbian–feminist emphasizes that 'lesbianism is a necessary political choice, part of the tactics of our struggle, not a passport to paradise' (Leeds Revolutionary Feminist Group, 1981).

It is precisely this rejection of socially sedimented notions that generates so much incomprehension of, and hostility to, the political lesbian account, from both heterosexual social scientists and 'assimilated' lesbians manifesting a concern with in-group purification. The political lesbian–feminist is dismissed as a 'pseudolesbian' (Defries, 1976), suffering from 'a chronic attitude of resentment against society' (Scharfelter, 1980) and adhering to 'a latter-day lesbian fascism' (Lewis, 1979, p. 175). She has a 'ghetto mentality' (Kenyon, 1978, p. 111) and exhibits an 'obsessive concern' with her 'problem', which, West (1968, p. 55) adds, 'recalls the obsessive concern of Jews and Negroes with race and colour'. And in both of the hierarchical models of identity mentioned above, the radical, political, version takes second place to the liberal humanistic account.

Conclusions

The argument of this chapter has been, in general, that identities are not primarily the private property of individuals but are social constructions, suppressed and promoted in accordance with the political interests of the dominant social order. In particular, I have argued that the oppressed are actively encouraged to construct identities that reaffirm the basic validity of this dominant moral order, and

I have demonstrated how liberal humanistic discourse serves this purpose and is widely promoted, while political lesbian or radical feminist accounts, which explicitly challenge existing social institutions and ideologies, are discredited and suppressed. Liberalism, which, as Gouldner (1968) argues, 'is not simply the conscientious and liberating faith of isolated individuals [but] verges on being an official ideology of wide sectors of the American university community as well as broader strata of American life', functions as an instrument of social control, dictating what identities are and are not appropriate for the oppressed (on the basis of what is convenient in maintaining the status quo), and rewarding, with a limited form of social acceptance, those members of the oppressed who present self-descriptive discourse in conformity with this ideology.

References

Bell, A.P. and M.S. Weinberg (1978) *Homosexualities: A Study of Diversity Among Homosexual Men and Women*. London: Mitchell Beazley.

Berger, P. and J. Kellner (1964) 'Marriage and the Construction of Reality: An Exercise in the Microsociology of Knowledge', *Diogenes*, 4: 1–24.

Berne, E. (1968) *A Layman's (sic) Guide to Psychiatry and Psychoanalysis*. Harmondsworth: Penguin.

Bieber, I. (1971) 'Speaking Frankly on a Once Taboo Subject', in R.V. Guthrie (ed.), *Psychology in the World Today: An Interdisciplinary Approach* (2nd edn). Reading, MA: Addison-Wesley.

Blumstein, P.E. et al. (1974) 'The Honoring of Accounts', *American Sociological Review*, 39: 551-66.

Brown, S.R. (1980) *Political Subjectivity: Applications of Q Methodology in Political Science*. New Haven and London: Yale University Press.

Buhler, C. (1971) *The Way to Fulfillment: Psychological Techniques*. New York: Hawthorn Books.

Caprio, F.S. (1955) *Variations in Sexual Behavior*. New York: Grove Press.

Cartledge, S. and S. Hemmings, (1982) 'How Did We Get This Way?' in M. Rowe (ed.), *Spare Rib Reader*. Harmondsworth: Penguin.

Cass, V. (1979) 'Homosexual Identity Formation: A Theoretical Model', *Journal of Homosexuality*, 3(3); 219–35.

Cohen, S. and L. Taylor (1976) *Escape Attempts: The Theory and Practice of Resistance to Everyday Life*. Harmondsworth: Penguin.

Coleman, E. (1982) 'Developmental Stages of the Coming-Out Process', *American Behavioral Scientist*, 25(4): 426–82.

Cooper, A.M. (1980) 'Homosexuality in Perspective', in C.R. Stimpson and E.S. Person (eds), *Women: Sex and Sexuality*. Chicago and London: University of Chicago Press.

Dannecker, M. (1981) *Theories of Homosexuality*. London: Gay Men's Press.

Defries, Z. (1976) 'Pseudohomosexuality in Feminist Students', *American Journal of Psychiatry*, 133(4): 400–4.

Dunbar, J., M. Brown and D.M. Amoroso (1973) 'Some Correlates of Attitudes

96   *The discursive construction of identities*

toward Homosexuality', *Journal of Social Psychology*, 89: 271–9.

Faderman, L. (1980) *Surpassing the Love of Men*. London: Junction Books.

Faye, C. (1980) 'Come Again', in S.J. Wolfe and J.P. Stanley (eds), *The Coming Out Stories*, Watertown, MA: Persephone Press.

Firestone, S. (1971) *The Dialectic of Sex*. New York: Meridian.

Freedman, M. (1971) *Homosexuality and Psychological Functioning*. Belmont, CA: Brooks/Cole.

Freedman, M. (1975) 'Homosexuals may be Healthier than Straights', *Psychology Today*, 8: 28–32.

Freedman, M. (1978) 'Towards a Gay Psychology', in L. Crew (ed.), *The Gay Academic*. Palm Springs, CA: ETC Publications.

Gagnon, J.H. and W. Simon (1973) *Sexual Conduct: The Social Sources of Human Sexuality*. Chicago: Aldine Press.

Gergen, K.J. (1973) 'Social Psychology as History', *Journal of Personality and Social Psychology*, 26: 309–20.

Goffman, E. (1961) *Asylums*. Harmondsworth: Penguin.

Goffman, E. (1963) *Stigma: Notes on the Management of Spoiled Identity*. Harmondsworth: Penguin.

Goodison, L. (1983) 'Really Being in Love Means Wanting to Live in a Different World', in S. Cartledge and J. Ryan (eds), *Sex and Love: New Thoughts on Old Contradictions*. London: Women's Press.

Gouldner, A. (1968) 'The Sociologist as Partisan: Sociology and the Welfare State', *American Sociologist*, 3: 103–16.

Greer, G. (1970) *The Female Eunuch*. London: Paladin.

Hall, R. (1928) *The Well of Loneliness*. Reprinted, 1981. New York: Bard Avon Books.

Hall, W.S., W.E. Cross and R. Freedle (1975) 'Stages in the Development of Black Awareness', in E. Krupat (ed.), *Psychology is Social: Readings and Conversations in Social Psychology*. Glenview, IL: Scott, Foresman.

Hansen, G.L. (1982) 'Measuring Prejudice against Homosexuality (Homosexism) among College Students: A New Scale', *Journal of Social Psychology*, 117: 233-6.

Hood, R.W. (1973) 'Dogmatism and Opinions about Mental Illness', *Psychological Reports*, 32: 1283–90.

Jahoda, M. (1958) *Current Concepts of Positive Health*. New York: Basic Books.

Jeffreys, S. (1982) '"Free from all Uninvited Touch of Man": Women's Campaigns around Sexuality, 1880–1914', *Women's Studies International Forum*, 5: 629–45.

Johnston, J. (1973) *Lesbian Nation: The Feminist Solution*. New York: Simon and Schuster.

Kelly, J. (1972) 'Sister Love: An Exploration of the Need for Homosexual Experience', *The Family Coordinator*, October: 473–5.

Kenyon, F.E. (1978) *Overcoming Common Problems: Sex*. London: Sheldon Press.

Kinsey, A.C. et al. (1953) *Sexual Behaviour in the Human Female*. Philadelphia: W.B. Saunders.

Kitzinger, C. (1987) *The Social Construction of Lesbianism*. London: Sage.

Kitzinger, C. (1988) 'Causes and Choice', *Lesbianism and Gay Socialist*, issue 15.

Kriegman, G. (1969) 'Homosexuality and the Educator', *Journal of School Health*, May: 305–11.

Larsen, K., M. Reed and S. Hoffman (1980) 'Attitudes of Heterosexuals toward Homosexuality: A Likert-type Scale and Construct Validity', *Journal of Sex Research*, 16(3): 245–57.

Leeds Revolutionary Feminist Group (1981) 'Political Lesbianism: The Case Against Heterosexuality', in *Love Your Enemy? The Debate between Heterosexual Feminism and Political Lesbianism*. London: Onlywomen Press.

Lewis, J. (1982) 'The Politics of Monogamy', in S. Friedman and E. Sarah (eds), *On the Problem of Men: Two Feminist Conferences*. London: Women's Press.

Lewis, S.G. (1979) *Sunday's Women: A Report on Lesbian Life Today*. Boston: Beacon Press.

Littlewood, R. and M. Lipsedge (1982) *Aliens and Alienists: Ethnic Minorities and Psychiatry*. Harmondsworth: Penguin.

Lumby, M.E. (1976) 'Homophobia: The Quest for a Valid Scale' *Journal of Homosexuality*, 2: 39–47.

MacDonald, A.P. (1976) 'Homophobia: Its Roots and Meanings', *Homosexual Counselling Journal*, 3: 23-33.

MacDonald, A.P. and R.G. Games (1974) 'Some Characteristics of Those Who Hold Positive and Negative Attitudes toward Homosexuals', *Journal of Homosexuality*, 1: 9–27.

Maslow, A. (1962) *Toward a Psychology of Being*. Princeton NJ: Van Nostrand.

Masters, W.M. and V.E. Johnson (1979) *Homosexuality in Perspective*. Boston: Little, Brown.

Mendola, M. (1980) *The Mendola Report: A New Look at Gay Couples*. New York: Crown Publishers.

Mills, C.W. (1940) 'Situated Actions and Vocabularies of Motive', *American Sociological Review*, 5: 904–13.

Minnigerode, F.A. (1976) 'Attitudes toward Homosexuality: Feminist Attitudes and Sexual Conservatism', *Sex Roles*, 2: 347-52.

Minton, H.L. and G.J. McDonald (1984) 'Homosexual Identity Formation as a Developmental Process', *Journal of Homosexuality*, 9: 91–104.

Moberly, E.R. (1983) *Psychogenesis: The Early Development of Gender Identity*. London: Routledge & Kegan Paul.

Pattison, E.M. (1974) 'Confusing Concepts about the Concepts of Homosexuality', *Psychiatry*, 37(4): 340–9.

Pearson, G. (1975) *The Deviant Imagination: Psychiatry, Social Work and Social Change*. London: Macmillan Press.

Pollner, M. (1975) '"The Very Coinage of Your Brain": The Anatomy of Reality Disjunctures', *Philosophy of the Social Sciences*, 5: 411–30.

Radicalesbians (1970) *Woman-identified Woman*. Somerville, MA: New England Free Press.

Rogers, C.R. (1959) 'A Theory of Therapy, Personality and Interpersonal Relationships, as Developed in the Client-Context Framework', in S. Koch (ed.), *Psychology: A Study of a Science*, Vol. 3. New York: McGraw-Hill.

Rorty, R. (1980) *Philosophy and the Mirror of Nature*. Oxford: Basil Blackwell.

Scharfelter, C. (1980) *General Psychopathology: An Introduction*. Cambridge: Cambridge University Press.

Schur, E. (1976) *The Awareness Trap: Self-absorption Instead of Social Change*. New York: Quadrangle Press.

Scott, M.B. and S.M. Lyman (1968) 'Accounts', *American Sociological Review*, 33: 46–62.

Shelley, M. (1972) 'I am a Lesbian – I am Beautiful', in J.S. DeLorea and J.R. Delora (eds), *Intimate Lifestyles: Marriage and its Alternatives*. San Francisco, CA: Goodyear.

Shotter, J. (1985) 'Social Accountability and Self-specification' in K.J. Gergen and K.E. Davis (eds), *The Social Construction of the Person*. New York: Springer-Verlag.

Siegelman, M. (1972) 'Adjustment of Homosexual and Heterosexual Women', *British Journal of Psychiatry*, 120: 477–81.

Smith, K.T. (1971) 'Homophobia: A Tentative Personality Profile', *Psychological Reports*, 29: 1091–4.

Socarides, C.W. (1965) 'Female Homosexuality', in R. Slovenko (ed.), *Sexual Behavior and the Law*. Springfield, IL: Charles C. Thomas.

Socarides, C.W. (1972) 'Homosexuality – Basic Concepts and Psychodynamics', *International Journal of Psychiatry*, 10: 118–25.

Star, S.L. (1978) 'Lesbian Feminism as an Altered State of Consciousness', *Sinister Wisdom*, 5: 83–102.

Stone, G.P. and H.A. Faberman (1981) *Social Psychology through Symbolic Interaction* (2nd edn). Chichester: John Wiley.

Stricker, G. and M. Merbaum (1973) *Growth of Personal Awareness: A Reader in Psychology*. New York: Holt, Rinehart & Winston.

Szasz, T.W. (1970) *The Manufacture of Madness: A Comparative Study of the Inquisition and the Mental Health Movement*. New York: Harper and Row.

Thompson, G.H. and W.R. Fishburn (1977) 'Attitudes toward Homosexuality among Graduate Counselling Students', *Counsellor Education and Supervision*, December: 121–30.

Toll, B.J. (1980) 'Strong and Free: The Awakening', in S.J. Wolfe and J.P. Stanley (eds), *The Coming out Stories*. Watertown, MA: Persephone Press.

Weeks, J. (1981) *Sex, Politics and Society: The Regulation of Sexuality since 1800*. London: Longman.

West, D.J. (1968) *Homosexuality*. Harmondsworth: Penguin.

Wilbur, C.B. (1965) 'Clinical Aspects of Female Homosexuality', in J. Marmor (ed.), *Sexual Inversion: the Multiple Roots of Homosexuality*. New York: Basic Books.

Wilson, M. and R. Greene (1971) 'Personality Characteristics of Female Homosexuals', *Psychological Reports*, 28: 407–12.

Wolff, C. (1971) *Love Between Women*. London: Duckworth.

7
Narrative Culture and the Motivation of the Terrorist

Khachig Tölölyan

The social sciences are all too eager for models that will enable generalizations suitable to their empirical discourse and to the instrumental aims that all too frequently guide and constrain such discourse. In that two-decade-old subfield of political science that studies terrorism, the search for a schematic and exhaustive typology of terrorism and for the factors affecting it has been frustrated even as the field has grown rapidly. It has been acknowledged that terrorism occurs as the result of an enormously complex and hetero-geneous conjunction of sociocultural, psychological and political factors; what has not yet been confronted fully is the possibility that a conceptually satisfying schema of terrorisms will remain elusive until we take into consideration social and psychological factors not responsive to the usual methods of political psychology.

One way to begin is to address the problem of the terrorist's self- image and motivation, a problem neither purely psychological nor even psychological and political, but rather one that compels us to consider the cultural construction of individual motives under certain circumstances. The problem of motivation is a particularly interesting one because of the difficulty that immediately confronts us as we grapple with it: we encounter the persistence and inad-equacy of the ethnocentric Western will to generalize from notions of ego psychology implicit in current analyses. For example, Joseph Margolin's dismissal of crude beliefs that 'the terrorist is a psychotic' or a 'highly irrational individual' rejects some common pitfalls, only to revert to the search for a generalizing behaviourist model: 'It must be assumed that the terrorist is human. Whether rational or irrational, he is governed as we all are by the same laws of behavior' (Margolin, 1977, p. 271). I would not dispute that terrorists are human. Because they are, they are socially produced, out of a specific cultural context; consequently, their behaviour cannot be understood by the crude – or even by the careful – application of general laws of psychological behaviour. Even William Ascher's nuanced psychological evaluation of the 'rationality' of beliefs supporting or endorsing terrorism avoids dealing with the collective, cultural context in which terrorism develops. It seeks instead to base its findings on individual-oriented formulations: 'In long-standing confrontations, even proviolence *individuals* can select or develop relatively coherent belief structures (Ascher, 1986, p. 408; my italics). Though helpful, this and other studies in political psychology[1] consistently pay mere lip service to the cultural construction of a terrorist's motives, quickly reverting to individual-oriented modes of analysis. In this chapter – the latter part of which focuses on Armenian political culture and Armenian terrorists – I want to begin with a consideration of the specific mediating factors that lead some societies under pressure, among many, to produce the kinds of violent acts that we call 'terrorist'. A universalizing model may in fact be applicable to *some* of the factors that belong in the explicitly political realm, but I shall be concentrating on culturally specific factors which resist such generalization.[2]

Whereas the imperative of a cultural analysis is frequently acknowledged, the acknowledgement too often takes the form of lip service. For example, Walter Laqueur (1977, p. 120) speaks eloquently against 'generalizations about the terrorist personality' which he deems of 'little validity', and insists on the importance of 'the historical and cultural context' of terrorism. He then proceeds to do two things: he lists dozens of different organizations and instances of terrorism, and then, the gesture towards heterogeneity completed, he moves on in one mighty leap to make those general statements and analyses of terrorism for which his work is best known. This pattern is very widespread. Elsewhere, H.H. Cooper, an analyst of wholly different background and attitudes, remarks that 'terrorism is not a discrete topic that might be conveniently examined apart from the political, social and economic context in which it takes place ... Terrorism is a creature of its own time and place (Cooper, 1985, p. 95). That is exactly right, and leads immediately to considerable difficulties all too easily evaded by most students of the topic, including Cooper. The *time* relevant to a particular terrorist act or group might be the day, the month, the decade or the century previous to the event. What is more, it can be the time that is embedded in the historiography, traditional narratives, legends and myths with which a society constitutes itself as a temporal entity.

The specific forms of narrative for which I shall be making large claims are the projective narrative and the regulative biography.[3] The precise meaning of these terms will emerge as I turn my attention to an analysis of Armenian terrorism. For the present, a projective narrative is one that not only tells a story of the past, but also maps out future actions that can imbue the time of individual lives with transcendent collective values. In a sense, then, projective narratives plot how ideal selves must live lives: they dictate biographies and autobiographies to come. They tell individuals how they would ideally have to live and die in order to contribute properly to their collectivity and its future. They prescribe not static roles but dynamic shapes of the time of our lives.

Similarly, the 'place' of terrorism, which is, in Cooper's terms, a 'creature of time and place', is no simple geographical locale. It can be the irredentist's vision of a land that he has never seen or the aspiration of the alienated ecologist seeking a land unmarked by society. Not only times and places that exist at this moment, but absent times and places, as well as times and places projected in utopian narratives shared by the social group, can all provide that context which is the domain in which a cultural vision can produce terrorists.

I take as my point of departure Professor Paul Wilkinson's brief survey 'Armenian Terrorism', which begins by contrasting the Baader–Meinhof gang, among others, with Armenian terrorists, among others. Wilkinson is especially concerned with terrorists who 'claim to be authentic champions of a whole ethnic community'. He cites the Irish, Croatians and Armenians as having produced such terrorists, who are said to secure 'a broader and more loyal base of political sympathy and support' than groups like the Baader–Meinhof (Wilkinson, 1983, p. 344). The way in which Wilkinson establishes authenticity is directly relevant to my argument: he cites historical precedents. Whereas there are no roots of valid grievance and reactive terrorism reaching down into the German past of the Baader–Meinhof, he points out, the Armenians have a history of both. Oppression, pogrom, genocide and then terrorism as a response to them are said to be 'part of a very long tradition' of Armenian history; as a result, the 'well-springs of ... terrorist violence' lie 'deep in national psyches and traditions' (p. 344). Committed as I am to notions of the social construction of individual motivation through narrative, I find a great deal that is appealing in this respect for history and tradition. It is therefore all the more disappointing to find Professor Wilkinson writing, two pages later, that 'the roots of modern Armenian terrorism lie in ... tragic events of sixty-eight years ago', namely in the Genocide, and in the examples provided by earlier terrorism. 'Young Armenians are ready to go on suicide missions', he writes, 'because they have both a grievance and an exemplar of terrorism as a proper response to that grievance' (p. 346).

What seems striking about both Professor Wilkinson's otherwise very good analysis and a legion of less creditable discussions of the same topic is the disciplinary rush to the politicization of terrorism. By 'politicization', I mean that the profession of political science seems powerfully impelled to turn enormously complex events into mere, or only, or just, *political* facts, which can then be seen as motivating other political acts, including terrorism. This reduction happens despite frequent and sincere genuflection in the direction of the complexity of social phenomena. The history of certain nations is seen as a series of basically political events which, as though moving through a vacuum of social life, become links in a chain of other politico–diplomatic events, and eventually stretch across the decades to cause yet more political events. Whether the causes be genocide, loss of sovereignty or loss of land, when they result in terrorism the model is the same at its core: one set of events, described as 'political', functions as a 'cause', creating among its victims a set of agents who are motivated, either by politics or by pathology, to commit another set of acts described as 'terrorist'.

What is crucially lacking in such a model is the concept of *mediation*, or a serious consideration of the possibility that past events, including the rare purely political events, are perpetuated, disseminated and experienced in a particular culture not as political events, but as narratives that transcribe historical facts into moral or immoral acts, vehicles of social values. Such acts sometimes become symbols, models or paradigms of behaviour, especially when they are internalized, when the narratives no longer exist 'out there' in the culture, to be sampled occasionally, but in the minds of individuals, as part of the mental equipment with which they are raised to perceive the meaning of events, to interpret them and to initiate new ones. Whether we are speaking of the tale of the forty-seven masterless samurai made so popular in interwar Japan, or of the Armenian projective narratives I shall be discussing shortly, we can venture one relatively safe generalization: *terrorism with an authentically popular base is never a purely political phenomenon.* A few other commentators have said this in general terms. Moshe Amon, significantly a professor of religion, writing as an outsider for an audience of political scientists, suggests that 'the legitimacy of terrorist movements may stem from a mythological model adopted by the terrorists and endorsed by large segments of society' (Amon, 1982, p. 82). All too often in writings on terrorism, the word 'mythology' lacks the complex meaning implied in Amon's sentence; rather, it comes to refer to that set of mystifying beliefs which happen to provide the underpinnings of national liberation movements that employ terrorism. To one reading through the professional literature with the outsider's eye, it sometimes seems that the entire question of cultural difference or specificity is handled by the ritual invocation of the tired truism that 'one man's terrorist is another man's freedom fighter'. Under the aegis of this cliché, the whole set of questions that I want to consider is then overlooked, shunted aside.

One explanation for the inability of commentators to carry through with the insight that they need culturally specific accounts of terrorism is the potency of the analytical model which was developed in the study of, and found its early illustrations in, groups close to home, like the Baader–Meinhof gang. The vocabulary and categories with which such terrorists are described in the literature are remarkably consistent. The pivotal terms are 'ideology', 'alienation' and 'pathology'. Such terrorists are correctly said to be better educated than the average Western citizen, with greater access to abstract theory and ideology. They are said to suffer from 'biographical deficits' (Rupprecht, 1985, p. 73) and psychopathologies ranging from sadism to 'a desire to express hate and revenge, to smash, to kill and to disrupt – or simply to feel big' (Clutterbuck, 1977, p. 94). Finally, they are seen as alienated from the mainstream of their society, forced to find shelter, for a time, among relatively alienated populations of student radicals, and in time to lose even that base of passive support.

It is not my intention to dispute this characterization, which may be adequate in certain contexts. But it too often persists even when the analysis moves on to consider groups like the Irish or Armenian terrorists. Endowing these movements with more authentic, perhaps even legitimate, grievances is something that the more thoughtful analysts, like Professor Wilkinson, are willing to do. But the model of personality, of relations with the rest of society, and therefore of motivation, which is grafted on to the descriptions of terrorists in these movements remains unchanged. The persistence of the model of the individual terrorist as an alienated Western youth is remarkable, and not without serious consequence. It disables any effort to give a culturally specific description of the way in which different societies maintain their vision of their collective selves with different projective narratives, and so produce different terrorisms and different terrorists. The act of terrorism may well continue to have identical legal status in the courts of Western governments (though even this can be disputed to some degree). Yet if our aim as scholars is not merely to dismiss the complexity of an act by reference to its legal classification, but rather to understand it, we must acknowledge the ways in which cultural meanings and culturally inscribed motives are relatively autonomous of legal codes.

At this point, I must invoke Clifford Geertz's well-known phrase, 'thick description', and move from my more general theoretical critique to a case study that will illustrate what I see as the promise of an alternative mode of enquiry. I will take my examples from the terrorist group whose writings in the native language I know best, and who are products of Middle Eastern Armenian society. I mean to lay equal stress on both elements, writings and society. It is not enough to know the dates of pogroms and Genocide, or to scan the English-language communiqués of the rather prolific terrorist groups, especially the Armenian Secret Army for the Liberation of Armenia (ASALA). Their vehement, error-laden English and French, or Arabic and occasionally even Turkish broadsides, allow an observer to develop a fairly clear sense of their explicitly acknowledged programmes and activities, and of the extent to which the PLO, say, or Kurdish guerrillas, or an oddly interpreted tradition of Marxism–Leninism, have influenced them. But their Armenian writings do not merely recapitulate this material. They also reveal minds steeped in a recognizable Armenian idiom that has roots not in a sixty-eight-year-old Genocide but in fifteen centuries of both learned and popular discourse, in ecclesiastical ritual and popular narrative and, perhaps most importantly, in living song. Alone among the commentators I have read, Professor Wilkinson acknowledges, in one sentence, the importance of literature and religion to the tradition of Armenian resistance (1983, p. 344); I want not only to confirm that, but also to enlarge greatly the claims that may be made about their significance.

The traditions and texts that constitute Armenian social discourse cannot simply be set up against the ideological pamphlets of terrorists; nor can the terrorists simply be seen as being in opposition to Armenian society, as alienated, fringe elements of their culture. The Armenian writings of terrorists' pamphlets are thoroughly intertextual, in the sense of being explicitly allusive to and continuous with mainstream Armenian social discourse. This stands in sharp contrast to the texts and situations that have thus far provided the models for the study of terrorists' self-image and motivation. It is easy to mock and dismiss the turgid theoretical pronouncements of groups like the Baader–Meinhof gang by pointing to the chasm that separates them from the discourse of ordinary life and ordinary Germans. Reinhard Rupprecht, for example, has observed that German terrorists often 'retreat from family and the ordinary way of life' as a prelude to coming 'under the influence of ideologies' (1985, p. 73). The Armenian situation very nearly requires that we reverse this observation. Armenian youth in the post-Genocide Diaspora, when they retreat from family, tend to do so in the direction of assimilation: they do not become terrorists. Those who *do*, speak in the accents of parents and grandparents, in the language of sermons and of the dominant political party, even when furiously rejecting the latter's more cautious platforms. The 'biographical deficits' of Armenian terrorists are usually the slaughter of most of their grandparents' generation, an event conveyed to them vividly through detailed narrative. Yet such memory is never by itself enough to cause terrorism. There are always more grievances that guerrillas, revolutionaries or terrorists. The catalyst here is the coupling of the vivid collective memory of injustice with traditional and valued paradigms for action, paradigms embodied in projective narratives. To be an Armenian in an 'ordinary' way in many Middle Eastern communities means, first, that one understands the present experience of injustice in terms of familial stories and national narratives that are deeply intertwined and, second, that one anticipates any confrontation with such injustice in terms of narratives of earlier resistance. These are projected upon both the present and the future as morally privileged patterns for action and for interpretation of that action; hence the term 'projective narrative'.

Before I give an account of the ways in which Diaspora culture is shaped by the master-narratives involved, and of their effect on Armenian terrorism, I must further qualify certain of my terms. In an Armenian Diaspora that numbers nearly 1.5 million people in some thirty countries, a typical Armenian is a fiction, not unlike that of the typical international terrorist. Not all Diaspora Armenians are relevant to a discussion of terrorism. Only one Armenian terrorist captured or otherwise identified is American-born; another is French-born; the remainder were all born in the Lebanon, Iran, Syria or Turkey. Both the ordinary Armenian and the terrorist of my analysis come from a certain stratum of Middle Eastern Armenian communities, a stratum that makes up a minority of the Armenian population of Iran, possibly a plurality in Syria and arguably a majority in the Lebanon. In most of these cases, the terrorist and the relevant stratum both live in a common cultural reality. The foundations of this cultural reality are not just endogamy or cuisine: they are religious, linguistic, rhetorical and mythic. This primarily verbal and narrative reality is maintained through a network of churches, schools, athletic unions and youth and student groups. Obvious, none of these institutions has the production of terrorism as its aim: their purpose is to reproduce and perpetuate a certain culture in a Diaspora under the pressure of assimilation. Of the elements that give the Armenian cultural tradition its cohesion and shape, perhaps the most central is a ubiquitous cluster of stories. Among those I shall now turn to, two are part of the cultural experience of every Armenian in the Diaspora; others are specific to the strata mentioned above.

The first of these is the story of the Genocide, which is always articulated at two levels, the national and the familial. On each level one encounters both a story of traumatizing events and an invocation of place. The first story is of the planned slaughter of a Nation and the appropriation of a Fatherland; the other is the tale of how family members died and a reminiscence of the ancestral village or town. Those familiar with older Armenians anywhere in the Diaspora and with Armenian life in the relevant Middle Eastern communities will know the importance of compatriotic associations and of the frequent question, Where are you from?, which always has a double import: Where in the Diaspora are you from? and Where in the lost Fatherland were your grandparents from? This concern is reinforced by a resurgent practice of naming children after lost places and landmarks: Ani and Ararat, Van and Masis, Daron and Nareg.

The second ubiquitous narrative dates from the second half of the fifth century, and is the story of Vartan and the 1036 martyrs, whose memory is commemorated by a Saints' Day in the calendar of the Armenian Apostolic Church. Armenian children encounter their story at church, in Sunday school, in kindergarten and in elementary school. More advanced students in the parochial school systems of the Middle East encounter it in extended narrative form, usually in contemporary Armenian but sometimes even in the classical Armenian, in which it was written down by the monk Yeghishe. This narrative has been ably translated and controversially edited by the Harvard scholar Robert Thomson (1982), who believes that the historically accurate residue in the narrative is small, and that the model for the heroic resistance and martyrdom of Vartan and his men derives more from the biblical books of the Maccabees than from reality. However, the debate about the historical accuracy of the work is beside the point. The invocation of the model of the Maccabees only serves to underscore the ways in which the Vartan story enables and sanctions certain kinds of resistance, endowing it with a mantle of traditional and religious authority. While this religious dimension was vital in the period extending from the fifth to the nineteenth centuries, it has steadily become less so since. In the nineteenth century, the increase of literacy, the revival of Armenian literature and the accessibility of secular education combined to spawn a dozen versions of the tale. The first important Armenian romantic poet, Alishan, composed one of his most important poems about the battlefield where Vartan and his followers fell in battle against the Sassanid Persians. Two of the most important early romantic historical novels authored by Raffi (the Armenian equivalent of Sir Walter Scott and Victor Hugo combined) invoke Vartan as model, while a third takes related figures from the same era for its heroes and villains. In the process of secularization of the tale and proliferation of its versions, two words have remained in play: *martyros*, from the Greek 'martyr', and *nahadag*, its Armenian synonym. In many recountings of the tale, in speeches, sermons, laments and funeral orations, the formulaic line most frequently invoked is '*mah imatzyal anmahootyun e*'; that is, 'death knowingly grasped is immortality'. The line is pivotal to Yeghishe's book, and refers to the willingness of Vartan and his followers to risk all in defence of Armenian Christianity, conceived then (as now) as a crucial component of national identity.

The crisis that provoked the remark was brought on by the Persian Empire's insistence, in AD 450/1, on converting the Armenians, who had been Christian since AD 301, to militant Zoroastrianism. Defiant Armenian princes and clergy were summoned to Ctesiphon, the capital of the Sassanid empire, where they submitted to forced conversion. Upon their return to Armenia they vacillated about imposing a similar conversion on the mass of their subjects until events took matters out of their hands: proselytizing Persian priests forcibly converted altars to fire-altars; they were attacked by enraged Armenians led by a priest, and the conflagration spread. The Persian army invaded; Vartan (the hereditary commander of Armenian armies) and his troops met it in unequal battle. He and over a thousand of his followers fell, and there followed thirty years of passive resistance punctuated by minor uprisings until AD 484, when Vartan's nephew obtained a favourable treaty of peace and autonomy from an otherwise embattled Persian Empire.

Such are the bare bones of the story. What matters to my analysis is the way in which what was originally a struggle for religious tolerance, local autonomy and feudal privilege became an exemplary narrative of virtuous action, in defence of national identity and personal honour, simultaneously. Today it retains the most potent aspects of martyrology without any longer being a tale that inspires religious piety as such; it has been reinterpreted, through its many nineteenth-century retellings, primarily as a struggle for national identity. Its exemplary status can be made clearer by a comparison with a medieval parallel. As Christ's life, narrated in sermons and pictured on cathedral windows, constituted an invitation to *imitatio Christi*, and functioned as an exemplar revealing the way in which to live one's life so that it confirmed to the highest ideals of the community as embodied in the New Testament narratives, so also Vartan's life and death are endlessly narrated with a passion that establishes them as models of exemplary courage and virtue. Today, even in Sunday schools in the USA, the grandchildren of pacific third-generation Armenian-Americans still learn to recite a rhyme that declares: '*Hye em yes, hye em yes/Kach Vartanin torn em yes*', namely: 'I am Armenian, I am Armenian/the grandchild of valiant Vartan'. The first and second statements are equal, and they imply a regulative autobiography: to be Armenian is to acknowledge Vartan as ancestor. To acknowledge as ancestor one who is not a blood relative is to acknowledge his moral and symbolic authority. In an ethnically pluralist America, the lines and the tradition have no further import. In the Middle East, where Armenians are less assimilated and much beset, the statement and the Vartan stories as a whole come into play as projective narratives.

The omnipresent narratives of the Genocide and of Vartan provide a frame for a series of more specific narratives of Armenian heroism and sacrifice, whose currency is more local, less pan-Diasporic. The most popular form in which these are embodied is song, learned in early childhood in schools and clubs, and in formal and informal public occasions where they are spontaneously sung. In the USA, where the music of Elvis Presley, say, is relegated to 'oldies' radio programmes, it is difficult to imagine the musical practice of a culture in which disco music coexists with the lyrics of Sayyat Nova (an eighteenth-century court composer), and with songs composed mostly in the period 1890–1920 in honour of executed revolutionaries and guerrillas fallen in combat. In the USA, of course, only a very small portion of Armenian-Americans retains this musical and narrative culture; records, cassette tapes, television and video dominate both musical and non-musical narrative for Armenians as for other ethnic groups. But in the Middle East, in the countries whence most Armenian terrorists have come, at least a plurality of the people retained this traditional culture until very recently. In the Lebanon, confessional warfare is temporarily reviving its fading vitality.

Armenian bookstores still sell songbooks containing such songs. Of these, one has the status of a national anthem. The quatrain inevitably included in all versions ends with the lines, 'Amenayn degh mahe me e/Mart me ankam bid merni/Paytz yerani oom ir azki/Azadootyan ge zohvi' – 'Death is the same everywhere/and a man dies only once/Lucky is he/ who dies for the freedom of his nation.' Another, composed in 1896, honours the revolutionaries who occupied the Franco-Turkish Banque Ottomane in Istanbul: they held hostages and demanded access to the European powers and press in the hope of publicizing the plight of the Armenians during a moment of persecution and pogrom particularly vicious even by the Sultan Abdul Hamid's high standards. Nearly a century later, the song is still sung spontaneously, with something of the ease with which an American might put a 'golden oldie' on the turntable as a party winds down.

Of course, this and other songs do not explicitly affirm the legitimacy of terrorism. Their sentimental melodies and depictions of suffering, daring, rare partial success and heroic death perform something other than legitimization: they establish the willingness to act against very high odds, and to accept violent death, as essential elements of the character of those who would honourably live out socially approved projective narratives. Literally dozens of other songs from this period celebrate small victories and large, heroic defeats that testify to Armenian endurance in what Wilkinson calls their 'very long tradition of resistance' (1983, p. 344). This tradition is alive in the web of culture, and is not just a matter for the learned, the books, the museums. It is inscribed into the minds of a certain proportion of Diaspora Armenians as they grow up; it partially but importantly constitutes their Armenianness.

The final cluster of traditional narratives I want to mention consists of stories of the Armenian assassins who, in 1921–3, after the Genocide, struck down several members of the Young Turk junta responsible for its organization, chief among them Talaat Pasha. Other stories concern the killing of Armenian traitors, or even particularly oppressive tsarist officials in eastern Armenia. These stories have been restricted to a more narrow audience, because they are not enshrined in song. Still, they are familiar to many. They were invoked in countless discussions and articles in the first few years of the contemporary revival of Armenian terrorism, which began with Kourken Yanikian's revenge-killing of two Turkish officials in Santa Barbara, California, in 1973. Of course, to a detached observer, there is a clear sense in which the earlier assassinations do not provide appropriate models for thinking about terrorism directed against officials whose guilt could be established only after extended moral and philosophical argument, if at all. Direct participation in a genocide is a different order of crime from working for the civil service of the contemporary Turkish state, however much that state continues to benefit from the crimes of the Young Turks while distorting the historical record. The point here is that the fact that phrases like 'The avenging arm of Talaat's assassins can strike again' were used to discuss such complex issues provides one measure of the saturation of Armenian culture by this narrative idiom of persecution and revenge. The persecution has been very real, of course, and revenge is not to be lightly dismissed as a value or motive; what must be underscored is that they are not political facts that are politically institutionalized in Armenian life, but complex cultural and psychological phenomena woven as narratives into the matrix of what passes for ordinary life in certain Middle Eastern societies.

Since my aim has been to depoliticize the discussion of terrorism, that is, to counter the tendency of political science to reduce terrorist acts to mere disturbances of the political order caused by political motives, I have so far avoided the exposition of Armenian political realities. By no means all, but certainly much of the maintenance of the narrative traditions has been the work of intellectuals, teachers, artists, organizers and activists who are or were, at one time or another, under the influence of the Hye Heghapokhaganneri Dashnagtzootyun, the Federation of Armenian Revolutionaries, founded in 1890, in the Tsarist Empire, as a confederation of existing student radical groups heavily influenced by the Narodniki. In the Diaspora, since the Sovietization of the short-lived independent Armenian Republic, this party, known in English by the acronym ARF, has struggled for dominance, which it achieved in the Lebanon, Syria and Iran to a considerable degree in the 1920s and then again between 1948 and 1967. There are very few card-carrying 'Dashnags' in the Diaspora: there are tens of thousands of sympathizers, and as many ex-Dashnags. As with members of the Roman Catholic Church, so with Dashnags the imprint of its culture is not easily removed, even in rebellion against its specific political dogma. That dogma has been a rhetorically potent but politically ineffective declaration of the rights of the Armenian people to a restored homeland, not accompanied by action. It has been difficult, for Armenians scattered in a Diaspora, to conceive of a course of action likely to result in the recognition of Genocide, let alone the restoration of their lost homeland.

The gap between rhetoric and action has been all the more underscored by the nature and origins of ARF culture. Since it was the dominant party in the resistance against Turkish persecution from 1890 onwards, a very large proportion of the songs, tales, memoirs and formal literary narratives from this period are about its cadres and heroes. It is not an exaggeration to say that the political entity called the Dashnag Party in the Diaspora has been, above all else, a cultural institution, even as it has exercised a serious measure of political power in the Armenian quarters of Beirut. Almost everywhere, its prestige and capital have been its past achievements and defeats, as commemorated in the narratives I have been discussing. From Papken Suny at the Banque Ottomane to Kevork Chavoush,

Aghpyoor Serop and his wife Soseh, and to Antranig Pasha, the larger than life heroes of Armenian projective narratives, men and women both, have been predominantly members or former members of the ARF. Until 1973, its cultural institutions were the chief custodians of the projective narratives I have described. Ironically, the first generation of terrorists spoke insistently of the bankruptcy of ARF rhetoric and of its failure to live up to its own narrative traditions as a motive for the formation of their own units. Many of these terrorists had broken away from ARF-dominated youth groups after being saturated by their unacted projective narratives. The frequency of indignant or ironic citation of these heroic models in the early pamphlets of the ASALA is readily apparent to anyone familiar with the relevant strata of Armenian culture.

My argument rests, of course, on several interdependent claims. One is that it is reductive and finally inadequate to think of terrorist acts as only a political response to political facts, past or present. Neither political not psychological explanations can compensate for a lack of analysis of the cultural milieu that provides the medium in which political facts are interpreted and engender new acts. Discussions of motivation and self-image that depend primarily on the manipulation of psychological and behaviouristic categories inevitably trivialize the cultural matrix. Second, I have made large claims for the power of socially approved narrative to shape individual perceptions and behaviour. I believe that, when 'narrative accounts are embedded within social action', events can then be 'rendered socially visible through them', and that such narratives can then be 'used to establish expectations for future events' (Gergen and Gergen, 1987). Third, narrative is a major conceptual category of my analysis because I am claiming that, in cultures like the Armenian, terrorism is not the product of a particular individual's alienation, but the manifestation of a desire to give one's individual life an iconic centrality in the eyes of the community, which professes to value certain forms of behaviour articulated in narratives. I say 'professes' because, of course, only a very tiny proportion of the many people sentimentally moved by either popular or high-cultural fictions are actually tempted to enact them. Life imitates art and other fictions only rarely; but imitate it does. I have given a detailed account of the dominant narratives and the socio-political structures that mutually sustain each other in the Armenian Diaspora because these narratives animate 'the example[s] set by predecessors', which Martha Crenshaw sees, in another context, as 'contribut[ing] to make the terrorists' purpose salient' (Crenshaw, 1985, p. 18). It remains to demonstrate that a direct link exists between the narratives, on the one hand, and the terrorists and their Diaspora audience, on the other.

Such a demonstration requires textual analysis of Armenian writings by the terrorists, by the sympathetic interpreters of their words and deeds, and even by their critics. Over the past five years, I have read some 4000 pages of such texts. Clear evidence of the links we seek is abundant in them. Space requires that I limit myself to only a few examples. These were obtained by my *random* scanning of five issues of the ASALA periodical, *Hayasdan*, and of one not randomly selected ARF publication.

The Genocide is massively present everywhere. It is constantly referred to as the double crime of mass murder and dispossession that can justify any terrorist act, which is inevitably seen as minor in comparison with this crime. The Genocide is denounced as the reason why the Diaspora exists and why assimilation can ravage most Armenian communities. Known as 'white massacre', assimilation is portrayed as inevitable in the Diaspora, and as the completion of the Genocide, which is invoked by photographs that stud many texts whose actual content is not the Genocide. Thus, a communiqué about a terrorist operation, or a theoretical piece on Third World Marxism, can be 'illustrated' by poorly reproduced photographs of Armenian dead from the Genocide. Typically, no more direct relation need be established, because internalized social discourse can be counted upon to do that work. The cover of one issue of ASALA's periodical features a photograph of a pile of skulls and a caption (in French) that translates as: 'that the 24th of April may become a day of struggle' (*Hayasdan*, 24 April 1981, special issue). That date, in 1915, marks the day when mass arrests of Armenian intellectuals in Istanbul 'officially' launched a genocide already begun in late March in the plains of Anatolia. The thought is elaborated in a longer Arabic caption and embroidered upon elsewhere in this as in all issues. Elsewhere, killings of Kurdish civilians and guerrillas in south-eastern Turkey are viewed as a continuation of the Armenian Genocide and part of the age-old dream of Turkification – which is perhaps true, but is hardly argued carefully by means of ordinary evidence. All is told as part of the narrative of an ongoing genocide: first the Armenians, then the assimilative cultural Genocide of the Diaspora, then Kurdicide. The implication is that we know this story, and we know its awful outcome, and we also know what must be done in response to it. All this does not remain at the level of the generalized story; there are practical details which reinforce it. Whereas an American military operation might be named Rolling Thunder, the ASALA often names its attacks after lost comrades and also after lost territories. The attack on Ankara Airport was named Garin, the Armenian name for the city of Erzerum; other 'commando groups' bear the names of the old and new heroes of projective narratives – 'Antranig Pasha', say, or 'Yanikian'. It's as if the terrorists' actions are responses to the double question I alluded to earlier: Whom did you lose? and What place did you lose?

The Vartan narrative is not as ubiquitous, but is present in ways both direct and indirect in the periodicals examined. The ASALA publications are illustrated with the photographs of fallen terrorists; the captions include an incongruous coupling of the Christian and the Marxist; all the dead are *nahadag-ungers*, that is, martyr-commandos. One issue has a paragraph describing the death of a terrorist that reads, in part (in my own translation), '*Fedayee* Megerdich Madurian completed his mission before he exploded a grenade he carried attached to his waist, thus showing that the Secret Army is determined to continue in the path of "death knowingly grasped" – of "*imatzyal mah*" – cited in the original classical Armenian from Yeghishe's Vartan narrative' (*Hayasdan*, 16 June 1983, p. 47). Such an explicit identification of ASALA cadres in 1983 with the Vartan of AD 451 constitutes a rejection of the simplifying Western notion of a suicide mission. Vartan and his men did not commit suicide; they went to do battle against large odds that in fact proved fatal to some of them, but their act was not suicidal, their defeat did not lead to extermination, and the word 'suicide' is not associated with their action. This is the narrative logic applied even to acts that are, in fact, inevitably fatal to the perpetrators when carried out in Turkey proper. Yet they are represented as standing and fighting to the death for Armenia, and those who fall are martyrs, like Vartan, not suicides.

Even opponents and critics of the terrorists, who (whatever the impression given by the popular press) are legion in the Armenian community, invoke the Vartan narrative. Khachig Pilikian, an artist living in London, recently published privately his own critique of terrorism, in which he attacks terrorists who refuse the challenge of enduring creatively as a Diaspora and instead resort to violence. In doing so, he refers to ASALA cadres as 'new *fedayeen*, little lefties of brave Vartan (Pilikian, 1984, p. 21). The clause is incoherent but significant. The ASALA terrorists are dismissed, but precisely in the terms they proudly claim for themselves: as leftists, as heirs of the Armenian *fedayee*s of the pre-Genocide resistance, as descendants of Vartan, as youthful and therefore daring (and therefore unwise, according to Pilikian).

The terrorists of the Secret Army see themselves as the heirs of the 'abandoned' and even 'betrayed' traditions of the early ARF; they neglect the historical context in which the ARF organized resistance against Turkish oppression of Anatolian Armenians who then were living on their ancestral territories, not scattered in a Diaspora. Thanks to the very narratives they have inherited from ARF-dominated culture, they find it possible to shoulder the goals of ARF rhetoric without examining too closely why those goals remained unfulfilled. The logic of ASALA analysis in the end owes more to the logic of the dominant narratives of Armenian culture, to the employment of sacrifice on the altar of national identity, than to Marighella or Lenin or Naief Hawatmeh. Despite the radical changes in that historical context over the centuries, the projective narrative that dictates the logic of action and projects that action and its agents into the future retains its stubborn structure, inherited from textualizations of history that began in the Vartan narratives and have continued since. Thus, the blinding by an accidental bomb explosion of ASALA leader Yenikomshian is compared to the death, under similar circumstances but a full seventy five years earlier, of Krisdapor Mikayelian, a member of the founding trinity of the ARF (*Hayasdan*, December 1980, p. 16). This comparison recurs throughout the early 1980s publications of the ASALA, even in some of the most vituperative essays attacking the contemporary ARF. The deep structure of such discourse has its own pre-analytic logic. It resembles most what scholars of literature and religion call typological–prefigurative narrative, in which historical and contextual changes intervening between two events do not necessarily create a discontinuity of meaning-making, of interpretative procedure. Just as Abraham sacrificing his son Isaac prefigures God sacrificing his son Christ, so also the whole of the Old Testament prefigures the New, and the book of Apocalypse the end of the world in nuclear holocaust, all proclaimed by parsons who think with the same narrative 'logic' as the ASALA.

Regulative biographies are retrospective manifestations of a similar logic. Kourken Yanikian's killing of two Turkish diplomats in 1973 was the isolated act of a solitary individual, a classic example of the work of the lone assassin. ASALA became active in early 1975, and from the beginning it appropriated Yanikian's action as something it was not, and has reinscribed it within the narratives of continuity and repetition as an instance of 'rebirth'. That this can be done to an action that has no relation to organized terrorism, either early or late, is testimony to the hold that the master-narratives have on collective thought. Thus, the April 1981 issue of *Hayasdan* features a photograph of Yanikian. The caption reads: '*verkerov li jan fedayee*' – a nearly untranslatable address to the *fedayee* bleeding, like Christ or Saint Sebastian, from many wounds, but more importantly a quotation from the first line of a famous song of the early 1900s. Although he was neither wounded nor a *fedayee*, Yanikian is nevertheless not understood in the context of his life, of his real biography, or even in the context of the brief autobiography we can glean from his utterances. He is assigned a regulative biography, and understood through it.

What the ASALA does in this instance with Yanikian, it often does with its own cadres. After the fact of the terrorist act, cadres are depicted in regulative biographies that interpret their actions in terms of past narratives and of the values that living tradition assigns to actions in those narratives. Even in more general essays about their own actions, they represent the design of their political project in terms of these narratives. Thus, an article occasioned by Shahan Natali's death, in the August 1983 issue of *Hayasdan* (p. 14), eulogizes this long-since expelled member of the ARF as 'the first Armenian Nemesis' along with other famed avengers from the same organization – Tehlirian, Torlakian, Yerganian – who assassinated Talaat Pasha, Behaeddin Shakir and Jemal Azmi, three architects of the Genocide. These names are intoned together with Yanikian's, and to them is added the phrase, 'the martyrs and imprisoned warriors of the ASALA', all enlisted in a resonating toll-call that blurs history, context and nuance. All become actors of the same master-narrative. The device of the roll-call that erases individual motives and historical detail is not, of course, unique to the Armenian situation. To glance for a moment outside my purview, at a context where my approach might be relevant in the hands of a seasoned observer of Irish culture, let me cite what seems to me the most Armenian of William Butler Yeats' poems, 'Easter 1916'. He ends that famed poem with a similar short list:

> And what if excess of love
> burdened them til they died?
> I write it out in a verse –
> McDonough and MacBride
> and Connolly and Pearce,
> Now and in time to be wherever green is worn
> are changed, changed utterly:
> a terrible beauty is born.

We might endlessly debate the terrible beauty of the events referred to, but the potency of the intoned list is indisputable. The list enlists; it tells us little about the different individuals and their different motives, but rather inscribes them in a past and future narrative, valid wherever green is worn, wherever, the poem implies, the sacrifice and resurrection of Christ which we celebrate at Easter are known as narratives of salvation. This is what it is to be a martyr, or a *martyros* or a *nahadag-unger*, a martyr–comrade whose death is always represented as a choice of enlistment in the narrative of national salvation, which requires the individuals' death as the price of the national collectivity's resurrection.

To cap this brief sampling of the intertextuality that obtains between terrorist discourse and the master-narratives of the culture in question, let me glance at the ways in which other Armenians have interpreted Armenian terrorism. One of the best-known acts of recent years was the seizure of the Turkish Embassy in Lisbon by Armenian Revolutionary Army (ARA) terrorists. It ended when an explosion killed all five terrorists. Some believe an accident caused the detonation of explosives brought in by the ARA cadres; others believe it was a group suicide committed when the terrorists realized they were about to be captured by Portuguese commandos reputed to be well trained by the British SAS. While the facts are in dispute, the interpretation of it by a segment of ARF-dominated Armenian society is not. Throughout that part of the community, the reach of regulative narrative is unchallenged. What is more impressive, even to a scholar accustomed to its power, is a poem composed in Soviet Armenia by a poet who was born, lived and recently died there, in the USSR, and who most probably knew of the terrorism only through Voice of America broadcasts and tourists' stories. He wrote a celebration of the heroism of the 'Lisbon Five', as they are generally known, in which the refrain is:

> Hishek, Hyer, inchbess Tizbon
> Yereg Tizbon, aysor Lisbon ...

and continues with:

> Yeg, vor Vartann Avarayri
> Anedzk tarna Turkin vayri

In Armenian, 'Tizbon' is the pronunciation of Ctesiphon, the capital of the Sassanid Empire where Vartan and others were forced into a conversion they later renounced. The rhyme with Lisbon ushers in the whole Vartan-narrative in the lines which mean, translated loosely (as they must be), 'Come, Armenians, [and recall] how it was in Tizbon./Yesterday Tizbon, today Lisbon'. To make his point even more unmistakable, the poet writes in the latter lines: 'Come, let the Vartan of Avarayr/Become the curse of the savage Turk'. This poem is found reprinted in an Armenian-language weekly published in Canada (Shiraz, 1984, p. 6), read entirely by recent immigrants from the Middle East, who can be counted upon to see the logic of narrative: the Sassanid Empire is dead; Ctesiphon is a heap of ruins that some tourists to Baghdad may visit; but the struggle is the same. The narrative of AD 451 still applies in 1985.

At a certain level of analytical abstraction, there is some sense to this logic. Armenians continue to struggle for cultural identity, which is perceived by them, and by so many other ethnics, as a self-evident value in its own right. That culture was produced by centuries of resistance in unequal struggle. Given the presence of some 'political' factors beyond the range of this analysis, such a culture, I have been trying to suggest, is able to produce and sustain a certain level of terrorist activity, even in Diaspora conditions, perhaps especially in Diaspora conditions. For the Armenians in the Diaspora, there is no state that can conduct their political life for them; that can challenge, for example, Turkish misrepresentations of Armenian history, or claim the legitimate use of force. The absence of a state and a country means that there is no possibility in the Diaspora for enacting a classical narrative of social revolution on either the Marxist or another model: neither Angolan revolution nor Afghan guerrilla war is possible. Under such circumstances, and in the conditions that have prevailed in the Middle East since 1967, the dominant cultural narratives overdetermine conditions that help to produce terrorism and are in turn reanimated by it. Such terrorism produces new heroes for old stories. It would be a mistake for political scientists to delude themselves into believing, as the terrorists themselves have, that the true audience and target of Armenian terrorism is Turkey and its NATO allies. Neither of those is likely to be moved; at most, a few nations might express a desire to set the record straight on the Genocide. But the true audience of Armenian terrorism remains the Armenian Diaspora, whose fraying culture is constituted to a remarkable degree by old stories, and who see in contemporary terrorists Vartan's refusal to abandon cultural identity and national rights.

Notes

*This is the revised version of an article which appeared in the *Journal of Strategic Studies* in December 1987. I am grateful to Professors David Rapoport of UCLA and Martha Crenshaw of Wesleyan University for inviting me, a humanist, to contribute to the deliberations of an APSA panel where the first version of this paper was given, and for providing me with references to relevant work. My thanks also to Professor Ellen Rooney of Brown University for her careful reading of earlier drafts.

1. See, for example, Rapoport and Alexander (1982), especially Louch (1982) and Glick (1982).

2. To resist such universalization is not to devalue the political realm, which remains indispensable, and indeed central, to the study of terrorism. However, the core assumption of my argument is that Armenian terrorism in particular (along with some others, such as Kurdish and Northern Irish, which emanate from long-standing grievances and enduring confrontations) cannot be fully understood simply by reference to the political objectives it announces and the antagonists it identifies. One must always take into account the embeddedness of such terrorism in the political

118   *The discursive construction of identities*

culture from which it emanates, and which it seeks to renew and transform by action even when the announced aim is solely to inflict damage on the target group. That political culture requires the mode of analysis developed here.

3. I derive the latter term from 'regulative psychobiography', a location I encountered in Spivak (1984). It has a somewhat different meaning in her work than that given to it here.

References

Amon, M. (1982) 'Religion and Terrorism: A Romantic Model of Secular Gnosticism', in Rapoport and Alexander (1982).

Ascher, W. (1986) 'The Moralism of Attitudes Supporting Intergroup Violence'. *Political Psychology*, 7(3): 403–25.

Clutterbuck, R. (1977) *Guerrillas and Terrorists*. London: Faber.

Cooper, H.H.A. (1985) 'Voices from Troy: What Are We Hearing?' in *Outthinking the Terrorist: An International Challenge*, Proceedings of the Tenth Annual Symposium on the Role of Behavioural Science in Physical Security. Washington, DC: Defense Nuclear Agency.

Crenshaw, M. (1985) 'Incentives for Terrorism', in *Outthinking the Terrorist: An International Challenge*, Proceedings of the Tenth Annual Symposium on the Role of Behavioural Science in Physical Security. Washington, DC: Defense Security Agency.

Gergen, K.J. and M. Gergen (1987) 'Narrative and the Self as Relationship', in L. Berkowitz (ed.) *Advances in Experimental Social Psychology*. New York: Academic Press.

Glick, E.B. (1982) 'Arab Terrorism and Israeli Retaliation: Some Moral, Psychological and Political Reflections', pp. 154–9 in Rapoport and Alexander (1982)

Hayasdan (various dates) (*Armenia*: in Armenian).

Laqueur, W. (1977) *Terrorism*. Boston: Little, Brown.

Louch, A.R. (1982) 'The Immortality of Belief' pp. 8–16 in Rapoport and Alexander.

Margolin, J. (1977) 'Psychological Perspectives in Terrorism', in Y. Alexander and S. Finger (eds), *Terrorism: Interdisciplinary Perspectives*. New York: John Jay Press.

Pilikian, K. (1984) *Refuting Terrorism: Seven Epistles from the Diaspora*. London: Heritage of Armenian Culture Publications.

Rapoport, D. and Y. Alexander (eds) (1982) *The Rationalization of Terrorism*. Fredericksburg, MD: University Publications of America.

Rupprecht, R. (1985) 'Terrorism and Counterterrorism in the Federal Republic of Germany', in *Outthinking the Terrorist: An International Challenge*, Proceedings of the Tenth Annual Symposium on the Role of Behavioural Science in Physical Security. Washington, DC: Defense Nuclear Agency.

Shiraz, H. (1984) 'Lisboni Voghchangeznerin' (poem in Armenian), *Horizon* (Montreal), 29 July: 6.

Spivak, G.C. (1984) 'The Political Economy of Women as Seen by a Literary Critic'. Unpublished paper.

Thomson, R. (trans. and ed.) (1982) '[The Monk] Yeghishe', in *History of Vartan and the Armenian War*. Cambridge, MA: Harvard University Press.

Wilkinson, P. (1983) 'Armenian Terrorism', *The World Today*, September.

8
Individualizing Psychology

Nikolas Rose

My concern in this chapter is with the birth of knowledges of identity and their social consequences. I shall consider the conditions for the emergence of scientific knowledges of human individuality, in particular within psychology. I will examine two senses in which such knowledges have been constitutive. On the one hand, I argue that individualizing knowledges had a constitutive role within the new forms of political authority that took shape in nineteenth-century Europe and North America. On the other hand, I suggest that it was around the issue of individualization that psychology constituted itself as a scientific discipline in its own right, as distinct from biology, philosophy, medicine and ethics. In conclusion, I suggest that there is a third sense in which such knowledges may be considered as constitutive. To the extent that they are not merely confined within theoretical treatises, but organize practices of differentiation and individualization, practices for the government of citizens *as* individuals, such knowledges have entailed a transformation of our existence as subjects and have been bound up with the constitution of the human individual itself.

Governing Societies of Individuals

The national political territories in Europe and North America in the late nineteenth and early twentieth centuries were traversed by programmes for the governing of increasing areas of social and economic life in order to achieve desired objectives: security for wealth and property; continuity, efficiency and profitability of production; public tranquillity, moral virtue and personal responsibility. These programmes were not unified by their origin in the state, nor by the class allegiances of the forces that promoted them or the aims they set themselves. As we shall see later, they were as heterogeneous in conception and support as they were diverse in their strategies and mechanisms. What did characterize these programmes, however, was the belief in the necessity and possibility of the management of particular aspects of social and economic existence using more or less formalized means of calculation about the relationships between means and ends: what should be done, in what ways, in order to achieve this or that desirable result. The most instructive arguments on these lines were made by Max Weber (1978). We are probably most familiar with his analysis of capitalism as a system characterized by monetary calculations, in which capitalists make planned use of raw materials and human activities to achieve a profit on the balance sheet.[1] However, these programmes of government not only sought to calculate and manage financial flows, raw materials, the co-ordination of stages of production and such like, but also operated upon what Weber refers to as the 'psycho-physical apparatus' of human individuals, in the belief that achieving objectives depended upon the organization of the capacities and attributes of those individuals, the ways in which they were fitted to the demands of the tasks to be undertaken, the ways in which individuals could or should be co-ordinated with one another in space, time and sequence, and the means by which those lacking appropriate capacities could be identified and excluded.

These programmes of government needed to forge a number of new instruments if they were to operate. First, a new vocabulary was required. For the government of an enterprise or a population, a national economy or a family, a child or, indeed, oneself, it is necessary to have a way of representing the domain to be governed, its limits, characteristics, key aspects or processes, objectives and so forth, and of linking these together in some more or less systematic manner.[2] While others have conceived of the languages used in regulatory practices as legitimations of the relations of power they install, this is to pose the question wrongly. Before one can seek to manage an economy, it is first necessary to conceptualize a set of processes and relations as an economy which is amenable to management. The birth of the national economy as a domain with its own characteristic laws and processes, a sphere that could be spoken about and about which knowledge could be gained, enables it to become an element in programmes that seek to evaluate and increase the power of nations by governing and managing 'the economy'. Similarly, the construction of a language of the enterprise, its processes and functions, enabled the development of new forms of managerial authority over the work-place and the worker. Thus, such languages do not merely legitimate power or mystify domination; they actually constitute new sectors of reality and make new aspects of existence practicable.

Psychiatry, psychology and psychoanalysis may also be considered in this way. Two distinct but related contributions can be noted.

On the one hand, these sciences provided the means for the translation of human subjectivity in terms of the new languages of government of schools, prisons, factories, the labour market and the economy. On the other hand, they constituted the domain of subjectivity as itself a possible object for rational management, such that it became possible to conceive of desired objectives – authority, tranquillity, sanity, virtue, efficiency – as achievable through the systematic government of subjectivity (see Rose, 1985a, 1986).

For a domain to be governable, one not only needs the terms to speak about and think about it, one also needs to be able to assess its conditions (see Latour, 1986, p. 6). That is to say, one needs intelligence or information as to what is going on in the domain one is calculating about. Information can be of various forms: written reports, drawings, pictures, numbers, charts, graphs, statistics and so forth. It enables those features of the domain that are accorded pertinence – types of goods and labour, or ages of persons, their location, health or criminality – to be represented in a calculable form in the place where decisions are to be made about them: the manager's office, the war room, the case conference, the committee room of the ministry for economic affairs or whatever. The projects for the government of social life which developed in the nineteenth century depended upon and inspired the construction of moral topographies, and a statisticalization of the population or at least its problematic sectors. The mental sciences had a role here, in providing the devices by which human capacities could be turned into information about which calculations could be made.

Such calculative practices are not auto-effective. Vocabularies of calculation and accumulations of information go hand in hand with the development of techniques by which the outcomes of calculative practices – in the form of decisions as to what should be done – can be translated into action upon the objects of calculation. New practices of regulation need to be invented, and the mental sciences made possible a form of rational regulation of individuality.

The mental sciences thus play a key role in providing the vocabulary, the information and the regulatory techniques for the government of individuals. But we should not be misled into thinking that these features of psychiatry and psychology were invented at the behest of some all-powerful authority, or in the service of some general and more or less conscious programme for control of 'deviants'.[3] Aspects of conduct and behaviour emerged for theoretical attention as a result of the often idiosyncratic difficulties encountered in the functioning of specific bits of social machinery. The army, the prison, the factory, the schoolroom, the family and the community have each formed significant institutional locations in this respect. The figures around which concern centred often seem marginal to contemporary eyes: masturbating children and hysterical women, feeble-minded schoolchildren and recruits to the armed forces, workers suffering fatigue or industrial accidents, unstable or shell-shocked soldiers, lying, bedwetting or naughty children. Instead of trying to discover overarching strategies of the state or the professions at work here, we need to describe the contingent and often surprising places in which these issues emerged as problems for authoritative attention, and the ways in which a variety of forces and groupings came to regard them as significant. These resist explanation in terms of a logic of class, gender or profession. While many of these forces have pointed to political problems and made political claims, their objectives often concern virtue as much as profit; their interests are often public good or personal happiness as much as private advancement; through their activities and inventions, they actually transform the field of politics and our beliefs as to what aspects of life are administrable and by whom. Rather than bodies of professional expertise serving functions for the state, we can begin to see the way in which the very conceptions of the nature and possibilities of regulation by social authorities have been expanded and transformed.

We should not regard the role of the mental sciences here as one of *application* of conceptual advances made in the serenity of the study or the laboratory. The impetus did not flow from an academic centre to a practical periphery or from a knowledge of normality to an application to pathology. Those histories that draw us diagrams in these terms do so in order to free their subject from associations which they consider disreputable or to re-orient it away from directions they consider unpalatable. The mental sciences did not consolidate themselves into disciplines around the timeless project of understanding the human mind, but around contingent and historically variable problems of institutional life, the psychophysical capacities and behavioural phenomena which they required and sought to produce, and the variabilities and vicissitudes of the human subject to which they accorded a visibility and pertinence.

Disciplining Difference

In the light of these comments, let me return to the questions with which I began. What does differentiate the mental sciences that were born in the nineteenth century from those discourses on the human soul that preceded them, and how is this difference linked up with other social and political events? Let me stress that I am not offering a general characterization of psychology or psychiatry – indeed, quite the reverse. Faced with the evident heterogeneity of these disciplines, their fragmented character, their lack of agreement on theory, methods, techniques or even subject matter, and their overlaps and boundary disputes with other sciences, we need to ask ourselves how they came to be individuated as distinct disciplines. What intellectual, social, practical or professional forces led to their partial separation from medicine, biology, philosophy and ethics? What produced their 'disciplinization', the establishment of university departments, professorships, degree programmes, laboratories, journals, training courses, professional associations, specialized employment statuses and so forth? If the necessity of the mental sciences cannot be derived from an ontology of their object, how might we begin to understand it?

I would like to adopt a hypothesis put forward by Michel Foucault: the suggestion that all the disciplines bearing the prefix psy- or psycho- have their origin in what he terms a reversal of the political axis of individualization. In his book *Discipline and Punish*, Foucault writes:

> For a long time ordinary individuality – the everyday individuality of everybody – remained below the threshold of description. To be looked at, observed, described in detail, followed from day to day by an uninterrupted writing was a privilege ... [The disciplinary methods] reversed this relation, lowered the threshold of describable individuality and made of this description a means of control and a method of domination ... This turning of real lives into writing is no longer a procedure of heroisation; it functions as a procedure of objectification and subjectification. (Foucault, 1979, p. 191)

Following this hypothesis, I will suggest that one fruitful way of thinking about the mode of functioning of the mental sciences, and their linkages with more general social, political and ethical trans-formations, is to understand them as *techniques for the disciplining of human difference*: for individualizing humans though classifying them, calibrating their capacities and conducts, inscribing and recording their attributes and deficiencies, managing and utilizing their individuality and variability.

Foucault argued that the disciplines 'make' individuals by means of some rather simple technical procedures. On the parade ground, in the factory, in the school and in the hospital, people are gathered together *en masse*, but by this very fact they may be observed as entities both similar to and different from one another. These institutions function in certain respects like telescopes, microscopes or other scientific instruments: they establish a regime of visibility in which the observed is distributed within a single common plane of sight. Furthermore, these institutions operate according to a regulation of detail. Such regulations, and the evaluation of conduct, manners and so forth entailed by them, establish a grid of codeability of personal attributes. They act as norms, enabling the previously aleatory and unpredictable complexities of human conduct to be conceptually coded and cognized in terms of judgements as to conformity or deviation from such norms.

The formation of a plane of sight and a means of codeability establishes a grid of perception for registering the details of individual conduct.[4] These have become both visible – the objects of a certain regime of visibility – and cognizable – no longer lost in the fleeting passage of space, time, movement and voice, but identifiable and notable in so far as they conform to or deviate from the network of norms which begins to spread out over the space of personal existence. Behavioural space begins to be geometrized, enabling a fixing of what was previously regarded as quintessentially unique into an ordered space of knowledge. The person is produced as a knowable individual in a process in which the properties of a disciplinary regime, its norms and values, have merged with and become attributes of persons themselves.

The individual of the mental sciences is, to adopt a term used in another context by Michael Lynch, a 'docile' object, one that behaves

> in accordance with a programme of normalisation ... when an object becomes observable, measurable and quantifiable, it has already become *civilized*: the disciplinary organization of civilization extends its subjection to the object in the very way it makes it knowable. The docile object provides the material template that variously supports or frustrates the operations performed upon it. (Lynch, 1985, pp. 43-4)

We should not, however, think of this movement from the complexities of actuality to the objectifications of scientific reality as one from the concrete to the abstract. Indeed, quite the reverse: the scientific object is far more concrete, far more real, than its elusive 'real' referent. Persons are ephemeral, shifting; they change before one's eyes and are hard to perceive in any stable manner. The act of scientific observation – in the laboratory, in the clinic, in the consulting room or the psychoanalyst's office – makes the individual stable through constructing a perceptual system, a way of rendering the mobile and confusing manifold of the sensible into a cognizable field. And in this process of scientific perception the phenomenal world is normalized – that is to say, is thought of in terms of its coincidences and differences from values deemed normal – in the very process of making it visible to science. Where the mental sciences differ, perhaps, from other sciences in this regard is that the norms that establish pertinence become part of the scientific programme of perception as a consequence of having first been part of a social and institutional programme of regulation – and to such programmes they are destined to return.[5]

The development of institutions and techniques, which required the co-ordination of large numbers of persons in an economic manner and sought to eliminate certain habits, propensities and morals and to inculcate others, thus made visible the difference between those who did or did not, could or could not, would or would not learn the lessons of the institution. These institutions acted as observing and recording machines, machines for the registration of human differences. These attentions to individual differences and their consequences spread to other institutions, especially those that had to do with the efficient or rational utilization or deployment of persons.[6] In the courtroom, in the developing system of schooling, in the apparatus concerned with pauperism and the labour market and in the army and the factory, two sorts of problems were posed in the early years of this century which the mental sciences would take up. The first was a demand for some kind of human sorting-house, which would assess individuals and determine the type of regime to which they were best suited. The question was framed in precisely these terms in relation to delinquency, feeble-mindedness and pauperism, and later in projects for vocational guidance and selection for the armed forces. The second was the demand for advice on the ways in which individuals could best be organized and tasks best be arranged so as to minimize the human problems of production or warfare, which ranged from industrial accidents through fatigue to insubordination. And it took only a small shift to pose this problem in a positive way and to set the mental sciences the problem, or for them to seize the opportunity, of advising on methods of managing the human factor in social and institutional life: from minimizing problems to maximizing efficiency, happiness, profit, tranquillity, security, virtue and welfare.

Inscribing Identities

These practices required for their operation new modes of codifying human individuality; they entailed the invention of devices that enable human beings to be individualized, and to be differentiated from one another in terms of that individuality. The systematization of files, records and case histories is contemporaneous with the transformations in the organization of asylums, prisons, hospitals and schools in the nineteenth century. This routine notation and accumulation of the personal details and histories of large numbers of inmates identifies each individual through the construction of a dossier consisting of those features of his or her life that are accorded pertinence by the institution and its objectives. The individual here enters the field of knowledge not through any abstract leap of the philosophical imagination, but through the mundane operation of bureaucratic documentation.

The sciences of individualization take off from these routine techniques of recording, utilizing them, amplifying them and organizing them into systematic devices for the inscription of difference.[7] They are inherently tied to the invention of such techniques for the writing down of difference, for the transformation of the properties, capacities, energies of the human soul into various material forms – pictures, charts, diagrams, numbers. In their relation to such techniques of inscription, the psychological sciences share much with other forms of scientific activity. The activities to which we give the name of science do not work upon some external raw material but upon traces, images, graphs, measurements. It is these that form the focus of the scientific gaze and the material of scientific debate.

The traces produced and worked on by science have certain characteristic qualities. Latour describes them as immutable mobiles (1986, p. 7). Whatever the original dimensions of their subjects, be they rooms full of children or chromosomes invisible to the naked eye, the traces must be neither too large nor too tiny, but of proportions that can be rapidly scanned, read and recalled. Unlike their subjects, which are characteristically of three dimensions, and whose image is subject to variations of perspective, inscriptions are ideally of two dimensions and are amenable to combination in a single visual field without variation or distortion by point of view. This enables them to be placed side by side and in various combinations, and to be integrated with materials, notes, records and so forth from other sources. Inscriptions must render ephemeral phenomena into stable forms which can be repeatedly examined and accumulated over time. Phenomena are frequently stuck in time and space, and inconvenient for the application of the scientist's labour; inscriptions should be easily transportable so that they can be concentrated and utilized in laboratories, clinics and other centres of accounting, calculation and administration.

The first techniques of inscription and individualization in the mental sciences constituted the surface of the body as the field upon which mental pathologies were made visible. The visual image, which in the portrait had functioned as a monument to an honoured nobility, now was to become a means of grasping and calibrating the sicknesses of the soul. Doctors of the insane in the late eighteenth and nineteenth centuries, from Lavater through Pinel and Esquirol, Bucknill and Tuke and up to the theorists of degeneracy such as Maudsley and Morel, reworked and systematized the ancient arts

of physiognomy, utilizing the external proportions and characteristics of the body as the means of individualizing the pathological
person. Tables and arrays of visual images, from line drawings to
carefully contrived photographs, sought to establish a grammar of
the body. This system of perception strove for a language in which
the variations and combinations of the visualized body could be
systematically mapped on to invisible mental characteristics. As
Sandor Gilman (1982) has pointed out, the linking of these pictorial
representations with case studies in textbooks on insanity and
psychopathology through the nineteenth century performed a vital
cognitive function in linking up the theoretical and the observable,
materializing the theory and idealizing the object, instructing the
mind through the education of the eyes (see also Shortland, 1985).

In phrenology, criminal anthropology and other sciences of
the soul, systems were constructed which sought to make other
aspects of the individual similarly visible and legible to the trained
eye. Such systems had only a limited life-span, not because of
their internal inconsistencies or through a theoretical critique, but
because they failed to provide the individualizing techniques that
were to be demanded of them. The co-ordination and regulation of
large numbers of persons in the expanding apparatuses of penality,
industry, education and military life produced a demand for new
techniques and vocabularies for the managing of human difference
and the conditions under which they might be invented. There now
became evident capacities and attributes of the soul which, while
they affected performance at school, or predisposed persons to
crime, or had a bearing on the success of penal regimes, or were
related to efficiency in the factory or a liability to breakdown in the
army, were not clearly inscribed upon the surface of the body. The
discipline of psychology took shape around the problem of inventing
these new techniques of individualization.

Among the various mental sciences, the principal contribution of
psychology to the project of individualization was the psychological
test. The psychological test was a means of visualizing, disciplining
and inscribing difference which did not rely upon the surface of
the body as the diagnostic intermediary between conduct and the
psyche. The problem arose in exactly this manner in the early
years of universal schooling in both England and France. Suddenly
a group of children became apparent who, while looking normal
to the untrained eye, could not learn the lessons of the school.
They accumulated in the lowest classes, a financial burden on the
authorities, a source of concern to those who regarded the school
as a vital apparatus of moralization and an affront to those who
considered education to be the right of all citizens. In seeking to

discover these children, it was first the body that was scrutinized as a means of diagnosis. Children would parade before the doctor who would seek to find marks of pathology: stigmata, misproportioned limbs, unbalanced nerves and muscles. But it proved difficult to align the gaze of the doctor with the requirements of the institution. Difference no longer marked itself unmistakably on the body's surface. It would have to be made legible.[8]

This new legibility was to be made possible by a new form of normalization: the statisticalization of human variability through the use of the normal curve. Francis Galton, in 1883, was to produce this new technique, through the argument that the simple act of comparison of the respective amount of a particular quality or attribute possessed by two members of a group enabled the mathematization of difference. This could be represented in a simple visual form once it was assumed that all qualities in a population varied according to a regular and predictable pattern, and that the characteristics of this pattern were those established for the statistical laws of large numbers. Thus individual difference could be inscribed, and hence grasped in thought and managed in reality, by means of representing the cumulative acts of comparison in the smooth outline of the 'normal' curve. Intellectual abilities could be construed as a single dimension whose variation across the population was distributed according to precise statistical laws; the capacity of any given individual could be established in terms of their position within this distribution; the appropriate administrative decision could be made accordingly. The intellect had become manageable. Difference had been reduced to order, graspable through its normalization into a stable, predictable, two-dimensional trace (Rose, 1985a).

The psychological test materializes into a routine procedure, the complex ensemble of processes whereby the individual is made inscribable. Such tests, be they intelligence tests, personality assessments or vocational guidance interviews, seek to reproduce, in the form of technical apparatus, any aspects of social or personal life that have been accorded psychological pertinence. One no longer has to aggregate persons in large institutions and observe them for long periods of time in order to see if they manifest evaluatively significant features of behaviour. Codification, mathematization and standardization make the test a mini-laboratory for the inscription of difference. The technical device of the test, by means of which almost any psychological schema for differentiating individuals may be realized, in a stable and predictable form, in a brief period of time, in a manageable space and at the will of the expert, is a central procedure in the practices of objectification and subjectification that are so characteristic of our modernity.

Psychological tests now use essentially the same techniques for quantifying all the qualities of the human soul: character, aptitudes, dexterities, levels of development and so forth. Such tests are devices for production of difference in an ordered form. They render human subjectivity into science as a disciplined object. As the visualization techniques discussed earlier merge the propositions of the theory as to the characteristics of the body with those of the object itself in the form of a visual display, so the test enables the conducts that are considered evaluatively pertinent to be produced in a stable, regular and predictable manner, to be occasioned at will. As inscription devices form a perceptual system which enable the object to be visualized in such a way as it embodies the properties of the theory, so the test forms a realization system, which enables the properties of the theory to be embodied in the actions of the subject.

The psychological test, and indeed all the techniques of examination utilized within the mental sciences, produce a peculiar mode of inscription of the powers of the individual. It is a form of writing whose destiny and rationale is the dossier: a diagnosis, a profile, a score. Its results are directed towards any institutional exigency where a decision is to be made through a calculation in which the capacities or characteristics of an individual will figure. Accumulated in the file or case notes, pored over in the case conference, the courtroom or the clinic, the inscriptions of individuality invented by the mental sciences are thus fundamental to programmes for the government of subjectivity and the management of individual difference. The procedures of visualization, individualization and inscription that characterize the mental sciences reverse the direction of domination between human individuals and the scientific and technical imagination. They domesticate and discipline subjectivity, transforming the intangible, changeable, apparently free-willed conduct of people into manipulable, coded, materialized, mathematized, two-dimensional traces which may be utilized in any procedure of calculation. The human individual has become calculable and manageable.

The mental sciences transform the ways in which inscriptions of human individuality can be produced, ordered, accumulated and circulated. They provide techniques of visualization and inscription of individuality which objectify their subjects by inscribing their differences from one another. Such technological changes in the ways in which inscriptions are produced, ordered, accumulated and circulated are simultaneously transformations in the cognitive and conceptual universe (cf. Goody, 1977; Ong, 1982; Eisenstein, 1979). The development of techniques for visualizing and inscribing human differences transforms the intellectual universe of the scientist and the practical universe of objects and relations to which things can be done. In short, these technical developments make the individual thinkable and practicable.

Conclusion

I have argued that, over the last one hundred and fifty years, social efficiency, well-being, happiness and tranquillity have increasingly been construed as dependent on the production and utilization of the mental capacities and propensities of individual citizens. Regulatory systems have sought to codify, calculate, supervise and maximize the level of functioning of individuals. They have constituted a system of individualization in terms of measurement and diagnosis rather than status and worth (Rose, 1985b). The mental sciences contribute to the language, intelligence and techniques of these programmes. They objectify their subjects by individualizing them, denoting their specificity through acts of diagnosis or of measurement. These sciences render individuals knowable through establishing relations of similarity and difference among them and ascertaining what each shares, or does not share, with others. They render previously ungraspable facets of human variability and potentiality thinkable. In so doing, they also make new aspects of human reality practicable. As objects of a certain regime of knowledge, we have become possible subjects for a certain system of power, amenable to being calculated about, having things done to us, and doing things to ourselves in the service of our individuality.

It is not, however, a question of recycling the familiar humanist critique of psychology as a science of adaptation, providing administrative tools for the manipulation of subjects by the managers of social control. Increasingly in our own century psychology has participated in the development of regulatory practices which operate not by crushing subjectivity but by producing it, shaping it, modelling it, seeking to construct citizens committed to a personal identity, a moral responsibility and a social solidarity. Dynamic and social psychologies have provided new vocabularies and technologies for thinking about and intervening in group life, family affairs and interpersonal relations. Individuality is increasingly governed not by denying subjectivity, but by seeking to forge an identification between subjective fulfilment and economic advancement, family contentment, parental commitment and so forth. Rather than basing a critique upon the need to rescue individual responsibility and subjective fulfilment from social repression, we need to recognize the extent to which our existence as selves, our awareness of our individuality, our search for our own identity, is itself constituted by the forms of identification and practices of individualization by which we are governed, and which provide us with the categories and goals through which we govern ourselves.

Notes

Different versions of this paper were presented at a Symposium of the Group for the History of Psychiatry, Psychology and Allied Sciences at Cambridge University, September 1986, and at the International Conference for the History of the Human Sciences, University of Durham, September 1986. A longer version appears in *History of the Human Sciences*, 1988. In addition to the obvious debts to the writings of Michel Foucault, I would like to acknowledge my indebtedness to the papers by Bruno Latour and Michael Lynch cited below. Thanks also to Diana Adlam for comments and advice during the preparation of this paper and to Peter Miller for incisive criticism of an earlier draft. I have not thought it appropriate to provide an extensive bibliographical apparatus, but have cited secondary texts where the various aspects of my argument can be followed up in more detail. The material presented here forms part of a study of psychological transformations of social life and subjectivity in the twentieth century, published by Routledge and Kegan Paul in 1988.

1. See in particular the comments on discipline: Weber (1978, vol. 2, ch. XIV, pt. iii).
2. For what follows see Braudel (1985); Tribe (1976); Forquet (1980); and Miller and O'Leary (forthcoming).
3. The following two paragraphs draw on Rose (1985b).
4. This discussion is indebted to Lynch (1985).
5. I demonstrate this in detail in my as yet unpublished paper, 'Making Children Manageable', in relation to the developmental psychology of Arnold Gesell and his followers.
6. More details of these are given in Rose (1985a) and the chapters by P. Miller and myself in Rose (1986). See also Garland (1985).
7. For the notion of 'inscription devices' see Latour (1986).
8. I discuss this further in Rose (1985a).

References

Braudel, F. (1985) *Civilization and Capitalism*, vol. 2. London: Fontana.
Eisenstein, E. (1979) *The Printing Press as an Agent of Social Change*. Cambridge: Cambridge University Press.
Forquet, F. (1980) *Les Comptes de la puissance*. Encres: Editions Recherches.
Foucault, M. (1979) *Discipline and Punish*. London: Allen Lane.
Garland, D. (1985) *Punishment and Welfare*. Aldershot: Gower Press.
Gilman, S. (1982) *Seeing the Insane*. Chichester: John Wiley.
Goody, J. (1977) *The Domestication of the Savage Mind*. Cambridge: Cambridge University Press.
Latour, B. (1986) 'Visualization and Cognition: Thinking with Hands and Eyes', in H. Kucklick (ed.) *Knowledge and Society*. vol. 6. Houston, TX: Rice University Press.
Lynch, M. (1985) 'Discipline and the Material Form of Images: An Analysis of Scientific Visibility', *Social Studies of Science*, 15: 37–66.

132   *The discursive construction of identities*

Miller, P. and T. O'Leary (forthcoming) Management as a Moral Science.

Ong, W. (1982) *Orality and Literacy*. London: Methuen.

Rose, N. (1985a) *The Psychological Complex*. London: Routledge & Kegan Paul.

Rose, N. (1985b) 'Michel Foucault and the Study of Psychology', *PsychCritique*, 1(2): 133–7.

Rose, N. (1986) 'Psychiatry: The Discipline of Mental Health', in P. Miller and N. Rose (eds), *The Power of Psychiatry*. Oxford and Cambridge: Polity Press.

Shortland, M. (1985) 'Barthes, Lavater and the Legible Body', *Economy and Society*, 14(3): 273–312.

Tribe, K. (1976) *Land, Labour and Economic Discourse*. London: Routledge & Kegan Paul.

Weber, M. (1978) *Economy and Society* (2 vols). Berkeley: University of California Press.

9
Social Accountability and the Social Construction of 'You'

John Shotter

> The thou is older than the I.
>
> Friedrich Nietzsche

Central to all that follows is a certain vision of the world and of our knowledge of it, that both consist of *activities* of various kinds (Shotter, 1984; Wertsch, 1981), and also a certain stance towards the conduct of research into such activity – that of investigating its nature from a position of active involvement in it, rather than contemplative withdrawal from it. Such a stance immediately raises questions about how the nature of the involvements in which one finds oneself should be best characterized. I shall claim that they are best characterized not by reference to one's own characteristics, those of first-person actors, of 'I's', but by reference to the nature of 'you's', the second-person recipients or addressees of actors' or speakers' activities; and that a central feature of any such characterization must articulate the nature of the moral proprieties, the 'ethical logistics' of the exchanges between 'I's' and 'you's' – to do with who has responsibility for what activity in the social construction of the meanings of any communications between them.

Person and Voice

Ordinary language marks a number of important distinctions, to do with articulating the character of the situation in which an actual utterance is produced, in both the voice and the person of verbs. In the simple active voice, the subject of the verb, the agent, does something to someone or something other than or separate from itself. In the passive voice, the agent is de-emphasized and often goes unmentioned, so that an outcome can be described without it being necessary to indicate explicitly *who* or what was responsible for it. In other words, to talk in a different voice is not merely to say the same thing in a different manner or style: it is to represent, in one's way of speaking, the way in which the subject of the verb in one's utterance (which might of course be oneself) is actually involved in the process depicted by that verb – for instance, whether the subject is morally *committed* (or not) by its actions to those to whom its actions or statements are addressed. For it may be that, later, those others will appeal to the character and situation of the utterance in justifying their sanctions against the subject for failures to honour such commitments. Thus, quite different practical–moral consequences flow from one's speaking in different voices.

The device of voice, and that of person, functions both to 'locate' the subject in relation to a process, and to define what might be called the positional field of the subject (Benveniste, 1971, p. 150), that is, whether the subject is involved in a personal or a non-personal relationship, and the character of that involvement. And this notion of voice may be extended to encompass more than just the voice in which a verb is uttered, but instead to characterize the whole style of an utterance upon a much larger scale, in which one speaks in, or 'through', a particular 'speech genre' (Bakhtin, 1986; Voloshinov, 1986) – where to speak in a different voice is to posit a certain form of life in which, among other things, there is a certain apportionment of the 'managerial' and 'administrative' tasks and responsibilities among the communicative participants in constructing the meaning of utterances, that is, the different rights and duties as to who must do what in constituting communicative activity as effective. Wertsch (in press), for example, mentions the different expectations engendered in the addressee about how the speaker's utterances should be related to one another by questions asked in (or through) a voice of knowledgeable authority, compared with those asked in a voice of genuine ignorance. (See also Gergen Chapter 5 above as well as Gilligan, 1982.) Most importantly, the voice in which one speaks influences where authority is to be located when matters of definition are involved.

But let me turn now to the person of the verb. In situations of ordinary language use, at least, to address a person in a particular person grammatically is straightaway to say something about what you take their status to be – and to address them wrongly has serious practical consequences. Grammatically, at least, to be related as a second-person, rather than as a third-person, to a first-person is both to be situated quite differently and to be assigned a quite different set of privileges and obligations (Lyons, 1968). Indeed, as Harré (1983) points out, a whole set of subtly different statuses is marked out in pronoun systems more complex than our present Indo-European forms. First- and second-persons (plural or singular) are, even if in fact non-personal or inanimate, always personified (with all that that implies for the 'personal' nature of their relation), and are thus, so to speak, 'present' to one another, in a 'situation'. By contrast, third-persons need not be personified (they can be 'its'); nor are they present as such to other beings or entities; nor are they necessarily 'in a situation'. Indeed, the category is so non-specific that it may be used to refer to absolutely anything, so long as it is outside of, or external to, the immediate intra-linguistic situation jointly created in the communicative activities between first- and second-persons. While second-persons have a duty to attend only to what in their activities first-person performers intend them to attend to – and to be continually responding to a speaker's hesitations, uncertainties and failures, rather than to their intended meaning, is not only to be thought rude, but to run the risk of their sanction – third-persons have no such responsibilities. Hence one's unease, as a first-person attempting a tricky interpersonal encounter, to notice oneself observed by a third-person, 'outside', observer (Goffman, 1959; Sartre, 1958).

The Inattention to the Second-person

Thus the use in a behaviouristic and/or positivistic social science of third-person, passive voice talk fails to capture the character of important relations between those whom one studies (and hence leads to the misrepresentation of their social life); it also hides the nature of the ethical (and political) relations between them and the science studying them. As a corrective to the concern with only third-persons, with what in fact are grammatical non-persons, the recent history of social and developmental psychology has been marked by an increasing concern with personhood, with persons, agency and action (rather than with causes, behaviour and objects) (Harré and Secord, 1972; Harré, 1979, 1983; Shotter, 1975; Gergen, 1982). That concern, however, has been directed mostly towards the analysis of grammatical first-persons, towards what it is to be an active agent, an 'I', a subject doing something to something or someone else. Little attention has been paid to people's existence as the persons 'addressed' by first-persons, to whom or what it is one is embedded in when one is rooted or embedded in communicative activity. And thus the nature of the grammatical second-person has been ignored.

In what follows, I want to redress the balance: I want both to render the 'I' problematic, and to show how little of substance can be said about it, and also, perhaps surprisingly, to show how much of importance can be said about 'you', about the 'medium' in which one is embedded as an 'I' and how its nature and workings make us what we are. Thus, rather than attempting to account for ourselves and our world in terms of how we at present experience them, I shall be much more concerned to account for *why*, seemingly, we experience them as we do, for why, at this moment in history, we experience ourselves – or at least, why we *account* for our experience of ourselves – in such an individualistic way: as if we all existed from birth as separate, isolated individuals *already* containing 'minds' or 'mentalities' wholly within ourselves, set over against a material world itself devoid of any mental processes.

The Repudiation of 'Possessive Individualism' and the Cartesian Starting-point

Indeed, I want to say that we *talk* in this way about ourselves because we are entrapped within what can be thought of as a 'text', a culturally developed textual resource – the text of 'possessive individualism' – to which we seemingly must (morally) turn, when faced with the task of describing the nature of our experiences of our relations to each other and to ourselves. In that 'text', the individual is seen as

> essentially the proprietor of his own person or capacities, owing nothing to society for them. The individual [is] seen neither as a moral whole, nor as part of a much larger social whole, but as the owner of himself. The relation of ownership, having become for more and more men the critically important relation determining their actual freedom and actual prospect of realizing their full potentialities, was read back into the nature of the individual. The individual, it was thought, is free inasmuch as he is proprietor of his person and capacities. (Macpherson, 1962, p. 3)

Indeed, Macpherson's account could very well figure as one of the major texts of identity explored in this book, for he shows how the notion of 'possession', although clearly not the source of other important concepts – such as freedom, rights, obligations and justice – has none the less powerfully shaped their interpretations, and hence our notions of how we are (or should be) related to one another, and hence what and who we are.

However, it is not my purpose here to explore the extent to which we have been (and of course, in these Thatcher/Reagan years, *still are*) entrapped within the image of society as a market, and of individuals as all living in psychological isolation from one another, engaging only in commercial relations with each other. My purpose is merely to explore the general point that different ways of accounting (still a commercial metaphor?) for ourselves to ourselves cannot be assessed as being simply true or false. They are constitutive of our actual relations to one another, and, to the extent that we constitute ourselves in our relations to others, constitutive of ourselves, and must be studied as such. I want now to account for our entrapment in this text, not so much by examining the particular nature and historical background of possessive individualism itself, as by examining the general nature of what it is for us, in our social and psychological being, to be 'shaped' by the textual nature of our involvements with one another. I want to do this, essentially, by the formulation of what might be called a counter-text (i.e., counter to possessive individualism), a text that tells a quite different story about the nature of our individuality and psychological capacities, and about the nature of our relations to the others around us; a story in which it is 'you' rather than 'I' that assumes the leading role – which entails a shift from an individualistic to a communitarian perspective.

In other words, I want to repudiate the traditional 'Cartesian' starting-point for psychological research located in the 'I' of the individual – which assumes that all psychological problems are to do solely with the acquisition and utilization of objective knowledge – and to replace it by taking as basic not the inner subjectivity of the individual, but the practical social processes going on 'between' people. In other words, I want to replace a starting-point in a supposed 'thing', geometrically or geographically located within individuals, with one located (if 'located' is now at all the right word) within the general communicative commotion of everyday life at large – the stance I mentioned above.

The Disappearance of the 'I'

The Cartesian starting-point is deeply entrenched: it is implicit in many of the practices of current psychological research (as well as in the philosophical discourses concerned with their justification). Central to it is the apparently self-evident *experience* that one's own *self* (one's 'I', or ego, or whatever else it may be called) exists somewhere 'inside' one, as something unique and distinct from all else that there is – and it is *that*, its substantial existence, which guarantees one's personal identity (rather than it being a social or discursive construction, as I would like to argue). In this Cartesian sense, it is '*the self*' as a 'thing' which becomes the ultimate, unconditioned source of thought, meaning and, strangely, of language and speech also. It appears on the philosophical scene as the epistemological *subject*, as the knower distinct from what there is to be known, able to gain knowledge from the world (said to be *objective* and 'external' to the subject) in a wholly individual and autonomous way; that is, such a subject is said to be able to gain knowledge without, in principle at least, needing to learn anything from other people. Thus, the fact that one comes into the world as a *child* and develops only slowly to adulthood – which in any case is a morally tenuous status in which one is continually corrigible by others – is neglected as immaterial in this individualistic image of personhood. Indeed, in this view, what took humankind many thousands of years to understand and to develop – namely, how to be a self-conscious agent distinct from the activities in which one is rooted – is treated either as something one learns as an individual mostly in one's early years, merely by opening one's eyes to what is around in one's external world for one to *observe*, or else as something one is born already knowing *innately*; a third possibility, that one *ontologically* learns how *to be* this or that kind of person, how *to be* a self-determining thinker, perceiver, rememberer, imaginer, listener, spectator, speaker, actor and the like, is not even considered.

This is because, I think, the Cartesian starting-point seems to accord so well with what many of us now regard as 'our experience' – at least, those of us who, after the appropriate schooling or instruction, know how to respond intelligibly to the request to explain our sense of personal identity. Witness, for instance, Nick Humphrey, who, in expounding his theory that we understand others in analogy with ourselves, writes:

> When I reflect on my own behaviour I become aware not only of external facts about my actions but of a conscious presence, 'I', which 'wills' those actions. This 'I' has reasons for the things it wills. The reasons are various kinds of 'feeling' – 'sensations', 'memories', 'desires'. '"I" want to eat because "I" am hungry', '"I" intend to go to bed because "I" am tired'. '"I" refuse to move because "I" am in pain'. (Humphrey, 1983, p. 33)

And he goes on to claim (p. 33) that we only understand another as an 'I's because 'I naturally assume that he (or she) operates on the same principles as I do'.

But here, is the 'I' that refuses to move in the same logical category as the 'I' that finds itself in pain? Is there any *thing* as such at all to which the word 'I' refers, or for which it stands – an entity, substance, or principle of unity? Consider, for instance, the claim that 'I think my thoughts'. Rather than implying that 'I' can exist separately from my thoughts, and that I possess them as I possess other objects external to myself – as, indeed, cognitive psychologists do seem to imply – the implication of such a statement must be, as William James (1890, p. 401) put it, that the 'thought is the thinker'. For, as he argued, if my thinking is confused, *I* am confused: if my thought is blocked, *I* am blocked; and so on. While my 'me' – an empirical identity, a 'loosely construed thing' which *I* construct for myself – may consist in an aggregate of things objectively known, 'the *I* which knows them cannot be an aggregate ...' (pp. 400–1). But if we are to accept James's claims here, another *image* of our relation to our own mental capacities is required, an image other than that of the proprietorial or possessive self, to guide us in making sense of his claims. We must imagine ourselves to be not an object-like thing as such, but a mobile *region* of continually self-reproducing activity. Then it might seem sensible to say of ourselves that 'The kind of activity that I am at the moment is thinking activity.' But at present, this way of talking about ourselves lacks currency. Whether we can recognize our experience of ourselves in James's kind of description or not, like Nicholas Humphrey, most of us feel that there *must be* something, some 'thing', within us which functions as the causal centre of all our activities, the 'I' that wills our actions. But must there be?

In his analysis of his own experience, James refused, in formulating his description of it, to talk in this way, to say that what he *must be* experiencing is the experience of a central 'I', the transcendental thinker. Indeed, for James, the 'I' as any kind of substantial entity disappears. And in his very final conclusion to his chapter on 'The Consciousness of Self', he says:

> The only pathway that I can discover for bringing in a more transcendental thinker would be to *deny* that we have any direct knowledge of the thought as such. The latter's existence would then be reduced to a postulate, an assertion that there *must* be *a knower* correlative to all this *known*: and the problem *who that knower is* would have become a metaphysical problem ... [and] that carries us beyond the psychological or naturalistic point of view. (James, 1890, p. 401)

Hence, as James sees it, it is not our experience as such that forces the conclusion upon us that we possess an inner, central 'I', a unitary self: indeed, as a result of the particular forms of 'deconstructive' investigations he conducted, his *experience* denied it.

And such a conclusion accords well with Benveniste's (1971, p. 210) claim that *I* is a sign that is non-referential with respect to any extra-linguistic reality; that it does not name any lexical entry; that it is, as he puts it, an 'empty' sign which becomes 'full' in different ways according to its use by speakers in their utterances. And it refers then, each time, only in the instance of discourse in which it is used, while, as he says, each instance of the use of a noun may be referred to a fixed and 'objective' notion, capable of remaining potential or of being actualized in a particular object and always identical with the mental image it awakens. Instances of the use of 'I' do not constitute a class of reference, since, like James, he claims that there is no 'object' definable as *I* to which these instances can refer in identical fashion. Each *I* has its own reference and corresponds each time to a unique being who is set up as such.

What then is the reality to which *I* and *you* refer? It is solely a 'reality of discourse', and this is a strange thing. *I* cannot be defined except in terms of 'locution', not in terms of objects as a nominal sign is ... *I* can only be identified by the instance of discourse in which it is produced. But in the same way it is also as an instance of form that *I* must be taken ... There is thus a combined double instance in this process: the instance of *I* as referent and the instance of discourse containing *I* as the referee. The definition [of *I*] can now be stated precisely as: *I* is 'the individual who utters the present instance of the discourse containing the linguistic instance *I*.' Consequently, by introducing the situation of 'address', we obtain a symmetrical definition for *you* as 'the individual spoken to in the present instance of discourse containing the linguistic instance *you*'. (Benveniste, 1971, p. 218)

Thus, in Benveniste's account, pronominal forms do not work by referring to an extra-discursive reality, or to an already existing set of objective statuses or places in space or time, but function within an intra-linguistically constructed 'positional field', a field that is constructed and reconstructed, moment by moment, in and through one's utterances.

By their use, we can not only distinguish between whose activity is whose – distinguish, for instance, what I am saying from what you are saying, and what was said by others, or that you did this while I did that, and so on – but we can do more. Because they function to provide in their use what Benveniste calls a 'combined double instance', or, to put it another way, because they possess what others have called 'duality of structure' (Bhaskar, 1979; Giddens, 1979; Shotter, 1983) and appear both as structuring and as a structure, they can function to indicate not only *who* one is but also *what* one is at the same time. Thus, the problem of representing both the relative 'location' of different 'places' and their changing character, in a shifting and developing discursive 'space', is solved by the use of these 'mobile' signs which each speaker can *appropriate* to themselves and relate to their person. So, although I may say 'I feel this' and 'I desire that', and may claim that in so saying I experience a certain conscious presence – my 'I', which accompanies such claims, if Benveniste and James are right (and I think they are) – then those different uses of *I* do not in any unitary or total way refer to what we *are*. So why do we *feel* so strongly that there *must be* somewhere such an entity?

Social Accountability and Rational Visibility

We feel so strongly, I want to claim, because of what elsewhere (Shotter, 1984), I have called 'social accountability', the fact that we *must* talk only in certain already established ways, in order to meet the demands placed upon us by our need to sustain our status as responsible members of our society – where the 'must' involved is a moral must. For, even as adults, our status is a morally tenuous one, and if we fail to perform in both an intelligible and legitimate manner, we will be sanctioned by those around us. I suggest that it is because of this – the moral (or perhaps better, the moralistic) requirement that we express ourselves only in ways approved by others – that we *feel* that our reality *must be* of a certain kind. It is not our actual experience that demands it, but our ways of talking which make themselves felt when we attempt to reflect upon our experience, and to account for it. In other words, what we talk of *as* our experience of our reality is constituted for us very largely by the *already established* ways in which we *must* talk in our attempts to *account* for ourselves – and for it – to the others around us. What we think of and talk of as our 'intuitions' about ourselves are 'forced' upon us by the ways of talking that we must use in justifying our conduct to others (and in criticizing theirs). And only certain ways of talking are deemed legitimate. Why?

Even more than Wittgenstein (1953, 1980), it was C. Wright Mills (1940) who much earlier emphasized that the main function of language is not the representation of things in the world, or the giving of 'outer' expression to already well formed 'inner' thoughts, but its use in creating and sustaining social orders. It is not so much how 'I' can use language in itself that matters, as the way in which I *must* take 'you' into account in my use of it. 'We must approach linguistic behaviour', Mills says, 'by observing its social function of co-ordinating diverse actions. Rather than expressing something which is prior and in the person, language is taken *by other persons* as an indicator of future actions' (Mills, 1940, p. 904; my emphasis). Although events and states of affairs in the world are always open to further specification linguistically, and may be further specified this way and that within a particular medium of communication, we cannot just talk as we please. We must talk in accord not only with what the facts will permit, but also with the requirements of the medium of communication used – which often, in the case of our everyday public communications, is the reproduction of a certain dominant social ordering. But it follows from this that, if our ways of talking are constrained in any way – if, for instance, only certain ways of talking are considered legitimate and not others – then our understanding, and apparently our experience of ourselves, *will be constrained also*.

To reverse a phrase of Garfinkel's (1967), aspects of our experience will be rendered 'rationally invisible' to us; we will be incapable not only of accounting for them, but of perceiving and registering them *as intelligible*, that is, as being one or another kind of commonplace event. And this, I maintain, *is* our position at the present time: we are all embedded within a *dominant* social order which we must, to some extent at least, continually reproduce in all of the mundane activities we perform from our place, 'position' or status within it – and it is an order that is both *individualistic* and *scientistic*. This induces in us not only a feeling of necessity – that we must account for all our experiences in terms that are intelligible and legitimate within this order - but also, paradoxically, a kind of rational blindness to the fact of our involvement in such an activity: in other words we fail to register the fact of our involvement with others, and in taking them into account in all we do we continually reproduce a certain way of structuring *all* the social relations in which we are involved.

What I now want to argue is that such communally shared ways of, or means for, making-sense are constitutive of people's social and psychological being in quite a deep way. Among other things, they *enable* the members of a social order not only to account for themselves to themselves and others when required to do so, but also to act *routinely* in an *accountable* manner – their actions informed in the course of their performance by such procedures. In other words, they enable the performance of activities for which individual persons can be held responsible, which can be related to their 'selves', that is, to their appreciation of how they are placed in relation to the others around them (Shotter, 1984). Besides *enabling* accountable action, however, such methods or ways also work to *constrain* it, to limit members in what they feel they can say or do – for people, as mentioned above, if they are to avoid sanctions by powerful others, must talk and act only in ways appropriate to their momentary 'position' or status in relation to the others around them. In other words, in developing within a particular region of one's society, from a child to an adult, one learns from the other adults there how to be the kind of person required in that region of one's social order, in order to reproduce it; one learns how to act taking 'one's relations to others' into account in the performance of one's actions. That is, one learns the nature of other people as 'you's', as certain kinds of 'you', who afford different kinds of opportunities for one's action – who 'motivate' or 'invite' one to act in some ways rather than others.

But the paradoxical result of all this for us is that our established modes of discourse 'invite' us to treat people as the 'text' of possessive individualism suggests, as possessing all their psychological characteristics within themselves, owing nothing to society for them. And thus, in our researches, we have concentrated all our attention upon what is supposed to occur 'inside' isolated individuals studied 'externally', from the point of view of third-person observers, socially uninvolved with them. We have failed to study what goes on 'between' people as first- and second-persons, the *sense-making practices*, procedures or methods made available to us as *resources* within the social orders into which we have been socialized – procedures that have their provenance neither in people's experience not in their genes, but in *the history* of our culture. We have also completely ignored the nature and importance of second-persons.

Addressivity: The Constructing and the Construction of 'You'

This is yet another aspect of the rational blindness which our current modes of accountability have induced in us: not only have we ignored the *resources* made available to us by our social context, but we have also ignored the standpoint, available only within a discourse, from which people's meanings (not their movements) are perceived and understood as such. To compensate for this neglect, the remainder of this chapter will concentrate upon 'you', upon what it is for someone to *address* their communications to 'you' specifically as their proper recipient – or to observe 'you' as someone to whom later they might properly address a communication, perhaps in criticism or correction of what has seemingly been said or done by one in one's actions or utterances. And indeed, the notion of 'addressivity' will be one of my central concerns below. (See Clark and Holquist's (1984) account of Bakhtin's views on this most important issue.) From our beginning as children, and continuing on into our lives as adults, we are dependent upon being addressed by others for whatever form of autonomy we may achieve; thus, in this sense we can say that, as persons, we are always 'you's', always essentially second-persons. The 'thou' is older than the 'I' in the sense that the capacity to be addressed as a 'you' by others is a preliminary to the ultimate capacity of being able to say 'I' of oneself, of being able to understand the uniqueness of one's own 'position' in relation to others, and to take responsibility for one's own actions.

In other words, in this view, people are not eternal, unchanging entities in themselves (like isolated, indistinguishable atoms), but owe what stability and constancy, and uniqueness, they may appear to have – their identity – to the stability and constancy of certain aspects of the activities, practices, and procedures in which they can make their differences from those around them known and accountable. The aspects in question are those in which, like the authoring of a text, we shape, pattern and develop, in moment-by-moment changes, as new contingencies arise, the differing relations between our own 'position' or 'place' (who we are), and the positions of those around us. But the title of this chapter is purposely ambiguous: in allowing for this passive concern with 'addressivity', and with the way in which we are created as the individuals we are by the others around us, it allows for a rather more active interpretation also: a concern with the way in which an *audience* (either a singular or a plural 'you') affords, permits, motivates, allows or invites *only a limited* performance upon the part of first-persons. I act not simply 'out of' my own plans and desires, unrestricted by the social circumstances of my performances, but in some sense also 'in to' the opportunities offered me to act, or else my attempts to communicate will fail, or be sanctioned in some way. And my action in being thus 'situated' takes on an ethical or moral quality. I cannot just relate myself to the others around me as I myself please: the relationship is ours, not just mine, and in performing within it I must proceed with the expectation that you will intervene in some way if I go 'wrong' – only with a highly developed skill at anticipating and pre-empting such interventions, can I proceed as I please.

The Second-person: 'You'

There are thus a number of reasons why the second-person role is important. The most obvious – but perhaps not the most important reason – is that, to put the matter quite personally, I need, if not your actual presence, then an imagined surrogate now (at each moment in my writing), as an audience to evaluate my attempts to write. And if this writing were talk, then I would need 'you' as a context 'into' which to address my remarks, and into which I feel I must fit what I say (if I am to avoid at least embarrassment); without your attention, without your smiles and occasional nods of approval, I would find it very difficult to continue my speech. It is necessary continuously to co-ordinate the management of our sense-making practices as our communicative activities proceed. But more than the avoidance of embarrassment is at stake. 'You' constitute for me (or the surrogate I constitute in place of you) someone who is like myself, able to be a member of the (dominant?) social order, someone to whom it makes sense to *address* my remarks here, and whom I can reasonably expect to be moved by them in some way; in other words, you provide the motivation for my remarks. For genuine human communication is not (as depicted in the 'information theory' model of it) a simple matter of transferring information from point A to point B. 'I's', in addressing themselves to second-person 'you's' (either actual or implied), rather than to third-person 'it's', or even to 'him's', 'she's' or 'they's', always speak or act with an understanding of what a 'you's' anticipated response might be. It is a part of what it is for someone to attempt to mean something to someone else: they are addressed as being capable of responding to such an address in some way. And an understanding of *how they might respond* is a part of our understanding of *who* they are for us; and clearly, we compose ourselves differently according to whether we must address a child, a superior or inferior, an equal, a loved one, an academic critic, an enemy and so on. Indeed, 'the anticipated response' – the way in which what one does or says indicates future action (Mills, 1940), whether one's own or of others, is a crucial part of what it is for a person to be self-consciousness: people must understand what socially they are trying to achieve, in what individually they actually do.

This leads me to my next, slightly more important, point: that you might respond, not to what I am saying or doing, but to what I might have said or done but didn't. In other words, you are expecting me to perform (to write) with certain standards 'in mind' (to use a figure of speech), to answer to certain responsibilities in my conduct, and if I do not, you have a right to correct me. You are not just a source or sink of information, but a *judge* of it too (and thus there is a degree of apprehension in my addressing you). I treat you as operating according to standards, as being able to evaluate my performance critically and to sanction it if it should fall short in any way (particularly in its intelligibility; less so, perhaps, for its legitimacy – though that is, as I see it, the major hurdle that work of this kind has to overcome if it is to gain acceptance).

Neither of these two points, however, seems to me to be so important as the third one that I now want to mention: that when small children are addressed as 'you', rather than merely having information reported to them upon which to base (or not) their individual actions, they are being 'in-structed' in how *to be*. This is another sense in which human communication cannot be seen simply as a matter of information transfer from one location to another, it must be seen as ontologically *formative*, as a process by which people can, in communication with one another, literally in-form one another's being, that is, help to make each other persons of this or that kind. For instance, one is addressed in discourse as 'you' and in such discourse in-formed as to the use of all the other pronouns. Hence the child, who can understand its mother's admonition, 'Stop making so much noise, *you*'re shouting', and can respond by saying (as they usually do) 'No *I* wasn't', knows, among other things, that just as he or she is annoyed or distracted by noise, and has a right to object to it, so have others – that they try to deny that right to others is, of course, all a part of the microsocial power politics of growing up. In responding thus, the child knows that the 'you' spoken by others addressing it refers to itself, yet also refers to those others when the child addresses them. And in learning the 'architecture' of address, children learn not only a set of ideal, reciprocal rights and duties to do with an equality of access to communicative opportunities, but also the *actual* distribution of such opportunities in the region of their development, and hence the nature of the social structure there – that some people are most difficult of access that others.

This suggests a fourth point. To the extent that people are essentially beings produced by other such beings – and especially by their predecessors, who form and care for them until such time as they can be *accounted* independent – there are certain *developmental* facts about us which are essential to our being persons at all. I mean the fact that we grow up: that we go through recognizable phases from, for example, infancy to maturity, from dependency to relative independency, from ignorance to wisdom: that we find life a task: and that, whatever achievements of our predecessors we inherit, we have to reject (or rebel against) a portion of their learning, as history moves on; that the media of communication we live in are suffused with claims to authority which are not easily contested. Indeed, people not only have a *life history*: they are expected to be knowledgeable about it in some way, and that knowledge is expected to be influential in their actions. They have had (and are still susceptible to) traumas and triumphs, joys and regrets, delights and disasters, and what has happened to them in the past makes a difference to how they act now. They cannot just exist as ahistorical, atemporal beings. So, although Dennett, 1978, p. 267), to mention one of the many who ignore these 'developmental' conditions on the attribution of personhood, may be right in saying that one's dignity as a person 'does not depend upon one's parentage', he is wrong to claim (with computers in mind), that it does not depend upon 'having been born of woman or born at all': it clearly does. A human life devoid of any relations of dependency upon, and responsibilities for, as well as tensions with, those around one, both older and younger, and with those from different regions of social life from one's own (although conceivable), would not quality as a (ordinary) human life at all. The possession of a developmentally susceptible identity – in other words, the possibility of living of a life susceptible to a biographical account – is an essential part of what it is to be an ordinary person, and to play one's part in the history of ordinary persons.

Putting the matter of one's identity in this way suggests a fifth and final point: the fact that individual development is not a matter (as, I must admit, I myself once thought - Shotter, 1973) of children being merely helped by adults around them to bring the 'natural powers' innately in them, in virtue of their birth as human beings, under their own control, thus transforming them into 'personal powers'. In my earlier views I was clearly still in the thrall of the classic 'text' of identity, possessive individualism, enshrined in our more everyday forms of talk. The activity between first- and second-persons – elsewhere I have called it 'joint action' (Shotter, 1984) – is, however, activity of a very special kind, for at least the following two reasons. First, as human activity it has an *intentional* quality to it; it 'points to', or 'indicates', or 'makes a relation to', something other than or beyond itself. In other words, it works to relate 'things' (whether objects, events, states of affairs, procedures, methods or other activities) in some way to the *situation* between the participants; as 'things', they are given an intelligible 'place' within it and thus made available as resources, as means. And it is in this way that the continual activity constituting the general commotion of everyday social life at large makes available a body of cultural resources for general use – at least, to the extent that one can gain access to the communicative activities in which they have their being.

But not only are otherwise alien entities transformed in joint action between different individuals into resources for general use: they are also transformed into 'shared' resources, in the following sense. Whether the joint activity producing them is a matter of agreements or disagreements, when one person acts 'into' a jointly constructed setting rather than 'out of' his or her own plans or desires, an outcome is produced which is independent of any of the individuals involved and 'belongs' only to the collectivity they constitute. An argumentative exchange involving justifications produced in response to criticism is just as productive of joint, and hence individual-independent, outcomes as an activity involving only agreements; the disagreements we have are just as much 'ours' as the love we find ourselves in.

So it is in this sense that, even among quite different people, who may maintain their differences in their involvements with one another, shared 'entities' held in common can be formed. Indeed, certain of these, whatever their origins in conflicts, coercions, negotiations or agreements, must serve as stable and basic standards in terms of which all our other communications have their sense and significance: I mean the rights and powers, the duties and enablements, the basic communicative ethics which regulate our ways of making sense. While not incorrigible or indubitable (in a Cartesian sense), such (ethical) standards cannot in any practical sense be rationally denied. For rationally, in any context, one should not deny the 'foundations' in terms of which one's actions have their force in that context.

Conclusion

What, then, is involved in the social constructing and construction of 'you'? Well, not the construction of a certain kind of object or entity – that's for sure. There ain't no such 'things' as 'I's' or 'you's' – at least, not with anything more than a fleeting existence, changing moment by moment. However, in being addressed as a particular 'you', in certain particular settings, by certain particular people, you come to know yourself as a particular kind of person among other such persons; as someone whom you can (in both a naturalistic and an ethical sense) address as they address you. In Hegel's phrase, people must live as 'mutually recognizing themselves as mutually recognizing each other'. And such a knowledge shows itself in the ability to use *all* the pronouns appropriately, as none of them have sense except in relation to one another. For that is their function: to indicate the momentary and changing relations between the 'places' or 'positions' constructed in a discursive reality: to locate the source and the address of communications, the rights and duties of the communicants in managing meaning, and the rights of access they might have to one another.

This implies an approach to language which perhaps should now be stated explicitly: that the primary function of language is formative or rhetorical, and only secondarily and in a derived way referential and representational. It works by people materially moving one another by its use to behave in certain ways (Silverman and Torode, 1980): it can 'instruct' them in their practical activities (Vygotsky, 1962), where among such activities and practices, along with many others, is the socially negotiated fashioning and use of modes of representation and ways of reference (see Lee, 1985). The formative nature of language seems to be such that primarily vague and only partially structured events and states of affairs in the world, can be *specified further* within a medium of communication; in other words, people can be 'moved' linguistically into treating their circumstances in certain socially recognized and recognizable ways. (See Shotter, 1984, for an account of this 'specificatory' approach to the functioning of language.) This enables the crafting, the social construction, of certain devices, particularly *ways* of speaking, for use by people in managing the nature of their social relations; that is, people can construct, within the activity of speaking itself (and once having done so, continually reproduce in their speaking), devices or procedures for use in co-ordinating and sequentially ordering complex and intricate activities (and their outcomes) among large numbers of people over large distances and long times. Such devices help in administrating and co-ordinating the logistical problems involved in managing different ways of meaning – who has responsibility for what.

Such devices or procedures, although of course structured (at least partially), are used not primarily as pictures, as copies or representations of one's surroundings to which to refer in one's actions *instead* of to one's actual circumstances – as if *all* of one's activity had to take place in relation to surroundings not actually present – but as a structured *means* through which to act or to communicate with one's actual surroundings, where its *structured* nature allows one to discriminate, in the relation between the outflow of activity from oneself and the resultant inflow of activity from one's surroundings, the active nature of one's surroundings. In other words, by acting *through* differently structured means, one discovers different aspects of one's surroundings in relation to one's self – an approach to the acquisition of knowledge first put forward by Plato in *Theaetetus* (see Pred and Pred, 1985), but articulated recently by quite a number of writers (e.g. Bohm, 1965; Heidegger, 1967; Polanyi, 1958; Shotter, 1982; Vygotsky, 1962; Wertsch, 1985). In such a view of language as a means through which to act, the different ways in which it functions as such a means are just as important as the different meanings to which it gives rise; what one does linguistically determines the character of the results produced by one's utterances.

For us as social scientists, this means that our ways of talking (when used both as a means through which to co-ordinate our activities among ourselves as investigators, and as a means for relating ourselves to those whom we investigate) are not neutral in how we present our world and its problems to ourselves: as I have argued above, our different ways of talking work to 'propose' different forms of social relationship, different statuses, different ways of 'positioning' ourselves in relation to others, different patterns of rights and privileges, duties and obligations. And it is now possible to see how the claim – not just in psychology, but in the rest of science – that to be 'scientific' one must speak in a particular way, making use of only third-person, passive voice talk, is more than merely a matter of producing a self-effacing representation of oneself, as lacking interests, opinions and desires of one's own. It is also more than a matter of producing an account which (supposedly) allows states of affairs, as it were, to 'speak for themselves'. It also works to construct a particular ethical (and political) relation between oneself and the audience one addresses in one's communications. The ignoring of 'you', the failure to provide a place or a function for the grammatical second-person, in the idioms or 'speech genres' (Bakhtin, 1986) we use in our scientific communications, thus has a number of serious consequences, and it has been my purpose here to explore some of those consequences – especially, how the shaping and crafting of the relations between ourselves and those around us is done linguistically, and the special the part 'you' might play in such crafting.

References

Bakhtin, M.M. (1986) *Speech Genres and Other Late Essays* (ed. M. Holquist; trans. C. Emerson and M. Holquist). Austin, Texas: University of Texas Press.
Benveniste, E. (1971) *Problems in General Linguistics*. Miami, FL: University of Miami Press.
Bhaskar, R. (1979) *The Possibility of Naturalism*. Brighton: Harvester Press.
Bohm, D. (1965) *The Special Theory of Relativity*. New York: Benjamin Press.
Clark, K. and M. Holquist (1984) *Mikhail Bakhtin*. Cambridge, MA: Harvard University Press.
Dennett, D. (1978) *Brainstorms: Philosophical Essays on Mind and Psychology*. Brighton: Harvester Press.
Garfinkel, H. (1967) *Studies in Ethnomethodology*. Englewood Cliffs, NJ: Prentice-Hall.
Gergen, K.J. (1982) *Toward Transformation in Social Knowledge*. New York: Springer-Verlag.
Giddens, A. (1979) *Central Problems in Social Theory: Action, Structure and Contradiction in Social Analysis*. London: Macmillan.
Gilligan, C. (1982) *In a Different Voice: Psychological Theory and Women's Development*. Cambridge, MA: Harvard University Press.
Goffman, E. (1959) *The Presentation of Self in Everyday Life*. New York: Doubleday. (Penguin Books, 1971).
Harré, R. (1979) *Social Being: a Theory for Social Psychology*. Oxford: Basil Blackwell.
Harré, R. (1983) *Personal Being: A Theory for Individual Psychology*. Oxford: Basil Blackwell.
Harré, R. and P.F. Secord (1972) *The Explanation of Social Behaviour*. Oxford: Basil Blackwell.
Heidegger, M. (1967) *Being and Time*. Oxford: Basil Blackwell.
Humphrey, N. (1983) *Consciousness Regained: Chapters in the Development of Mind*. London: Cambridge University Press.
James, W. (1890) *Principles of Psychology*, Vols 1 and 2. London: Macmillan.
Lee, B. (1985) 'Intellectual Origins of Vygotsky's Semiotic Analysis', in J. Wertsch (ed.), *Culture, Communication, and Cognition: Vygotskian Perspectives*. London: Cambridge University Press.
Lyons, J. (1968) *Introduction to Theoretical Linguistics*. London: Cambridge University Press.

Macpherson, C.B. (1962) *The Political Theory of Possessive Individualism: Hobbes to Locke*. Oxford: Oxford University Press.

Mills, C.W. (1940) 'Situated Actions and Vocabularies of Motive', *American Sociological Review*. 5: 904–13.

Polanyi, M. (1958) *Personal Knowledge: Towards a Post-critical Philosophy*. London: Routledge & Kegan Paul (New York: Harper & Row, 1962).

Pred, R. and A. Pred (1985) 'The New Naturalism – A Critique of *Order out of Chaos*', *Environment and Planning D: Society and Space*. 3: 461–76.

Sartre, J-P. (1958) *Being and Nothingness: An Essay on Phenomenological Ontology* (trans. Hazel Barnes). London: Methuen.

Shotter, J. (1973) 'Acquired Powers: The Transformation of Natural into Personal Powers', *Journal for the Theory of Social Behaviour*. 3: 141–56.

Shotter, J. (1975) *Images of Man in Psychological Research*. London: Methuen.

Shotter, J. (1982) 'Consciousness, Self-consciousness, Inner Games, and Alternative Realities', in G. Underwood (ed.), *Aspects of Consciousness*, Vol. 3. London and New York: Academic Press.

Shotter, J. (1983) '"Duality of Structure" and "Intentionality" in an Ecological Psychology', *Journal for the Theory of Social Behaviour*. 13: 19–43.

Shotter, J. (1984) *Social Accountability and Selfhood*. Oxford: Basil Blackwell.

Silverman, D. and B. Torode (1980) *The Material Word: Some Theories of Language and its Limits*. London: Routledge & Kegan Paul.

Voloshinov, V.N. (1986) *Marxism and the Philosophy of Language*. Cambridge, MA: Harvard University Press.

Vygotsky, L.S. (1962) *Thought and Language*. Cambridge MA: MIT Press.

Wertsch, J.V. (1981) *The Concept of Activity in Soviet Psychology*. Armonk, NY: M.E. Sharpe.

Wertsch, J.V. (1985) *Culture, Communication, and Cognition: Vygotskian Perspectives*. London: Cambridge University Press.

Wertsch, J.V. (in press) 'The Role of Voice in a Sociocultural Approach to Mind', in W. Damon (ed.), *Child Development Today and Tomorrow*. San Francisco: Jossey-Bass.

Wittgenstein, L. (1953) *Philosophical Investigations*. Oxford: Basil Blackwell.

Wittgenstein, L. (1980) *Remarks on the Philosophy of Psychology*. Vols 1 and 2. Oxford: Basil Blackwell.

PART III

DRAMA AND NARRATIVE IN THE CONSTRUCTION OF IDENTITIES

10
Narrative Embodiments:
Enclaves of the Self in the Realm of Medicine

Katharine Young

> To write the body.
> Neither the skin, nor the muscles, nor the bones,
> nor the nerves, but the rest: an awkward, fibrous,
> shaggy, raveled thing, a clown's coat
>
> Roland Barthes

Persons are tender of their bodies as if their selves inhered in its organs, vessels, tissues, bones and blood, as if they were embodied. For us, the body is the locus of the self, indistinguishable from it and expressive of it. As the phenomenologist, Maurice Natanson, writes,

> The immediacy of my experience of corporeality should be understood as an indication of the interior perspective I occupy with respect of 'my body'. I am neither 'in' my body nor 'attached to' it, it does not belong to me or go along with me. *I am my body.* (Natanson, 1970, p. 12).

I experience myself as embodied, incorporated, incarnated in my body. To appear in my own person is to evidence this implication of my self in my body.

Medical examinations threaten this embodied self with untoward intimacies. The accoutrements of propriety are stripped away: I appear in nothing but my body. What follows has the structure of a transgression, an infringement, but one in which I am complicit. I disclose my body to the other, the stranger, the physician (see Berger and Mohr, 1976, p. 68). To deflect this threat to the embodied self, medicine constitutes a separate realm in which the body as lodgement of the self is transformed into the body as object of scrutiny: persons become patients. This transformation is intended to protect the sensibilities of the social self from the trespasses of the examination. Whatever the medical business of the examination, its phenomenological business is to displace the self from the body (see Young, in press). However, persons can perceive rendering the body an object as depersonalizing, dehumanizing or otherwise slighting to the self.[1] The disparity between the physician's intention and the patient's perception establishes the context for 'gaps', 'distortions' and 'misunderstandings' between patients and physicians (Mishler, 1984, p. 171).

Because of their sense of the loss of self – a well-founded sense if also a well-intentioned loss – patients can have some impulse to reconstitute a self during medical examinations. This reconstitution can be undertaken by the patient in one of two moves:[2] either by breaking the framework of the realm of medicine by disattending, misunderstanding or flouting its conventions[3] or by maintaining the framework but inserting into the realm of medicine an enclave of another ontological status, specifically, a narrative enclave.

Rules for producing narratives on ordinary occasions require that they be set off by their frames from the discourses in which they are embedded (see Young, 1982, pp. 277–315). Narrative frames – prefaces, openings, beginnings, endings, closings, codas – create an enclosure for stories within medical discourse. The discourse within the frames is understood to be of a different ontological status from the discourse without. In particular, the Storyrealm, the realm of narrative discourse, conjures up another realm of events, or Taleworld, in which the events the story recounts are understood to transpire (see Young, 1987, pp. 15-18). It is in this alternate reality that the patient reappears as a person. This move depends on the existence of what Alfred Schutz calls 'multiple realities' (1967, pp. 245–62), the different realms of being, each with its own 'metaphysical constants' (Natanson, 1970, p. 198), which individuals conjure up and enter into by turning their attention to them.

Embodying the self in a narrative enclave respects the conventions of the realm of medicine and at the same time manages the presentation of a self, but of one who is sealed inside a story. An inverse relationship develops between the uniquely constituted narrative enclosure in which a patient presents a self and the jointly constituted enclosing realm in which the patient undergoes a loss of self. Stories become enclaves of self over the course of an occasion on which medicine inhabits the realm of the body.

Erving Goffman argues that persons are in the way of presenting themselves, guiding controlled impressions, not necessarily to deceive, but to sustain a reality, an event, a self. Structurally, the self is divided into two aspects: (1) the performer who fabricates these impressions, and (2) the character who is the impression fabricated by an ongoing performance which entails them both (Goffman, 1959, p. 252). On ordinary occasions, then, persons do not provide information to recipients but present dramas to an audience (Goffman, 1974, p. 508). It is here that the theatrical metaphor for which Goffman is famous takes hold: talk about the self is not so far removed from enactment. We do not have behaviours and descriptions of them but a modulation from embodied to disembodied performances. Storytelling is a special instance of the social construction of the self in which 'what the individual presents is not himself but a story containing a protagonist who may happen also to be himself' (Goffman, 1974, p. 541). On the occasion investigated here, embodying the self in stories occurs in circumstances in which the self is being disembodied, a complication of the matter Goffman has called 'multiple selfing', that is, the evolving or exuding of a second self or several selves over the course of an occasion on which the self is being presented (Goffman, 1974, p. 521 fn.).

The natural occurrence of these 'texts of identity' in the course of a medical examination suggests implications about the uses of narrativity in social scientific discourse. Kenneth and Mary Gergen write that 'rules for narrative construction guide our attempt to account for human actions across time', both in making ourselves intelligible informally and in social scientific discourse (Gergen and Gergen, 1986, p. 6). Individuals use narratives, they argue, to reflexively reconstruct a sense of self. 'The fact that people believe they possess identities fundamentally depends on their capacity to relate fragmentary occurrences across temporal boundaries' (Gergen and Gergen, 1983, p. 255). What the Gergens call 'self-narratives' then 'refer to the individual's account of the relationship among self-relevant events across time' (p. 255). Kenneth Gergen's speculation that 'lives are constructed around pervading literary figures or tropes' (Gergen, 1986, p. 3) is an instance of his more general claim 'that scientific theory is governed in substantial degree by what are essentially aesthetic forms' (Gergen and Gergen, 1986, p. 20).

Note that two claims are being made here: that individuals use stories to make sense of events, and that so, in the same vein, do social scientists. The narrativity of social scientific discourse, then, takes its legitimation from storytelling in everyday life. This in turn warrants the application of narrative theory to social scientific discourse. However, discovering the structures of narrative in discourses about the self must be distinguished from imputing narrative structures to discourses about the self. The first is an ethnographic enterprise; the second an analytic one. To regard social scientific discourse as narrative is to treat it under a metaphor, in the same way that it is to regard cultures as texts or minds as cybernetic systems or reality as mechanistic. Analysts' uses of the devices of narrative to structure their approaches to discourses about the self render problematic the conventions that narrativity imports into the social sciences. My concern as a narratologist is to distinguish these approaches from persons' presentations of self in narrative modes. It is crucial to return to the social disposition of stories, to their linguistic coding, their contexts of use, to see how they illuminate the way individuals construe their lives. Doing so lays the groundwork for pursuing enquiries into narrativity as an interpretive structure for social scientific discourses about the self.

This is an analysis of a medical examination in the course of which the patient tells three stories in which he appears as a character. The links and splits between the realm of medicine and the realm of narrative illuminate the nature of narrative, the nature of medicine, and the nature of the self.

Medical examinations are divided into two parts: the history-taking, and the physical examination. These internal constituents of the realm of medicine are bounded by greetings and farewells which mark the transition between the realm of the ordinary and the realm of medicine. The shift from greetings, in which the physician emerges from his professional role to speak to his patient as a social person, to history-taking, in which the physician elicits information from the patient about his body, is the first move towards dislodging the self from the body. The patient's social person is set aside to attend to his physical body.

The patient on this occasion is Dr Michael Malinowski, a seventy-eight-year-old professor of Jewish history and literature. He has come to University Hospital to consult an internist, Dr Mathew Silverberg.[4] Dr Silverberg shakes hands with the professor and his son in the waiting room, escorts them to his office, and there begins to take the patient's history. The shift from the waiting room to the office reifies the transition between realms. The history-taking reorients the person's attitude towards his body in two respects: it invites him to regard his body from outside instead of from inside, and it invites him to see it in parts instead of as a whole. Dr Silverberg's enquiries direct the patient to attend to his body as an object with its own vicissitudes which he recounts with the detachment of an outsider. In so doing, Dr Malinowski suffers a slight estrangement from his own body. In making these enquiries, Dr Silverberg asks about the parts of the body separately, disarticulating it into segments. So Dr Malinowski's body undergoes a fragmentation. Since the self is felt to inhere in the body as a whole from the inside, these shifts of perspective tend to separate the self from the body. It is against the thrust of this ongoing estrangement and fragmentation that the professor sets his first story, the story of the liberation. Dr Silverberg has shifted from general enquiries about the whole body – height, weight, age, health – to specific enquiries about the eyes, the throat and the blood. He continues:

Story 1
The Liberation[5]

Dr S: Have you ever had any problems with your heart.
Dr M: No.
Dr S: No heart attacks?
Dr M: Pardon me?
Dr S: Heart attacks?
Dr M: No.
Dr S: No pain in the chest?
Dr M: No pain in the chest.
Dr S: I
        noticed that=
Dr M: I am a graduate from Auschwitz.
Dr S: I know— I heard already=
Dr M: Yeah.
        I went there when— I tell Dr Young about this
        and
        after Auschwitz
        I went through a lot of— I lost this
Dr S: Umhm.
Dr M: top finger there
        and
        I was in a—
        after the liberation we were under supervision of
        American doctors.
Dr S: Yeah?
Dr M: American doctors.
Dr S: Right.
Dr M: And it uh
        I was sick of course after two years in Auschwitz I was
           quite uh uh exhausted.
        And later I went through
        medical examination
        in the American Consul
        in Munich
Dr S: Yeah?
Dr M: and I came to the United States.
Dr S: Right?
Dr M: In nineteen hundred forty-seven.
        Nineteen forty-six—

<pre>
          about nineteen forty-seven.
          One day—
          I lived on Fairfield Avenue
          I started to spit
          blood.
Dr S: Right?
Dr M: Yeah?
          And I called the doctor
          and he found that something here ((gestures to his chest))
Dr S: Tuberculosis?
Dr M: Somethin— yeah.
          And I was in the Deborah
          Sanitorium for a year.
Dr S: In nineteen forty-seven.
Dr M: I would say forty-seven and about
          month of forty-eight.
              ...
Dr S: Back
          to your heart.
</pre>

The story conjures up a Taleworld, the realm of Auschwitz, which is juxtaposed to the ongoing history-taking. The preface, 'I am a graduate from Auschwitz', opens onto the other realm. Prefaces are a conventional way of eliciting permission to take an extended turn at talk in order to tell a story (Sacks, 1970, II, p. 10). In response to what he perceives as a divagation from the realm of medicine, Dr Silverberg says, 'I know – I heard already.' Having heard a story is grounds for refusing permission to tell it again (Goffman, 1974, p. 508). Dr Malinowski persists in spite of this refusal, thus overriding one of the devices available to physicians for controlling the course of an examination, namely, a relevancy rule: that the discourse stay within the realm of medicine. To insert the realm of narrative into the realm of medicine, the professor initially breaks its frame. But in so doing, he substitutes another relevancy rule: topical continuity. Like the history-taking, the Taleworld focuses on a part of the body, the chest. It is this part of the body that the professor uses to produce topical continuity between the history-taking and the story. However, it is not the chest but the heart on which the physician is focusing. When he returns talk to the realm of medicine with the remark, 'Back to your heart', he is at the same time protesting the irrelevance of the excursion.[6] As is apparent from this, the rule for topical continuity, the selection of a next discourse event which shares at least one element with a previous discourse event, permits trivial connections between discourses and, by extension, between realms. But there is a deeper continuity here. Both the realm of Auschwitz and the realm of medicine address the body.

In the realm of medicine, the dismantling of the body continues with Dr Silverberg's enquiries about the heart, breath, ankles and back; he recurs to whole body concerns with enquiries about allergies, habits and relatives; then he goes on to segment the body into the skin, head, eyes again, nose, throat again, excretory organs, stomach again, muscles, bones and joints. Into this discourse, the professor inserts his second story, the story of the torture. This story is also about a part of the body, the finger, and so again maintains a parallel with the realm in which it is embedded, although not the strict tie of topical continuity. Having created an enclosure in medical discourse for the Auschwitz stories earlier on, Dr Malinowski now feels entitled to extend or elaborate that Taleworld (see Young, 1987, pp. 80-99). This story is tied not to the discourse that preceded it but to the previous story in which he mentions his finger. As if in acknowledgement of the establishment of this enclosure, Dr Malinowski's preface, 'I was not sick except this finger', elicits an invitation from Dr Silverberg to tell the story: 'What happened to that finger.' The Taleworld is becoming a realm of its own.

Story 2
The Torture

Dr M:　No.
　　　　I don't know.
　　　　I tell you— I told you Dr. ((*to me*)) I don't—
　　　　during the twenty-three months in Auschwitz
Dr S:　Yeah?
Dr M:　I was not sick except this finger.
Dr S:　What happened to that finger.
Dr M:　I wa—
　　　　I tell Dr. Young
　　　　I was sitting
　　　　((*coughs*)) you have something to drink
Dr S:　Yeah.
　　　　I have for you.
Dr M:　Yeah.
　　　　I was sitting at the press—
　　　　the machine
　　　　I don't know how to say in English
　　　　[— a machine or]
Dr S:　[I understand.]
Dr M:　Anyway I had to put in this was
　　　　iron
　　　　and I had to put in— in here with the right hand to put
　　　　　　this which made a hole or whatever it did.
Dr S:　Made a hole in your finger.
Dr M:　No.
　　　　Made a hole here. ((*in the piece of iron*))

My finger got it.
And behind me was an SS man.
The SS was walking.
And he stood behind me
and at one moment he pushed me.
Just— this was a— a— a—
daily sport.
And instead to put the iron in I put my finger in.
/
But otherwise I wasn't sick.

The shift from taking the history to giving the physical examination involves moving to another space, the examining room, which is an even more narrowly medical realm. Dr Silverberg closes the history-taking by saying:

Dr S: I would like to examine you.
Dr M: For this I came.
Dr S: I will lead you into the examining room?
Dr M: All right.
Dr S: I would like you to
       take everything off
       Down to your undershorts.
       And have a seat on the table.

Dr Silverberg then takes his patient to the examining room down the hall and leaves him to take off his clothes. Clothes are the insignia of the social self. Their removal separates the body from its social accoutrements. This reduction of the social self along with the enhancement of the medical realm completes the dislodgement of the self. What remains is the dispirited, unpersoned, or dehumanized body.

During the physical examination, the body is handled as an object. When Dr Silverberg returns he finds the professor lying on the examining table in old-fashioned long white shorts that button at the top, with his arms folded across his chest. They speak to each other and then Dr Silverberg comes up to the examining table, picks the patient's right hand up off his chest, holds it in his right hand, and feels the pulse with his left fingertips. Here is the inversion of the initial handshake which enacted a symmetry between social selves; the physician touches the patient's hand as if it were inanimate. The examination is the rendering in a physical medium of the estrangement of the self and the fragmentation of the body. The external perspective is substituted for the internal perspective and the whole is disarticulated into parts. Of course, there is still talk – questions, comments, instructions; but now such remarks are inserted into interstices between the acts, the investigations, the physical manipulations that structure the examination. Henceforth, for the course of the physical examination, the patient's body is touched, lifted, probed, turned, bent, tapped, disarranged and recomposed by the physician. It is here that the absence of the self from the body can be intended as a protection: the social self is thereby preserved from the trespasses of the examination. These are committed only on an object.

The physical examination proceeds from the hands up the arms; then Dr Silverberg sits the patient up, looks at his head, ears, eyes, nose, mouth, throat, back, chest and heart; then he lays the patient back down on the table, tucks down the top of his shorts, examines his genitals, and folds the shorts back together at the top. He continues down the legs to the feet, then sits him up again and returns to the arms and hands. At this point, Dr Silverberg asks the patient to touch his nose with the tips of his fingers and as he does so the patient alludes to a bump on his skull: 'I have to tell you how I got that.' And the physician responds, 'How.' Despite this invitation, Dr Malinowski appears uncertain about the propriety of inserting a story into this realm.

Story 3
The Capture

Dr M: I have to tell you how I got that. ((*the bump*))
Dr S: How.
Dr M: Should I talk here?
Dr S: You
Dr M: Can I talk here?
Dr S: Sure.
      /
Dr M: You already know. ((*to me*))
      When I (s— try) to go the border
      between Poland and Germany
Dr S: Yeah?
Dr M: I wanted to escape
      to the border over Switzerland=
Dr S: Umhm.
Dr M: as a Gentile.
Dr S: Yeah?
Dr M: When they caught me
      they wanted investigation.
      /
Dr S: That it?
Dr M: (At)
      the table was (sitting) near me
      and (his arm) was extending behind me
      with— how the police ha— how do you call it.

```
        A police club?
Dr S:   Nightstick.
Dr M:   Nightstick.
Dr S:   Umhm.
Dr M:   And they—
        I had to count
        and they hit me twenty
        times over the head.
        And er— he told me zählen
        zähle means you count.
        And after the war—
        after the liberation shortly about two three days
        American Jewish doctors came
        they (examined us)
        and he told me
        that I have
        a nerve splint here?
Dr S:   Yeah.
Dr M:   And this made me be deaf.
```

The physician then examines the patient's ears, and finally his prostate and rectum. So here, suspended between the genital and rectal examinations, the two procedures towards which the displacement of the self from the body are primarily oriented, is the professor's third and last story. Once again, the story is about a part of the body, the ears, which maintains a continuity with the realm of medicine. But it is also about another part of the body, the genitals. As he mentions, Dr Malinowski has already told me this story when I talked to him in the waiting room to get his permission to observe and tape-record his examination. He told me that he and a friend had decided, boldly, to cross the border out of Poland into Germany and work their way across Germany to the Swiss border. They carried forged papers. He himself got through the border and was already on the other side when something about his friend aroused the border guard's suspicion and they called him back. To check their suspicions, the guards pulled down his pants and exposed his genitals. Jews were circumcised. This story is concealed as a subtext directed to me within a text directed to the physician. On this understanding, the positioning of the story between the genital and rectal examinations has a tighter topical continuity than is apparent on the surface.

Stories are sealed off from the occasions on which they occur – here, the realm of medicine – as events of a different ontological status. For that reason they can be used to reinsert into that realm an alternate reality in which the patient can reappear in his own person without disrupting the ontological conditions of the realm of medicine. Stories about the realm in which he appears, the world of Auschwitz, might be supposed to be inherently theatrical, on the order of high tragedy. But the boundary between realms insulates medicine in some measure from the tragic passion. The apertures along the boundary through which the realms are connected are here restricted to parts of the body. In telling these stories, Michael Malinowski is not intending to play on his hearers' emotions. He is rather reconstituting for them the ontological conditions of his world and, having done so, inserting himself into that realm as a character. Besides creating a separate reality, telling stories during a medical examination creates a continuity between the two realms which converts the ontological conditions of the realm of medicine precisely along the dimension of the body.

The stories are tokens of the man, talismans of the salient and defining history which has shaped him. They are not, on that account, unique to this occasion, but are invoked as touchstones of his presence (as they were, for instance, for me when we talked before the examination). They present a person whose life is wrought around an event of existential proportions. Auschwitz was a life-pivoting, world-splitting event: time is reckoned before-Auschwitz and after-Auschwitz; space is divided by it. Not only has he lost a country, a language and a childhood, but he has also lost a life-form. Before Auschwitz, he had a wife and child in Poland; the son who has brought him today is the only child of a second marriage made in the USA after the war. Dr Malinowski mentions once that he had two sisters: one perished, the other died a few years ago of cancer.

The sequential order of events in a story replicates the temporal unfolding of events in the realm it represents (Labov, 1972, pp. 359-60). This replication is supposed by social scientists to extend to the sets of stories which are strung together to make a life history. In this instance, the sequential order in which these stories are told does not replicate the temporal order in which the events they recount occurred. He tells about the liberation first, then the torture, and finally the capture. There are of course clear contextual reasons for this which have been detailed here in terms of topical continuity. But I would like to suggest a deeper reason for their array. These stories cluster around Michael Malinowski's sense of self. Auschwitz provides what I would like to call centration: life is anchored here, everything else unfolds around this. The set of stories that make up the Auschwitz experience could be told in any order. There is an implication here for the use of narrativity in the social sciences. In insisting either on the notion that temporally ordered events are presented sequentially in stories or on re-ordering stories to present them so, social scientists have misunderstood the shape of experience: a life is not always grasped as a linear pattern. Serious attention to narrativity in stories of the self will not force the sense of self into the pattern of narrative, but will deploy narrative to discover the sense of self.

In so presenting the man and reconstituting the ontological conditions of his world, these stories attain the status of moral fables and lend the medical examination a delineation which renders the etiquette of touch an ethical condition. Not that the stories are warnings to the physician against similar transgressions. Rather, in the existential context of these stories, what might otherwise be seen as indignities to the body are transmuted into honours: the physician is a man whose touch preserves just those proprieties of the body that are infringed at Auschwitz.

The body in the Taleworld is the analogue of the body in the realm of the examination, connected to it part for part, but inverted. The stories spin out existential situations in which the self is constrained to the body. In the first story, 'The Liberation', the part of the body is the chest and the mode of insertion of the self in the body is sickness. The self cannot transcend its absorption in its bodily discomforts: its sensibilities are sealed in its skin. In the second story, 'The Torture', the part of the body is the finger and the mode of insertion of the self in the body is pain. The self is jolted into the body, its sensibilities concentrated in its minutest part, the tip of a finger. In the third story, 'The Capture', the parts of the body are the head and the genitals, and the mode of insertion is humiliation. Here the body is emblematic of the man, literally inscribed with his identity. Its degradations are his.

The phenomenological cast of the Taleworld is set against the phenomenological cast of the realm of the examination in which the self is extricated from the body. The medical history of the tuberculosis, the severed fingertip, the deafness, which could be detached, is instead enfolded in the personal history of the concentration camp and recounted as a story. So Auschwitz is invoked not as the cause of these dissolutions of the flesh, but as the frame in terms of which we are to understand what has befallen the body and, it transpires, the frame in terms of which we are to understand what has become of the man. To see the fact that both the realm of medicine and the realm of narrative are about the body as topical continuity is a trivial rendering. The stories are transforms of the ontological problem that is central to the examination: the fragile, stubborn, precarious, insistent insertion of a self in the body.

Appendix: Transcription Conventions

Line-ends   Pauses

From Tedlock, 1978:

=	Absence of obligatory end-pause
/	One turn pause
Capital letters	Start of utterance
.	Down intonation at end of utterance
?	Up intonation at end of utterance
—	Correction phenomena
( )	Doubtful hearings
(( ))	Editorial comments
[[	Simultaneous speech
[ ]	Extent of simultaneity

Adapted by Malcah Yeager from Schenkein, 1972:
...   Elisions
Initials before turns are abbreviations of speakers
English spelling indicates English speaking

Notes

This paper was first given in 1985 at the American Folklore Society Meetings in Cincinnati, Ohio. The present version was clarified by a critical reading by Kenneth Gergen.

1. This sense of dehumanization is well attested to in both popular and social scientific literature. Elliot Mishler locates dehumanization in the discourse of medicine, where he describes it as the conflict between the voice of medicine, which is understood to dominate during medical examinations, and the voice of the life-world, which is suppressed in a way, he argues, that leads to an 'objectification of the patient, to a stripping away of the life-world contexts of patient problems' (Mishler, 1984, p. 128).
2. Mishler points out that the conventions could be shifted by the physician (1984, p. 162).
3. Mishler would say, by interrupting the voice of medicine with the voice of the life-world (1984, p. 63).
4. To protect confidentiality, the names of the patient, the physician and the hospital are fictitious.
5. The text is transcribed from tapes of medical examinations collected during my research on the phenomenology of the body in medicine in 1984. Transcription devices are appended.
6. Mishler notes that the struggle between voices for control is associated with disruption of the flow of discourse (1984, p. 91). As he says, to see departures from the medical paradigm as interruptions is to privilege the physician's perspective (p. 97). 'I am proposing an interpretation of the medical interview as a situation of conflict between two ways of constructing meaning. Moreover, I am also proposing that the physician's effort to impose a technocratic consciousness, to dominate the

voice of the life-world by the voice of medicine, seriously impairs and distorts essential requirements for mutual dialogue and human interaction. To the extent that clinical practice is realized through this type of discourse, the possibility of more humane treatment in medicine is severely limited.' I should like to reiterate my point that the objectification of the body can be intended to protect the sensibilities of the person. To see the dominance of the medical paradigm as an imposition is to privilege the patient's perspective. The rhythm of interplay between perspectives, discourses or realms is my concern here.

References

Barthes, R. (1977) *Roland Barthes*. New York: Hill and Way.
Berger, J. and J. Mohr (1976) *A Fortunate Man: The Story of a Country Doctor*. New York: Pantheon.
Gergen, K. (1986) *If Persons are Texts*. New Brunswick, NJ: Rutgers University Press.
Gergen, K. and M. Gergen (1983) 'Narratives of the Self', in T.R. Sarbin and K.E. Scheibe (eds), *Studies in Social Identity*. New York: Praeger.
Gergen, K. and M. Gergen (1986) 'Narrative Form and the Construction of Psychological Theory'. Unpublished paper, Swarthmore College/Pennsylvania State University.
Goffman, E. (1959) *The Presentation of Self in Everyday Life*. New York: Doubleday.
Goffman, E. (1974) *Frame Analysis*. New York: Harper & Row.
Labov, W. (1972) 'The Transformation of Experience in Narrative Syntax', in *Language in the Inner City*. Philadelphia: University of Pennsylvania Press.
Mishler, E.G. (1984) *The Discourse of Medicine: Dialectics of Medical Interviews*. Norwood, NJ: Ablex.
Natanson, M. (1970) *The Journeying Self: A Study in Philosophy and Social Role*. Reading, MA: Addison Wesley.
Sacks, H. (1968) Unpublished lecture notes, University of California, Irvine, 17 April 1968.
Sacks, H. (1970) Unpublished lecture notes, University of California, Irvine, 17 April 1970.
Schenkein, J. (1972) *Foundations in Sociolinguistics*. Philadelphia: University of Pennsylvania Press.
Schutz, A. (1967) *On Phenomenology and Social Relations*. Chicago and London: University of Chicago Press.
Tedlock, D. (1978) *Finding the Center: Narrative Poetry of the Zuni Indians*. Lincoln and London: University of Nebraska Press.
Young, K. (1982) 'Edgework: Frame and Boundary in the Phenomenology of Narrative Communication', *Semiotica*, 41(1/4): 277–315.
Young, K. (1987) *Taleworlds and Storyrealms: The Phenomenology of Narrative*. Dordrecht: Martinus Nijhoff.
Young, K. (in press) 'Disembodiment: The Phenomenology of the Body in Medicine', *Semiotica*.

11

Complex, Ontology and Our Stake in the Theatre

David Holt

This chapter begins in Jung's theory of complexes. The complex provides a text for the exploration of identity in this sense: as Jung saw them, our complexes have us as much as we have them. Put this way, his theory of complexes poses a question: Which comes first, life or meaning – the activities we perform or the meanings we think of ourselves as enacting? Who (or what) is the 'I' which is presented to an audience? Is it an entity generated in a larger flow of activity of which it is only a part, or is it itself one of the sources of that activity? Two orders of reality would seem to be involved, or, better, two ways of ordering reality: one is as if we are embedded in a process that generates its own meaning; in the other, we live as if meaning depends upon our enactment. Unless we attempt to ignore one or the other, we cannot avoid committing ourselves to both; but that is hazardous, lest we fall between the two. We are left unsettled, insecure, at risk, with the choice of either adopting some strategy of evasion, or staking our lives on the hazard, and attempting to accept both. What might be a model for exploring the relation between these two orderings?

Theatre is one of the ways in which we celebrate that 'staking', the riskiness of giving ourselves up to a larger process in order to become more ourselves. I illustrate this with reference to Sophocles' play *Oedipus the King* and Aristotle's interpretation of its effect on its original audiences. From its beginnings, theatre has explored the discrepancy between character and action, and the conflict between the rival claims of meaning and life to explain one another. It is in the enactment of dramas that we can find, not a coherent resolution of the two, but paradigms for possible 'workings-out' of their relation. One such working-out is suggested by the history of our word 'hypocrite', which leads to recognition of the human face as the most familiar of all texts of identity.

Complexes and the Selection of Meaning

When we consider how 'having an analysis' fits into the whole shape of someone's life, there is one fact that we should not overlook. However often, for however long a period of time, we go to an analyst, he is never going to know more than a fraction of what we know about our lives; and what we know ourselves is never more than a fraction of the whole. If we have lived for thirty years before we get into an analyst's consulting room, and if we live for another thirty years after we've said good-bye, whether we spend twenty, or two hundred, or two thousand hours there, we can never hope to tell all about ourselves. Inevitably, selection, and selection of a minute fraction of our total experience, is a fundamental factor in determining the nature of psychoanalytic practice.

This kind of selection is familiar to students of drama and of the novel. Whatever we need to know about Hamlet in order to understand and respond to the play is enclosed within the limits of the play; similarly with whatever kind of understanding an analyst can acquire of the life presented to him. It is not the understanding of an outside observer contemplating a more or less complete causal sequence leading up to the present situation (though the unhappily chosen name 'analyst' suggests just that): it is the understanding of someone who has tacitly agreed to accept an implicit principle of selection, in the same way as the audience agrees to accept the convention of the theatrical limits in time and space.

But if this selection is such a fundamental factor, who or what selects the things we talk about to our analyst? Is there anything in the analytical situation that corresponds to the role of the playwright in the theatre?

We can look at this question from the point of view of the so-called presenting situation. Here it is obvious that the analyst has not had any say in the selection of the problem we want to discuss. But is it true to say that 'I' have selected it? It usually feels more as if life has in some way presented us with some intractable dilemma which we have to get help with. The problem has been selected *for* us, rather than *by* us.

Or we can look at this question of selection in terms of what happens in those first crucial interviews. There is that strange process so often commented on, by which the initial problem gradually drops away, and in its place quite other subjects occupy the analytic sessions. What is happening here? Who is selecting these new questions? How can we understand this process of selection, which allows of such a shift of interest away from what I was convinced was my real problem?

Various answers to such questions have been proposed. The one I want to consider is Jung's concept of the complex. Here, it seems to me, we have an idea which places this fundamental fact of selection where it belongs – at the heart of psychoanalytic theory and practice – while also suggesting connections with cognitive and behavioural studies. The word 'complex' has passed so easily into our general vocabulary that it has lost the special meaning that Jung tried to give it. But this meaning is central to an understanding of Jung's work, and has a wider relevance today when analysts from various backgrounds are feeling their way to a more comprehensive hermeneutic than was available to either Freud or Jung.

Jung selected the complex as the theme for his inaugural lecture as Professor at the Swiss Federal Polytechnic Institute in 1934. In this lecture he made two points relevant to our question, Who, or what, selects the subjects we talk about with the analyst?

> 1. The unconscious would in fact be ... nothing but a vestige of dim or 'obscure' representations, or a 'fringe of consciousness' ... were it not for the existence of complexes. That is why Freud became the real discoverer of the unconscious in psychology, because he examined those dark places and did not simply dismiss them, with a disparaging euphemism, as 'parapraxes'. The *via regia* to the unconscious, however, is not the dream, as he thought, but the complex, which is the architect of dreams and of symptoms. (Jung, 1960, p. 101)

And, elsewhere in the same lecture:

> 2. Everyone knows nowadays that people 'have complexes'. What is not so well known, though far more important theoretically, is that complexes can *have us*. (Jung, 1960, p. 96)

What are the implications of this for my experience in analysis? It means that the analyst's attitude to my problem is going to be infuriatingly equivocal. On the one hand, he appears to treat me as a person who knows what he is doing and what he wants, that is, to be rid of this 'thing' which is making a thorough mess of my life. At any rate, he is accepting my money, and unless he is dishonest that should mean that he is accepting me as a legally responsible person, who knows what I want. But on the other hand, I quickly sense that for him the problem is not a problem in the same sense as it is for me. Sometimes I have the uneasy feeling that, far from helping get rid of this incubus that has settled on me, he is more interested in it than he is in me. When I get this feeling, I have mixed reactions. On the one hand, I am furious. That is not what I am paying money for. But on the other hand, I probably would not have gone to an analyst in the first place unless I had myself felt that there was more to this problem than met the eye. If I have this feeling, then, besides anger at the analyst being apparently more interested in my problem than in me, I will also feel that, precisely for that reason perhaps, he can help where others cannot. I am beginning to sense that I am 'had' by something greater than myself: that the thing of which I was so anxious to be rid may be much more interesting and full of life than I am. In Jung's language, I am beginning to recognize the value of the complex. Another way of putting it would be to say that I am beginning to realize that life is not merely something that I live, but is also something that I enact.

The idea behind Jung's phrase about the complex as having me, as well as my having it, is one that we meet in many places in his work. In a sense, this is an idea we can grasp easily. But my experience over twenty years of practice is that it needs more than psychology for its understanding. It involves us in philosophical, and perhaps theological, problems which have gone out of fashion. How are we to train ourselves to deal with them properly?

Ontological Hazard

This brings us close to what for many is the central 'scandal' of Jung's psychology, that cause of offence and stumbling which gives his work its special quality and which is probably the reason for its exclusion from the main stream of university teaching and research. I cannot open up that whole issue here. All I wish to do is to try to extend our awareness of what is involved in the idea of the complex so as to introduce my main thesis: that the psychoanalysis of complexes implies a view of the world that is both ontological and dramatic.

If we want to explore more deeply what Jung meant with this idea of 'complexes having us', we have to turn to his writing on that most difficult area of experience, which he has named, not very happily, 'archetypal'. It was out of reflection on the experience of the complex that Jung developed his theory of archetypes, and it was in his writing about the archetypes that he developed the wider implications of this sense of being had by a complex, as well as ourselves having a complex.

Here are two passages – again, derived from a lecture given in 1934 – which open up wider horizons round our questions: Who, or what, selects what we talk about with the analyst?

1. Life is crazy and meaningful at once. And when we do not laugh over the one aspect and speculate about the other, life is exceedingly drab, and everything is reduced to the littlest scale. There is then little sense and little nonsense either. When you come to think about it, nothing

has any meaning, for when there was nobody to think, there was
nobody to interpret what happened. Interpretations are only for those
who don't understand; it is only the things we don't understand that
have any meaning. Man woke up in a world he did not understand,
and that is why he tried to interpret it. (Jung, 1959, p. 31)

and

2. It always seems to us as if meaning – compared with life – were
the younger event, because we assume, with some justification, that
we assign it of ourselves and because we believe, equally rightly no
doubt, that the great world can get along without being interpreted.
But how do we assign meaning? From what source, in the last
analysis, do we derive meaning? The forms we use for assigning
meaning are historical categories that reach back into the mists of
time – a fact we do not take sufficiently into account. Interpretations
make use of certain linguistic matrices that are themselves derived
from primordial images. From whatever side we approach this
question, everywhere we find ourselves confronted with the history
of language ... (Jung, 1959, p. 32)

Jung is here describing the human predicament as existing
between two worlds, the world of life and the world of meaning.
The question of selection with which we started is seen to be one
special case of a wider problem: the need to distinguish between
two ways of ordering reality, in one of which life seems to generate
meaning, while in the other meaning generates life. He is setting
the narrower problem we sensed behind the complex – that of
both having and being had by some experience, of 'I'-ness as
both subject and object – in this much wider context of the
relationship between life and meaning.

Perhaps there are better ways of making Jung's point. But I
want to emphasize how radical and yet familiar his formulation
is. He is reopening philosophical questions which a large number
of our more influential teachers insist are either finally closed and
answered, or else meaningless, and at the heart of these questions
he sets the individual man or woman suffering under the sense of
being both the subject and the object of experience.

However difficult and strange these questions may seem, we cannot avoid them if we want to understand what complexes are about.
But we must make it clear that we are not simply talking psychology.
We have to own the fact that we are talking about something that
has gone out of fashion, something in which we are not trained,
and in which it is difficult to get proper tuition. This is why I have
given the word 'ontology' an important place in my vocabulary: to
stake out my ground while also admitting to ignorance.

Jung uses language in ways that can be properly appreciated and
criticized only within a frame of reference that allows questions of

Being with a capital B to arise. He is saying that that mystery that we call language flows, as it were, in two opposed directions: from life into meaning, and from meaning into life. We can illustrate this if we wish by saying that the first direction of flow, from life into meaning, is what we have got used to with the development of the natural sciences in the last three hundred years, while the second direction of flow, from meaning into life, is familiar to (some of) us in the theological idea of the creation of the world by the Word. But such illustrations should not be allowed to obscure the familiar immediacy of the dilemma with which Jung confronts us: that we have to live as both the subjects and the objects of meaning, that 'I is'.

That is easy to say. But it is not easy to account for it in our living. If we take this experience seriously, it is very, very hard to fit both sides of it into a coherent whole. We have to make room for uncertainty of a very radical kind. For if we wish to accept and work with experience of the 'I is' in its completeness, then we have to allow that, at the source of all our human attempts at understanding, there lies a kind of ontological hazard (or, to point up certain historical connections, a kind of 'semantic original sin').

By which I mean this: if we hope to understand and direct our lives in terms of some meaning generated by life, which it is our job to recognize and then learn to apply, we are up against the risk that this whole endeavour will prove futile and self-defeating should it turn out that life is an explanation of meaning, rather than the other way round. And conversely, for those who hope to live their lives as the explanation of a meaning prior to life, a meaning that is revealed in holy writ, in the teaching of a tradition, in prophecy, oracle or a great dream, there is the ever open question: How can we know that this meaning is not of our own making?

Between the two we find ourselves unsettled, insecure. We hesitate, recognizing a choice that seems to ask too much of us. We can draw back into some strategy of evasion. Or we can come out to meet it in the only way open to us: 'Aha, so we have to take risks do we? Well, if that is the case, what am I willing to wager?'

The practice of psychotherapy is carried on between those two positions. That between is a place of uncertainty, oscillation, cross-purposes. Twenty years there has convinced me that, if I am to render an account of the work I do, I need the help of theatre.

The Celebration of Hazard

Theatrical experience is manifold. It is all relevant to our theme. If one example is to be chosen, it is best to go to the beginnings, to Aristotle's reflections on how theatre works. This has the advantage of keeping us close to the theatrical event which more than any other has captivated the psychoanalytic imagination, Sophocles' play, *Oedipus the King*.

Aristotle says (1) that tragedy is an imitation not of human beings but of action and life; and (2) that the stage figures do not act in order to represent their characters, but include their characters for the sake of their actions.

I am no Greek scholar, and cannot pretend to give more than a second-hand explanation of these statements. But I think we can all recognize that what seems to be implied in these strange remarks of Aristotle disturbs us. They do not fit our assumptions as to how human being and life, character and action, are related. I believe this disturbance is theatre's way in to the experience of ontological hazard.

Much has happened in the theatre since Aristotle wrote, and I do not want to claim all-inclusive authority for his explanation of how it works. His thought has, however, the advantage of standing close to the ritual origins of the theatre, when the idea of a play as merely a pretence which we watch was unimaginable. Aristotle could still feel the play as a communal activity in which actor, chorus and spectators were all engaged together. If we want to use our experience of theatre to bring a sense of ontological hazard to the study of behaviour, it is worth trying to recover the freshness, the originality, of what Aristotle is saying.

Let us try and flesh it out with reference to the figure of Oedipus. It is clear that for Aristotle it is not the character or fate of Oedipus that is important in Sophocles' play. He is drawing a distinction between the action of the play and the stage figures enacting it which it is very hard for us, who are brought up on the modern theatre, and especially modern cinema and television, to appreciate. But if theatre is to help us understand and account for the way complexes have us as well as we them, this distinction is crucial.

Aristotle is saying that the person shown on the stage is of no significance in himself: he merely carries his share of an action whose interest does not lie in personality. There is something that needs to be acted through. The actors carry that need, and the mask they wear underscores the fact that, precisely because they are *merely* acting, they can represent an action which cannot be included within their personality.

It is this idea of the representation of action as what carries personality, rather than the other way round, that I have found so helpful in learning to tolerate and work with the uncertainties and oscillations of ontological hazard. It makes room for doubt of a kind that can remain unsure as to which comes first, life or meaning, while still celebrating the need for action.

What is the action that is being imitated in Sophocles' play? On one level it is like a detective story: the uncovering of the guilt, with the surprising twist familiar from so many dreams within analysis, in which the guilty one is found to be identical with the detective. But the motive that really drives the action along is the problem of the oracles. At the beginning, before ever the play begins, both Laius and Jocasta, and Oedipus, try to undo, contradict, the truth of oracular prediction. Jocasta by giving her child to be exposed, Oedipus by fleeing from the city where the man and woman he took for father and mother reign. At the moment of greatest relief of tension, that brief interlude when Jocasta and Oedipus imagine themselves safe, they both exult in the exposure of the oracles as untruthful, as unfulfilled. But in the end, the truth of the oracles is justified, and it is shown that it was the blind Teiresias who saw truly, while the king who insisted on knowing in spite of Teiresias' resistance must blind himself once he too sees the truth.

In short, the imitation of action has to do with the interaction of two worlds – the world of human affairs, and the world of dream and oracle and prophecy. The humanly more comfortable attitude which would like to insist on a one-order world has been refuted, and in its place the interdependence of two worlds has been celebrated. Or, if we look at this interaction of the world of human affairs with the world of oracle in terms of Jung's question: Which is the younger event, meaning or life?, we can perhaps better see them not as two worlds, but as two ways of ordering one reality.

This is one theatrical response to ontological hazard. It implies a profoundly dramatic attitude to human life. But it does more than that. It grounds the contradictions of human emotion (joy in grief) in a sense of the world's eventfulness as necessarily in a state of ontological insecurity. Events are as they are because they cannot settle between the rival claims of meaning and life as to which comes first. They resonate in ontological discomfort. What is interesting about human beings is how they react to that discomfort.

Masks and Faces

A common example of how we react to this discomfort is given in what we call hypocrisy. This example can serve to return us to our book's theme, in recognizing the human face as a text of identity.

The word 'hypocrisy' derives from a classical Greek word, 'Hypokrites'. Originally, in the Ionian dialect used by Homer, the relevant verb meant something like: to express a decision, based on deep reflection, knowledge and intuition, in reply to a question – and the question is to be thought of not as a cold, logical question, but as informed with urgency, as much a challenge from one person to another as a question. From this meaning grew the further sense of 'to explain, expound, interpret'; and the word was specifically used of the interpretation of dreams and oracles in Homer, and much later in the Attic of Aristophanes and Plato.

A further sense of the word then developed, to mean 'to speak in dialogue, to play a part on the stage'. Thus, the noun 'Hypokrites' was used of the stage actor from about 500 BC. By the end of the fourth century BC, in the speeches of Demosthenes, it was beginning to acquire a pejorative sense of 'to play a false part, to deceive'. It was this sense of the word that was picked up in the Greek translation of the New Testament, and with which we are familiar in our modern English word 'hypocrite'.

We can use the history of this word to amplify our understanding of how mask and face are related.

If theatre is indeed an imitation of action in which two ways of ordering reality come together, the actor's face becomes the inter-face on which the two orders meet. This is why, in all manner of theatre, we have resource to masks. To move from Aristotle to the present day, here is how one critic describes the dilemma of the actor at this interface.

> The farther drama leans towards farce and tragedy, the more the actor assumes the mask. It lends impersonality to the experience, frees the spectator from the need to sympathise, frees him to laugh, all without the tiresome restrictions of everyday life. A play needs only a germ of probability to begin, but once begun it can soar with the madness of hysteria or race faster than nightmare. Since at the extreme the movements of either tragedy or farce border on dance and its tones on song, the language of colloquial prose dialogue can barely satisfy the needs of its stage. Yet, either in tragedy or in farce, the actor immersed in its spirit stands outside his role while seeming to believe utterly in its reality: both are the drama of the straight face. (Styan, 1975, pp. 82-3)

The change in the meaning of 'Hypokrites' helps us appreciate what is at stake in this drama of the straight face. Masking is how we face the ontological discomfort of events. We have, as it were, a continuum of experience: at one end, hypocrisy in our modern sense; at the other, a powerfully felt call to interpret. As we move up and down that continuum, the mask changes its nature. It can be a means of retreat from facing hazard, or a medium by which far more can be faced than would otherwise be possible. On that continuum there are many resting places between the two extremes.

This is how we manage the discrepancy between character and action. In pretending to be otherwise, the hypocrite does one kind of thing with that discrepancy, the Hypokrites another. We can begin to combine the two when we realize where that discrepancy is grounded: in a discomfort, an unsettledness, which is given in the make-up of our world's eventfulness.

To appreciate the human face as the most familiar of all texts of identity, we need to own that grounding. Concealing and revealing in one, the face responds to the constitution of an eventfulness of which we are part. It responds in taking up the 'dare' of events. We are dared to decide which comes first, life or meaning, and in taking up that dare we find that disappointment and expectation are kept constantly in play together.

How we wear our faces bears witness to what it is like to be in play between disappointment and expectation. Living both as subject and object of meaning shows itself in our faces. They are texts in which interpreter and interpretation are always having to make room for each other.

I hope that what I have said in this chapter will encourage us to risk more in that 'wearing'. There are times for the straight face, and times for losing face. We need to make room for both. Our research programmes would tell us more if we would do so. I believe, with Polanyi, that conviviality is necessary for true scientific community. Such conviviality will be more resourceful in the presence of ontological hazard if we bring to it more of the theatre. As a contribution to developments in my own field of psychotherapy and social work, I hope this chapter will help coax psychoanalysts, behaviourists and cognitive psychologists into more experiment, more give and take, with one another. My own preferred starting-point would be in shared exploration of the hazards of dramatic performance.

References

Jung, C.G. (1959) *Collected Works*, Vol. 9, Pt 1: *The Archetypes and the Collective Unconscious*. London: Routledge & Kegan Paul.

Jung, C.G. (1960) *Collected Works*, Vol. 8: *The Structure and Dynamics of the Psyche*. London: Routledge & Kegan Paul.

Styan, J.L. (1975) *J.L. Styan: Drama, Stage and Audience*. Cambridge: Cambridge University Press.

12
The Construction of Identity in the Narratives of Romance and Comedy

Kevin Murray

The business of this chapter is to explore the thesis that both personal and social identity are constructed by finding stories to tell about the self. Harré's theory of personal being is recruited as the theoretical base for this assertion. Popular psychology and conversation are seen as providing access to the resources necessary for the construction of identity. How these resources are employed in the lives of individuals is investigated in the choices to run a marathon and to travel. Before commencing this task, though, I will introduce some of the issues that make the thesis of the narrative construction of identity significant.

Narrative and Life

The relationship between narrative and life has been subject to much questioning in contemporary culture. An example of this is a recent film[1] which tells of an affair between two characters. The woman is a member of a cinema audience, and the man has escaped from the world of the screen to enter real life. As romance between these characters builds, they embrace for their first kiss. After a few seconds, though, the woman notices the man's growing hesitancy. She asks him what the matter is. His reply is that he is only accustomed to kissing in films, and the lovers' kiss always fades out on screen; he does not know how to go any further. The film continues to explore the misreadings of the real world that occur when acting according to its supposedly mimetic representation on the screen. This play on the intersection between the real and the fictional world indicates at a popular level a similar concern with the status of narrative in the way our world is actually lived as is found in some recent developments in the social sciences.

Narrative representation as a way of making sense of the world has become an issue in various disciplines. Many literary critics have seen the realm of literature as allowing for the construction of models of the world of experience in ways that guide our actions (e.g. Frye, 1957; Hernnstein-Smith, 1978; Price, 1983). In the discipline of history, Hayden White's *Metahistory* (1973) proposes the general thesis that, when historians provide an account of the past, they are partly concerned with finding a plot according to which the events can be ordered in a meaningful sequence. Exploring this notion further, philosophers such as Paul Ricoeur (1983, 1985) have been concerned with the manner in which our very experience of time is dependent on the narrative structures that we impose on experience. In political science, Frederic Jameson (1981) has proposed an interpretive scheme which claims that ideological systems are produced in part by the workings of narrative structures. Even in architecture, one finds the concern with fiction expressed in the young London-based group called Narrative Architecture Today (NATO), which, rather than attending to the formal properties of design, focuses on the possibilities of experience created by buildings. In each of these cases, theorists are concerned with the way our mode of living reflects the representational structures that are imposed on our experience. As such, these approaches reflect a post-modern concern with the nature of reflexivity: how our worlds are governed by our designs, and the abysses in time and space created in this process.

Although much of contemporary psychology still concerns itself with mechanistic models of human behaviour, there are fields of research such as action psychology (see Harré et al., 1985) which allow reflexivity to be entertained as having a role in individual lives. Later this entrance for narrative into psychology will be considered, but we should begin with its initial entry through the back door of psychoanalysis. Roy Schafer (1976) claimed that psychoanalytic therapy involved the restructuring of a person's sense of the past so that it would make a more cohesive narrative. The aim of the therapy was to find a place for the analysand at the centre of this reconstructed life narrative.

While Schafer's approach is instructive, it is constrained in a way that this chapter seeks to avoid. This limit is found in Schafer's account of the factors that govern the process of employment in therapy. Apart from the agreement between the constructed story and certain ungrounded 'visions of the world', such as the ironic focus of psychoanalysis,[2] his theory lacks a detailed exposition of the dynamic process of finding a place for the self in a narrative.

How a *storied* sense of self plays a part in development is explicated more fully in recent approaches to this issue. Theodore Sarbin (1986) proposed that mechanism as a root metaphor in psychology be replaced by narrative. Sarbin draws on both literary and psychological material to demonstrate the fundamental role of narrative in our making sense of the world, especially when this activity is sensitive to context. And, as Kenneth and Mary Gergen propose, it is regarding the construction of self in a social context that the use of narrative has much to offer (Gergen and Gergen, 1988). Here, stories seem to enable others to share one's point of view. As a recent writer in this field states, 'when we understand someone, we understand his or her stories' (Keen, 1986). It is this concern with how one's story relates to the social order that allows us to progress beyond the individualistic account of narrative construction provided by Schafer. Later in the chapter, I will attempt to establish how two forms of narrative enable this social construction of identity.

Why narrative should be the medium in which a social sense of self is constructed can be explained by contrast to the other modes of understanding. Jerome Bruner (1986) distinguishes the *narrative* mode of understanding from the more abstract scientific mode, which he calls the *paradigmatic*. While the paradigmatic mode is best for making sense according to principles that abstract from context, narrative understanding carries the weight of context, which therefore makes it a better medium for relating human experience and the contradictions that that entails. According to Bruner's argument, therefore, encapsulating experience in the form of a story enables it to make sense in the interpersonal sphere. A further enquiry into the dynamics involved in this process, although of great interest, is beyond the scope of this chapter. Rather, my analysis will assume that narrative adapts experience to the social context of meaning, and will pursue the implications of this in theories of identity.

Theory and Identity

A theory of identity is required which can accommodate the narrative construction of self. Initially, one might look to a branch of attribution theory. Implicit Personality Theory (Wegner and Vallacher, 1981) seems a good candidate because of its emphasis on the *constructive* processes involved in identity formation.

Implicit Personality Theory concentrates mainly on the ways in which individuals create and test hypotheses concerning the behaviour of others. It is assumed that these individuals use theories about other people as a means of predicting and therefore controlling their social environment. In the practice of assigning certain traits to people, the individual differs little in nature from the psychologist. Both use tested theories of the world to predict consistent patterns of behaviour. The sense of self that follows from this is simply a reflection of one's own theories about others. However, rather than attempting to predict one's behaviour, one attempts to create information about oneself that will fulfil one's self-theory. In discovering a match between self-theory and information about oneself, one gains self-esteem. The notion of self as autonomous creator of theories that predict others' behaviour and make sense of one's own identity would seem to be a pure example of a *paradigmatic understanding of identity*. Thus, despite the constructivist assumptions of Implicit Personality Theory, the processes it posits as the logic of identity formation are unsympathetic to the narrative mode.

A different type of constructivist theory of identity is presented by Rom Harré (1983). In contrast to Implicit Personality Theory, Harré's conceptualization of personal being imbeds the self in the social context, which suggests a greater role for the narrative understanding of self. Although Harré is concerned with the relation between self and theory, he does not see the self as *origin* of theory. Rather, self is a *product* of theory. Harré thus reverses the relation between self and theory proposed by Implicit Personality Theory. At the same time, he uses in a different sense: he employs the term "theory" not as an abstract principle, but as a rule derived from the moral order. Given the different logical statuses of 'is' and 'ought' statements, therefore, these theories should be selected not on their testability, but on their place in the wider social context. An example of such a 'theory' is the medieval moral principle that those who help themselves will find that they can achieve more than if they rely on others. This theory is less successful in predicting the actions of others than in providing a guide to living a 'good' life. Harré extends this argument to account for the Western sense of self, not in the autonomous consciousness of one's thoughts and actions, but in the referential grid of social time and space to be found first in the grammatical relations between persons. Persons are therefore made partly by the modes of 'talk' found in the social order.

To gain a sense of identity in Harré's scheme, one needs to find a place for oneself in the social order. Harré maps this process out on a two-dimensional grid (see Figure 1) which contains axes of display and realization. The development of identity begins in the *appropriation* of 'theories' from the social order. This process is enabled by a psychological symbiosis between the future person (child) and a competent social actor (parent) – so 'theories' contained in the collective–public quadrant are incorporated into the private world of individual thoughts and action. The sense of identity provided by these 'theories' is found in the *metaphoric* relations between them

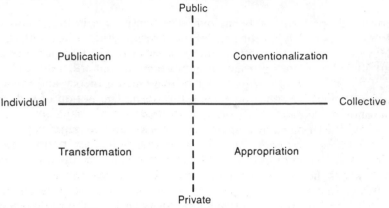

Figure 1. *Rom Harré's psychological dimensions*

and one's own experiences; thus, these theories are transformed, from their realization in the collective realm, into becoming part of the individual sense of identity. Yet to achieve social and personal being, one needs to find ways of making these metaphoric relations *public*. The realization of one's experience in public display carries experience over into the social order. It is here that tests of hazard are found and moral careers are made. Finally, individual paths through the social order become *conventionalized* into accepted forms of biography.

According to Harré, finding a place for oneself in the world involves two projects. One must find a *social identity* – an honoured place in the social order – yet also attempt to maintain a *personal identity*, in the sense of a biographical uniqueness. Whereas social identity is a problem for marginal individuals such as migrants who have no place in the established social order, personal identity becomes difficult for people who have achieved a successful moral career to the point where it is hard to distinguish oneself from the official social order. To illustrate the dilemma of personal identity, Harré uses the example of tycoons during the Victorian era who constructed autobiographies based on their humble origins.

Harré's work on personal being reflects the paradox that a sense of self is gained only through social meanings. This paradox is resolved in the way social meaning is *lived*. Although experience – that which provides a source of resistance to the social order and therefore the stuff from which a personal identity can be hewn – is more difficult to account for purely within Harré's theory, it is the space allowed for experience that makes his theory more consistent with a narrative sense of self than Implicit Personality Theory. The paradigmatic sense of self denies the relevance of point of view – the focus of the subject that coheres storied experience. In Harré's framework, it is the necessity of living out the appropriated social meanings that reserves the place for point of view, and therefore the narrative sense of self.

Narrative and Experience

One of the primary functions of narrative is to relate theory to experience. It achieves this not through testing theories according to systematic procedures of data analysis, but through finding a *point* to a series of events. This point ranges from the kind of moral statements found in fables, to the simple declarations of astonishment found in such expressions as 'amazing' and 'unbelievable'. Such resolutions indicate that experience in narrative has the potential of resisting theory.[3] This potential is governed by the interplay of metaphoric and metonymic relations of meaning in the story (see Brooks, 1984). In terms of identity, metaphor deals with the similarities and differences between one's own situation and what one knows of others'. Its partner, metonymy, is an experiential domain of meaning which relates events according to their contiguity in time and space rather than their relationship to similarly placed events in different contexts. It is the metonymic axis of meaning that most strongly contrasts the narrative mode of understanding with the paradigmatic. And it is the concern of narrative with a specific time and space that qualifies it as a medium for finding a unique identity in the social order. This qualification is supported by consideration of the predominance of narrative in the conventionalization of one's unique appropriations of the social order. It does not require much examination to be certain of the inappropriateness of scientific theories in the representation of personal experience in the public realm of newspapers and television, etc. It is here that Schafer's statement, 'self is a telling', becomes interesting.

Harré's conceptualization of personal being is rich in empirical possibilities. This chapter attempts to explore several in an attempt to identify some of the narrative structures governing the instantiation of self in the social order. As a guide to types of narrative structures, I will follow the lead of many theorists in narrative studies and employ the terms 'comedy', 'romance', 'tragedy' and 'irony' to represent different types of narrative.[4] These terms refer to narrative structures that govern much of the telling of stories in the Western tradition. Briefly, 'comedy' involves the victory of youth and desire over age and death. Conflict in comedy usually deals with the repression of desire in a society, which is released in the course of an adventure or festivity by means of which a healthier social unit is restored. By contrast, 'romance' concerns the restoration of the honoured past through a series of events that involve a struggle – typically including a crucial test – between a hero and forces of evil. Conflict is resolved by battle rather than sociality as in comedy. In 'tragedy' the individual fails to conquer evil and is excluded from the social unit. The nobility of this failure is contrasted with the satire of 'irony', which deals in the discovery that comedy, romance and tragedy are mere schemes of mortals to control experience: individuals are not so pure, nor is the social order so healthy.

Such narrative structures have been described schematically in order to loosen their tie with a specifically *literary* tradition. These structures do not presume to represent the 'real' state of affairs, but rather to structure the social world according to certain moral relations between society and the individual, the past and the future, and theory and experience. With regard to the epistemological status of these structures, this chapter takes Ricoeur's (1985) position that they are *sedimented* forms which are subject to the vicissitudes of history and specific to the Western narrative tradition. Their appropriation into the issue of identity formation is thus best conducted under the aegis of an *historical* social psychology (see Gergen, 1984), rather than a universalist model of socialization.

There will be two rounds of relating theories about self with individual experience in this chapter. Each will explore the way theories of self contained in the public–collective domain are appropriated in identity projects. In the first case, theories found in popular psychology are demonstrated in the decision to run a marathon: in the second, theories used in the construction of persons in conversation are related to accounts of travel. In each round we are looking for two relations: a metaphoric linkage between the theories and individual accounts, and a contextual reading of the employment of those theories. As such, this chapter represents an attempt to discover some of the dominant theories in the social order, as well as an investigation of the dynamics involved in engaging these theories in the process of establishing a social and personal identity.

Narrative

Popular Psychology

Popular psychology has affinities not only with the existing academic theory used for explaining actions, but also with the tradition of life manuals written by people such as Epicurus, Castiglione, Samuel Smiles and Dale Carnegie. This conjunction is illustrated in one of the most successful of recent authors in popular psychology, Gail Sheehy.[5] Readers are advised by the packaging of her books that they are to be used as a resource for understanding one's life and choosing a better course of action. Her basic theory of development maps a romantic course over an individual's biography. Sheehy begins her description of life with the dreams of future achievement formed in adolescence. These are lost sight of in the bitter experience – gained in adulthood – of the limits imposed by the world on oneself. This disillusionment leads to a crisis (the mid-life crisis) when the old enemy of self-confidence (the 'inner custodian') takes command. At this point, Sheehy advises her readers to face the conflict squarely with hope of eventual victory. As long as the battle with the 'inner custodian' is engaged in wholeheartedly, the person will emerge with renewed potential to realize past dreams as well as a sense of purpose beyond their own desires. In addition to the metaphor of battle and the victory of good, Sheehy's scheme reflects a romantic narrative structure in the way she emplots the mid-life crisis as containing three events: confrontation, struggle and recognition of transcendental meaning. These events in classical romance are termed *agon*, *pathos* and *anagnorisis*. Sheehy's theory, therefore, is that those who face their conflict squarely, and engage seriously in battle with the evil within themselves, will successfully navigate their passage through difficulty. Entailed by this theory is a firm commitment to individuality as a mode of being and self-reliance as a valued goal. The narrative structure of romance indicates how Sheehy believes such values may be instantiated in the life-course.

The Decision to Run a Marathon

The emergence of the mid-life crisis as a narratable hazard in the life-course is concurrent with other developments in the social order. About the time that Sheehy's theories became public, there was a popular movement concerned with individual responsibility for physical health. One of the most obvious displays of this movement was the emergence of jogging as a popular pastime. This had its dramatic apotheosis in the transformation of the marathon from an event restricted to elite athletes to an occasion for the participation of the whole of society. People hitherto excluded, such as women, children, paraplegics and the elderly, were encouraged to participate. Contrary to what one would expect of the increasing demands placed on time by the responsibilities of adulthood, in the marathon studied here[6] half the participants were over thirty, and most of these were entering the event for the first time. Because the marathon involves a test of one's strength as well as a necessary separation from the daily concerns in the lengthy training necessary to complete the event, the decision to enter it would seem to be a candidate for the romantic structuring of life as proposed by Sheehy.

A collection of the accounts of first-timers over thirty confirmed this. Part of the shared mythology concerning the marathon were notions such as the 'wall'. Runners expected to encounter the 'wall' near the end of the event, when their supplies of body energy would be exhausted and they could continue only by sheer will and commitment. If the will was sufficient, then entrants expected to be able to conquer this obstacle and experience the 'runner's high', a euphoric feeling of invulnerability and transcendence of bodily limits. As such, then, the common meaning attached to the marathon is of a test, with possible romantic associations. How this relates to the renewal of past dreams, though, can be ascertained most directly by examining the marathon as part of accounts by the participants, where its meaning is embedded in life concerns.

A closer look at the accounts revealed an interesting divergence in the context and construction of the decision to run a marathon. The group of entrants classified as 'Born Again' contained elements of the restoration of past ambitions and struggle between good and evil within the self. For instance,[7] Kate, a thirty-two-year-old student, related her current interest in the marathon to her sporting past and the hopes that her father had then placed in her future. In contrast, her twenties had been a time when 'I became very average. I just sort of joined in. There was nothing exceptional in my life at that stage. No aim. No goal.' This experience of lack of distinction from others was associated with feelings of confusion, weakness of will and lack of control. This led eventually to a 'nervous breakdown', which Kate eventually overcame by taking up running. Running was a means of gaining control of her existence by providing a locus outside of the confused and dependent self. In describing the probable reaction of her father to her completing the marathon, she said, 'He probably thinks I'm mad ... but underneath, I reckon if I finish the marathon, word would get round the golf club pretty quickly.' Like nearly all entrants, Kate believed that others saw her decision as 'mad', yet at the same time she anticipated that she would win respect by its completion.

Many entrants generalized this recognition from specific individuals to the public realm as a whole – one of the reasons for entering was 'just to say I've done it'. While entrants such as Kate perceived that they could win honour in the social order by changing their life-style – to fashion it in greater consonance with the value of physical responsibility – their individuality was maintained by the particular route chosen for the expression of this value. From feelings of sameness arise a distinguished place for the self in the social order. To achieve this, the individual must *test* herself in a situation that demands the sorts of virtues that are lauded by society – endurance, individual autonomy, strength, and so on. In the discovery for the self of a respected place in society, the decision of runners like Kate to enter a marathon corresponds to what Harré describes as a *social identity project*. The 'theory' she appropriates to gain honour involves the restoration of past ambition through a test of the self involving clearly identifiable forces of good and bad whose result is dependent on the hero's commitment to the good. This is a *romantic* narrative structure. Finding a way in which one's own life might resemble such a structure seems a dominant part of many runners' decision to enter the marathon.

However, the narrative structure of revival of ambition applied to only a part of the total number of accounts. Many of the men – found in the 'Repossessed' group – entered the marathon in order to *withdraw* from these tests of character. The event for these men was related to easing the frustrations of work while at the same time releasing a youthful spirit that had lain dormant during young adulthood.

For example, a thirty-five-year-old advertising executive, David, described being 'intolerant' and 'irritable' as a result of responsibilities at work. The effect of this was to make family life more difficult. David became involved in running during a family holiday at the beach, when he discovered 'how terrific it was to feel fit again'. Since then, running had provided a convenient release after the tensions at work and so had led to a 'better family life'. The marathon was a 'logical progression' in running, and David liked the 'challenge'. Unlike Kate, David did not structure the elements in his account in an antagonistic manner. For instance, when training conflicted with the family, this was a matter of lack of consideration; if David missed a run because of home commitments he felt guilty – 'I still get a conscience after it, because although I know I've done the right thing by my family, I've sort of overlooked myself.' The justification of the decision to enter the marathon was in terms of easing conflict. This served to strengthen the family as a social unit while at the same time allowing David's youthful energies to re-emerge.

David seems quite secure in the official role that he plays in society, yet he feels that he has overlooked himself in the drive to be a successful person. His decision appears to be an example of what Harré would call a *personal identity project*. The issue is not to improve the stakes in his moral career, but to find expression for his free and spontaneous self. In common with similar male entrants, David saw the release of self as occurring within the interests of the social unit. Some male entrants differed from David in this by emphasizing the camaraderie of the running events above the benefit to the family, but they shared the feeling of amused distance from the possible competitive role they might take in the event, and this lightness distinguished them from those pursuing a social identity project. The discovery of a sense of identity outside of his roles is managed by David through the construction of account involving the rediscovery of youthful energies in the escape from responsibilities which leads to the renewal of the social unit. As such, David was making his decision take the form of a *comic* narrative structure.

Identity Projects and Distance

Despite the difference in accounts of marathon entrants, there was a common belief that their actions could be construed by others as 'mad' or 'insane'. This should spur us to question the isomorphism it is possible to maintain given Harré's scheme between social meaning and individuality. It seems odd that, in spite of their concern with establishing a sense of identity, these runners would take pride in their lack of integration in normal society. Reference to the treatment of this paradox in other disciplines may be helpful here. The relationship between identity projects and distance from the norms of social life is something that has been an issue to anthropologists such as Victor Turner (1969), who studied the ritual practices governing identity change and found that these 'rites of passage' typically remove participants from normal space and time into a 'liminal' sphere. The liminal sphere serves as a transitional place in which normal expectations of behaviour are suspended, allowing participants to take on new roles. This division of cultural life is based on a more fundamental dichotomy between the *structure* of society – the ordered hierarchies of roles and meanings – and its *anti-structure*, which inverts and subverts these established meanings. Two types of rite of passage correspond to Harré's two identity projects. Rites of *status elevation* concern ascendancy of one's social identity – one's place in the structure. On the other hand, rites of *status reversal* concern elements of self-denied expression in the structure and so are sympathetic to the construction of personal identity. Kate's concern was with her lack of social distinction: for her, the marathon became a rite of status elevation involving separation from others through a *test* of character. (Conversely, David's worry was that the work which grants him distinction also represses his humanness. Holiday was the initial release from work.) This escape from the 'burdens of office' then found fuller realization in the free release of aggression in training for the marathon. This relaxation of social hierarchies makes his participation in the marathon a rite of status reversal. In short, while Kate's involvement in the marathon is part of a plan to secure a respected place among others – with the accompanying sense of stability and independence – David's decision plays a part in a narrative of expanding communality which encourages the release of youthful energy entailed in this.

The inclusion of Turner's work on identity change fills some of the space for anthropological detail made available by Harré's scheme. As identity is perceived to be constructed through certain social practices which regulate the assignment of meaning to individuals' sense of selfhood, it is fitting to turn to anthropology to discover these. As we have seen, Turner's framework accounts for the necessary separation involved in identity change, as well as the different movements in identity. But the inclusion of Turner's theory has its problems. It raises the issue of the status of narrative in the process of identity change. How is *story* related to rites of status elevation and inversion? As we saw when examining the suitability of Harré's theory, the space allowed for experience outside the social order necessitates a process which mediates individual biography and collective representations: while the result of this is a metaphoric transformation of the self, the mediating process involved is that of narrative. What place does narrative have in Turner's account?

The emphasis on ritual in Turner's work underlines a processional model of social life. This processional approach is not antipathetic to the idea that individuals find ways of making their experience conform to certain narrative structures. In Turner's later work (1980), he saw the ritual practices involved in social dramas such as identity change as related in a reciprocal manner to the stories that govern their representation. The basic narrative structure of breach–crisis–redress reflects the ritual structure of social drama. And it is in such genres of cultural performance that modes of self-understanding are found.

The narrative structure of breach–crisis–redress identified by Turner is a superordinate form of which romance and comedy are species: such a form requires a disruption of the normal order which leads to a decisive instant after which order is restored. This scheme allows for the central role of narrative in identity: narrative is seen to govern the *transgression* of the social order, which is necessary for the creation of personal being. What this scheme adds to Harré's concept of identity project is the emphasis taken from ritual on a single event as the focus for change: either the 'test', as in romance, or the 'release', as found in comedy. Stories in Turner's scheme serve in the process of conventionalizing ritually governed patterns of events. So, in terms of the two narrative structures identified here, romance is a suitable structure for recording an individual's successful negotiation of certain hazards encountered in rites of status elevation, while comedy is more appropriate for inscribing rites of status reversal in which communal bonds are reaffirmed through individuals who act outside of their prescribed roles. Narrative in these cases enables the experiences of struggle and release to be inscribed in individual and collective memory.

A Person Constructed through Talk

An alternative way of approaching Rom Harré's notion of the 'person' as constructed through talk is to take his approach literally: to ask a group of people to *actually* perform the task of constructing a person. Such an exercise aims to gain access to collective goals and strategies through the intragroup negotiation involved in completing the task. It is expected that this makes explicit the expectations that govern the practices of biographical construction in everyday life. (Such an approach resembles research in action psychology: see von Cranach, 1982.)

I asked ten groups of between three and four people to construct the life of a person. They were given the freedom to decide the type and amount of information necessary for this purpose. Generally, the groups took their time at the start in deciding on the basic characteristics of their person, but once they were agreed upon these most groups made steady progress. The groups tended to finish with this person when they had lost interest in the life they had constructed.

The life of 'Nicola' is a typical construction which expresses most of the themes of other lives while including clear justifications within the group of the information included. Nicola was created by three women and one man, all in their early thirties and pursuing professional careers. After a brief examination of the constructed person, key points in the life will be interpreted in the light of the group's discussion.

Looking initially at the finished story of Nicola (see Appendix), one can see that her life is divided into two parts. In the first there is a conflict between her desire to become independent of her family and her responsibilities at home. This conflict is made clear when her wish to escape the family by travelling overseas and exploring her artistic potential is thwarted; while away, her father dies and she realizes that she is needed back in Australia to maintain the family. As a result, her desires are not able to be fully realized. Eventually, the affair with the archaeologist enables her to escape these demands and as a result her career flowers in New York. Having established her personal career, she then goes on to do good for others in the suffering world of Africa and South America. This new life structure is made possible by the liberating role that the community of New York plays in restoring her denied self.

What is the narrative structure governing Nicola's life? On the one hand, her life follows Sheehy's scheme of development: Nicola's adolescent dream of success is lost in adulthood and then regained owing to the adventures following the mid-life crisis when a sense of social mission is gained. Nicola's path to selfhood diverges from Sheehy's, though, in that her ambition in architecture is realized not through struggle, but through the free spirit of New York.

The dominant plot in Nicola's life seems to concern the vicissitudes of her ambition: the initial conflict in her life, release in New York, and its metamorphosis into an altruistic pursuit. The analysis of the story will examine the group's goals governing the life structure, especially at the turning points of Nicola's ambition. The theories that inform this discussion are taken as representative of the moral order which governs biographical discourse in the society to which the group belongs.

First, why was Nicola given an ambition? Nicola's ambition was born in the group's attempt to make their character 'interesting'. Initially this was made possible by introducing elements of conflict into her life.

F: I quite like the idea of her coming from somewhere like St Albans or Footscray,[8] cos now she's ... the struggle to overcome.
P: It's the battler syndrome. [*Laughs*]
F: Well, otherwise, what's her struggle going to be? Let's say she comes from Kew, or wherever, say, gone to the private school – whichever one it was – and she's gone through Uni and she's done all the obligatory things. Well, maybe she has, maybe she has gone through the obligatory things.
J: What's going to make her interesting?
F: Maybe she has no struggle? Everything ... her life goes extraordinarily smoothly.
J: Do we want her to have a struggle?
T: I want her to be interesting.
F: Well, you create something that's interesting about her.
T: Okay, [*Pause*] I think she's got really pushy parents who have high aspirations, 'cos they had to work really hard.

In order that their character appeals to a curiosity about human nature, the group placed her initially in a scenario where her freedom is being limited by the aims of others.

The group later reviewed this question of how to make Nicola interesting, and decided to achieve this instead by creating a cultural and intellectual gap between Nicola and her parents. The gap arises in the conflict between her status as second-generation immigrant and her desire to grow as a person. So that Nicola can be both distanced from her parents and given ambition, the group decided that she wants to be an architect. The source of this goal is the experience she had when growing up of her father going with her over the plans for the sites that he was contracted to build on. This was given narrative plausibility by making Nicola the eldest in the family, with a much younger brother who lacks ambition. And Nicola's mother is made sickly to explain the smallness of the family and the dominant role of the father in Nicola's life. Having established that giving Nicola an *ambition* will provide the break with the social order that enables the struggle which is necessary to make her 'interesting', this fact about her character then became the major feature around which other facts of her life were mustered. What is important is that, although her ambition plays a major role in the narrative to follow, it was initially granted to Nicola to separate her from her family and thus involve her in some kind of 'struggle'. As shown in Figure 2, the group set themselves the goal of creating an *interesting* character, which for them meant a person who was engaged in some *struggle*, and for this, extraordinary *ambition* was necessary.[9] The initial situation of Nicola's life follows from this.

Nicola's eventual release from the demands of family is made possible by an affair with an American archaeologist in the free atmosphere of New York. In this process of release, her hidden abilities are allowed to emerge. At this point, the group had constructed a life for their character which is basically comic: Nicola overcomes the responsibilities that restrict her so that she may live a life of freedom. Although the catalyst for this is the affair, the real context for it is *New York*, it is the city where she can begin a 'wonderful new life'. New York is a magical city where she can explore her varied artistic potentials free from the

Interesting

↑

Struggle

↑

Extraordinary ambition

↑

Eldest daughter, sickly mother, contact with father, etc.

Figure 2.   *Goal hierarchy for an 'interesting' life*

bounds of responsibility. So, for instance, when her lover is away on a dig in Africa, the fact that she is in New York means that she is liberated from the dependencies that previously would have made her situation miserable and constrained her range of actions.

F: She's been practising architecture for some time, but she's in New York, the guy she's with is an archaeologist which means he goes off anyway. Even if he's not off on his digs or trying to raise money for them, he's an intellectual so he's doing his studies. He's not really a social human being as such.
J: As she finds out.
P: So what does she do?
F: That in fact might be okay for her, you see, because New York is one of the most fascinating cities in the world.
T: By then [the year 2000] it's degenerating into a gigantic ...
J: No, maybe she loves the fact that she can look at a city and enjoy it and just enjoy people. And she doesn't have responsibilities.

New York functions in Nicola's life as a haven where none of life's problems intrude. In the terminology of literary criticism, the narrative function of New York would be as a 'utopic space' (Barton, 1985), or a 'green world' (Berger, 1965).

The function of such spaces as a means of escape from repressive forces in the real world is most noticeable in the forest of Arden in Shakespeare. They provide the social interaction that is necessary in the comic scheme for the resolution of conflict. The 'green world' is inhabited by an *including* community who make few demands on the subject, but instead provide an enabling environment for fulfilment of her desires. In the story of Nicola, it is New York that provides the magical setting for the comic resolution of the contradictions in her life. In it she can resolve the conflict between her desire for independence and her network of dependencies. New York enables

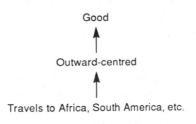

Figure 3.   *Goal hierarchy for a 'good' life*

this to happen by providing a world inhabited by individuals whose spontaneity and undemanding acceptance enables the hitherto denied potential within Nicola to be released without conflict.

Having provided a comic fulfilment of Nicola's quest for independence and creative potential, the group then proceeded to work on making her a 'good' person. Her life at this point changes from being a comic escape from responsibility to being a discovery of suffering: the narrative goal of being an 'interesting' person is supplemented by that of being a 'good' person (see Figure 3). This involves the adventure of travel with her lover. For the group, the basic purpose of Nicola's philanthropic journey was to make her a character who can be called 'good',[10] and this was achieved through her not only gaining an awareness of suffering, but also attempting to relieve it. This is part of the general drift in her life from being concerned with inner needs to being involved in causes outside of herself. As the group is deciding what to do with Nicola after New York, two members discuss how her character should develop.

> F: She's becoming not so self-centred; even if she's being responsible she's becoming outward-centred. She's looking at other people and their needs.
> T: I think that would be a normal development at that age.

What the group seems to be deciding is to return Nicola to the concern for others from which she had escaped in New York. Yet she has not lost everything in this return. Experience has intervened to make her a more rounded character than before. Her insularity has been transcended through the engagement with the people of New York, and this has opened her up to the world and its problems.

The story of Nicola thus can be seen as a comic escape from responsibility leading to the successful pursuit of individual ambition followed by integration of self into the concerns of the greater world. The group makes their character *interesting* by separating her from normal social life in the struggle of her ambition. And Nicola's *goodness* is granted by her witness of the suffering which extends her horizons beyond personal success. A remarkable feature of the story is the way travel overseas, specifically to New York, functions as a comic device for release from responsibility and harmony of conflicting elements of character. Having firmly established herself in the role of mother, the pursuit of ambition becomes a personal identity project – not so much to do with finding a place for herself in society as finding a medium for the expression of her individuality. This expression is eventually tied to the emergence of a society where conflict is healed between the West and Third World countries through the positive creative power of Nicola's thinking. Again, *the expression of individuality emerges from the context of the social.* Initially, this was through the sociality of New York, but it finds its fulfilment in the universal health of people in the world. Nicola's life therefore reflects a braided structure of personal and social identity projects which culminate in the realization of her individual talents in New York, and their social fulfilment in the work in Third World countries.[11]

Identity Projects and Travel

Escape from the responsibilities of the past was clearly granted a necessary role in the development of personal identity in four of the ten groups. The way in which travel enables this process would suggest that the decision to leave one's home environment to journey through foreign lands is sometimes an attempt to find that part of oneself that is denied expression by one's responsibilities to others. With such a possibility in mind, interviews were conducted with university students who had returned from travel. These interviews were designed to collect accounts of the experience in a similar fashion to the marathon study mentioned above. A brief examination of two cases will be used to demonstrate different ways in which travel is constructed.

Michael was a twenty-three-year-old student of agriculture when he left Australia to travel around Europe and America. The main reason he gives to account for this decision was the desire to see his Irish grandparents while they were still alive, so he spent four of his eleven months overseas in Ireland. It is this period that Michael sees as having made most impact on him during his journey. He found the closeness of the community in Ireland quite remarkable, and enjoyed greatly the camaraderie of social life, especially in the pub. This closeness became narratable in the story of his visiting his uncle.

> I think I liked, eventually I liked, the sense of community and the sense of the closeness, I found it claustrophobic at first. I remember one particular incident. I have an uncle who lived about 10 miles out of Cork and I was going to visit some cousins who lived about 15 miles away in another town and I was cycling along the road and I went and visited my cousins and I walked in the door and they said we knew you were coming, and it was because someone had seen me on the road cycling and thought this person is obviously such and such and it got back like that later.

The other impressions that Michael remarks upon concern the sublime landscape and being able to experience the presence of cultural sites and objects he had only read about before. Consistent with this is his emphasis on the elements of experience that are not found in mundane life. Given these expressions of anti-structure in Michael's account, it is reasonable to expect, on the basis of the persons constructed above, that a comic narrative structure is evident as well.

To discover if this exists, though, requires that we look beyond the specific happenings while away and examine the way Michael frames the journey as an event in time. When describing the sorts of changes that travel has produced, Michael refers to his feelings before departure. Besides anticipation of the journey, he mentions feelings of intolerance towards others, especially his father. He felt misunderstood – his family could not accept the way he had changed while at university. This independence was buttressed in travel by a pilgrimage to galleries and landmarks concerning literature. The interest in the arts separated him not only from his parents, but also from his fellow students.

According to Michael, though, the unsympathetic relationship with his family changed as a result of his travel experience. When talking about his feelings towards his parents, Michael says, 'I didn't get on very well with my father ... But now, definitely I'm closer to them.' And on his return to Australia, he admits to starting university with a 'new vigour', though this had not lasted. More certainly, travel strengthened the bonds between Michael and his family. In returning from Ireland to Australia, he felt he could understand better the frustrations and uncertainty his parents would have felt when they first moved to Australia. Again, paradoxically, to become close to his family, Michael needed to go away from them. He returned able to empathize with them, as well as having an independent set of experiences that enter the repertoire of stories he can tell about himself.

Like Nicola, therefore, Michael's travel is a time for realizing a unique identity in the extraordinary, and therefore free exchange between people. This leads to a renewed feeling of energy as well as a greater commitment to the world of people outside the self.

A contrasting case to Michael is Susan. Susan is a twenty-eight-year-old postgraduate student who has travelled to Europe twice, once with a girlfriend and on the last occasion by herself. She included two months in India and Nepal on her last journey. Susan's descriptions of travel mainly concern the moral characteristics of the foreign people. The French are beautiful people who adopt an easy-going Mediterranean attitude to life: they are 'nice'. At the opposite extreme, the Indian people are ugly and rude. The aspects of travel that Susan comments on deal mainly with the extraordinary – for example, the precocious politeness of a French boy, and where to obtain the 'best croissants in the world'. What stands out from this in its urgency, though, is her account of trying to survive in India.

This includes hanging on to the outside of a departing train while two young men tried to push their way out. Contrasted to Michael's stories of Ireland, Susan's travel narratives deal more with struggle than with sociality. Although both accounts are concerned with the extraordinary, Susan's fit more into a romantic narrative scheme than a comic.

Again, it is necessary to examine the frame of the travel account to verify this. Before travelling, the main problem Susan saw in her life was the conflict between her feeling of responsibility towards her boyfriend, and her desire to break off the relationship. Part of the reason for travelling was for her to gain the strength needed to be more assertive in her affairs with other people. Susan saw her experiences in India as certainly aiding this.

Yet it is not only with this personal perspective that Susan views travel. Being a traveller is importantly a *moral* business: it broadens one's horizons. Susan admits to feeling superior to those people who have not travelled. The moral substance of this scaffolding is the quality of 'niceness'. This is evident in her discussion of why she likes the politeness of the French.

> I wouldn't say that I like politeness just because it gives a structure that facilitates interaction, I just think it's nice ... I value politeness not because it gives you a structure. I see no reason to be rude to people. It's just as easy to be polite and it makes it all so much ... nicer.

Although politeness is related to the interaction between people, in Susan's case it is involved in the distinctions between people who are 'nice' and those who are not. It has the quality of an absolute value. This sharply contrasts from the feelings of greater tolerance reported by Michael on his return. Indeed, Susan broke off from her boyfriend on her return, rather than finding aspects of him that appealed to her, as would be the resolution of a comic narrative. Thus, the place for Susan in the social order – distinguished from ignorant and rude people – is gained through the experience of travel, in which she struggles not only against the uncouth behaviour of others (Indians), but also against the weak side of herself.

In this, Susan's experience of travel resembles Kate's social identity project of running a marathon, as does Michael's reparation with the family through his journey to Ireland follow a similar path to David's greater commitment to the family through rejuvenation in deciding to enter the marathon. In the case of social identity project, a place for oneself in the social order can be found in the discovery in one's own life of events that potentially fit a romantic narrative structure. Romance suggests *the honourable course by which established moral values may be realized in the individual biography*. And it follows that individuals may find in romance one of a repertoire of structures of meaning that grant their life social significance. A necessary component of this is the separation of the person from everyday life and the test of a certain quality of her character. This account is consonant with Rom Harré's notion of moral career as a history of success and failure in tests of hazard in which the contempt of others is risked for the sake of their respect. Similarly, it is not contradictory to the anthropological notion of rite of passage, although this emphasizes more the framing of the period of test as an event distinct from the conduct of mundane world. Engagement in these events may be what Harré describes as a social identity project.

This is contrasted, in the case of Michael, with the remarkable experience of community which granted him a travel story that would serve to distinguish him from others, while at the same time reconciling him to the social world. This project of personal identity has found itself in this chapter often framed within a comic narrative structure, making it resemble what Turner describes as rites of status inversion, rather than status elevation, and therefore placed more within the anti-structure of society rather than its structure. The implication of this is that the expression of individuality is something for which there is a certain time and place. Finding the right time and place remains a necessary part of the personal identity project, and leads people often to leave their homes for extraordinary adventure (Scheibe, 1986). The personal identity project – finding a recognizable characteristic of uniqueness from others – is discovered in the narrative structure of comedy. The central event in this is not a test of the self – requiring distance from oneself and others – but a *release of an aspect of the self denied expression, enabled by the extraordinary closeness of the community separate from the structure of normal society*. This specific context for the development of personal identity provides a valuable extension in Harré's theory of personal being. It leads to greater consideration for the role that the interpersonal contexts of friendship and carnival play in the 'fleshing out' of identity.[12]

Romance and Comedy in Identity Projects

What both the personal and the social identity projects share, as evidenced by the stories discussed in this chapter, is the importance of distance from the social order in the development of a sense of self. This distance has been evident in various ways: the necessary 'journey' of the mid-life crisis, the 'madness' of the marathon entrant, the travel to the 'utopic space' in constructed persons, and the 'extraordinary' events recounted by travellers. In romance, the hero ventures to the wilderness where tests are encountered. The very notion of a test indicates an event at the margins of the social order. As most of official life runs according to a routine in which contingency is avoided, a test, which involves the possibility of failure, necessarily occurs on the margins of everyday social order. And in comedy people are brought together outside of their normal relations in situations of extraordinary social gathering. In these cases, the familiar patterns of life are disrupted and new meanings explored.

In both the romantic and comic narrative structures, the possibility exists for forging an identity. This identity, whether in terms of one's honour or one's sociability, is necessarily found outside the social order. Thus, in terms of Harré's original grid, the sense of self is to be found removed from the public–collective domain, though maintaining a metaphoric link with it. What is evident from the range of stories examined in this chapter is the way this space is not necessarily defined as a private–individual domain. The place for the construction of identity need only be framed as belonging outside the boundaries of the normal social order (i.e., the 'liminal' sphere). A useful comparison may be found in the less individualistic societies which people this 'other world' with gods rather than selves. But, just

Table 1. *Romantic and comic narrative structure and details*

		Breach	Crisis	Redress
Romance				
Theory	Sheehy	Mid-life crisis	Psychological struggle	Self-reliance
Marathon	Kate	Nervous breakdown	Marathon as a test	Physical responsibility
Travel	Susan	Dependence in relationship	Physical struggle	Niceness
Structure		Lack of distinction	Struggle	Moral point
Comedy				
Theory	Nicola	Mid-life crisis	Escape to New York	Global welfare
Marathon	David	Denial of self	New York	Family
Travel	Michael	Intolerance of others	Holiday with family Closeness in Ireland	Family
Structure		Lack of communality	Release	Social utility

as the role of gods is bound up with the existence of social institutions, the liminal experience in the development of self is contained in a story envelope which relates the individual's life to the social order. Thus, the *separation* referred to above is complemented by the *return* to the moral values of self-reliance, physical responsibility and 'niceness' in romance, and to the social utilitarian values of global welfare and family in comedy. It is this process of separation and reparation of meaning that is enabled by the telling of stories.

As shown in Table 1, the narrative structures of comedy and romance share the basic ritual form of breach–crisis–redress which collectively manages deviations from the normal order. The crises in romance mediate this process through struggle, whereas in comedy this occurs through release. The resolution, or redress, as a normal order is re-established and functions to give meaning to the events by reference to a superordinate moral and social order. While the narrative allows entry into discourse of foreign elements, these are eventually granted meaning by the point that frames the story as a social act. To have a story filled with bizarre happenings without a point is to reflect the same confusion felt by people like Kate, who lack a distinctive social identity. And to have a story that is all point is like a self deprived of spontaneity, as in David's encasement in his social roles of father and manager. Without spontaneity, communality is robbed of the energy derived from the free exchange between people. The elasticity of meaning enabled by the narrative mode of understanding given in its point allows the departure of the individual from the normal social order to be only temporary. The construction of identity through narrative is thus necessary to deal with the paradox of individuality. There are some cases, however, when the paradox is unresolved in narrative.

When's the Fade-out?

The experiences of selfhood described and constructed in this chapter all concern the world of extraordinary happenings. Given that most people, most of the time, live in one ordinary world, it is necessary to raise the issue of how *real* these stories are. Like the fictional man in the film, we ask, 'When's the fade-out?' Two narrative structures not addressed in this paper – tragedy and irony – both deal with aspects of experience that miss out on the round of official narrative representation. Tragedy deals in the elements of self that have been discovered, yet are incapable of realization in the real world. The film *Elephant Man* is a tragedy about the inability of the contemporary social world to recognize a humanness beyond the abominable exterior of a deformed person. Irony deals with the less noble exposition of how reality often fails to live up to the expectations of it contained in its representations. In *Don Quixote* we attend more to the amusing inappropriateness of the hero's actions – led astray as he is by reading too many romances – than to the sad loss of hope for happiness on the part of the hero. In both cases, the audiences of these stories witness how fictional members of a social order are caught in a contradiction that leads them necessarily to transgress certain norms. The fate of these heroes – becoming martyrs or fools – serves to monitor those boundaries, just as the occasional failed escape attempt reminds us of the existence of the Berlin Wall. Tragedy and irony, although indicating that there are certain times and places where romance or comedy are inappropriate, can lead to depression and cynicism if taken to extreme. None the less, they help to instantiate the limits of the moral order in the government of human action.

That tragedy may sometimes be an appropriate structure for an individual's biographical identity challenges the commonsense assumption that people's actions are motivated by the desire successfully to achieve their individual goals. An alternative model consonant with the thesis of this chapter would propose that this assumption is itself partly a product of the narrative structures that govern its expression. The motivating force would instead become the desire to find a match between one's own biography and the socially recognized life-stories resembling romance and comedy, etc., but also including tragedy. Turner (1980, p. 155) views the possible participation of such 'action paradigms' as a guarantee of social status and certainty:

> Just to be in the cast of a narrated drama which comes to be taken as exemplary or paradigmatic is some assurance of social immortality.

When an 'action paradigm' begins to be discernible from the variety of narrative possibilities in one's life, when suffering begins to be considered tragic or when a change of script is considered, when the burdens of office outweigh the glory of romance, when self-deprecation and cynicism overtake generous communality – it is plausible that these moments are managed by framing devices similar to those found in transformations of outlook within literary narrative. While the identification of these devices is likely to be an uncertain process, it should be easy to appreciate their function in switching moods in dramatically recognizable ways: 'Things began to turn sour when ... '; or 'I had almost given up hope when ... '
The difference between change of fortune in real life and literature must be the necessary place of individual volition, perhaps mediated by negotiations in friendship and therapy, in choosing what makes

best narrative sense in one's own life. As emphasized earlier, when a lack of narrative fit is perceived and a change of design is desired, the individual must seek out those areas of social life set aside for transformations of identity, such as running a marathon or travelling overseas. The identification in this chapter of some of the traditional costumes for biography and recognized changing rooms should then lead us to examine the dynamics of the choice of clothing.[13]

The Narrative Self

Narrative has been depicted in this chapter mainly as a process for mediating between theories from the social order and individual lives. It is from such a mediation that identity is constructed: social identity through the instantiation of a romantic narrative structure of tests, and personal identity by means of the release of idiosyncracies allowed in a comic narrative structure. These story forms serve as prescribed ways for the instantiation of moral values such as self-reliance, and commitment to social units such as the family, into the life of the individual. They allow for the possibility that lives might contain a meaningful and honourable point. Although romance and comedy were taken as structures that enabled this process, there is no reason why they should exhaust the narrative possibilities of selfhood in Western culture. Different structures will probably be found in other discourses which govern the expression of individuality. One can, for instance, consider the serious retirement speech as emplotting the career in terms of an epic narrative structure.

The way the construction of identity through narrative has been represented in this chapter implies that the collectively represented social order is an integral part of the development of self. While this is in harmony with Harré's theory of personal being, it denies the validity of theories that lack the collective component, such as the Implicit Personality Theory and Schafer's theory. Implicit Personality Theory might well respond that romance can be viewed as a means of *testing* an element of one's character, while comedy can be seen as an *exploration* of one's personality, similar to, say, drilling for oil. These accounts would preserve the initial concern with sense of self as the product of practices of collecting data about the self. However, while such explanations might undoubtedly account for *part* of the narrative structures uncovered in this chapter, they have little to say about the central role played in each by values of morality and social life. The struggle and release described by romance and comedy concern our interaction with norms that are collectively held, and it is among these that the narratives of self find the point that grants them an eventual meaning. Finding a place for an individual in the concerns of the collective is thus a problem that a narrative formation of identity can manage better than a sense of self based on abstract informational procedures.

Conclusion

In terms of Harré's view of personal being as a product of the theories contained in the social order, it seems that narrative has a necessary role to play in the mediation between those theories and experience which permits the construction of identities that are more than mere transcriptions of the social order. To achieve this, individuals must leave the familiar everyday world and not only engage in tests in order to be granted a place in the status hierarchy, but also find release from normal controls in order to relate to those others, such as one's family, who exist outside of that hierarchy. And narrative is the means by which these departures are managed and inscribed in one's biography.

Appendix: The Life of Nicola

Nicola was attractive, gregarious, and ambitious. She was her father's girl.

Angelo, her father, was a bright and hard-working builder in East Doncaster of classical Italian background. His wife, Dimantina, was sickly and had many miscarriages.

Nicola went to a Catholic primary school, where she was very mischievous and got into trouble. Rather than continuing her Catholic education, she was forced to go to a government secondary school because her mother's illness had left the family in financial trouble. At her new school she was very popular and even became a prefect.

Nicola developed the ambition to become an architect while looking over plans for buildings which her father showed her when he was working at home. This ambition was strengthened during work experience when she met a spunky architect. Architecture inspired her as a symbol of the unattainable.

While studying architecture she was again very popular. She went out with a former prefect from her old school. Halfway through her degree, her father had a heart attack. This strengthened her resolve to do well, and she withdrew into her studies.

Once she had successfully completed her course, she was given a ticket overseas as a present by her parents. Nicola felt that it was time to break from her family. While she was overseas she developed an interest in fashion and discovered that she had a real creative flair. But when Nicola was twenty-three her father died and it became clear that she was needed back home. She realized then that it was up to her to hold everything together.

Back in Australia, she married her boyfriend. They had two children by the time she reached thirty years of age. By the age of forty-two she had still not reached her career potential, and this precipitated a mid-life crisis. While accompanying her husband on a business trip to New York, she had an affair with Peter, an archaeologist from Texas. Looking for a way of fulfilling her ambitions, Nicola decided to leave her husband and stay with Peter in New York. There she managed to set up a successful business practice. Peter would go away on digs, but that was all right for her because there was plenty to do in New York. Her children did not mind her leaving them, and they came to visit her.

At the age of fifty-two, Nicola went with Peter to Africa. She felt the need to contribute, and so designed cheap communal housing for the natives. The experience of poverty enabled her to realize what a comfortable life she had been living. When she was sixty-two Nicola travelled to South America. At this point she had become interested in a combination of archaeology and architecture. Unfortunately, her heart went in the heat. This complaint was in the family and she was given ten years to live.

At this point she went to live in Italy, where Peter died. Nicola decided then to return to Australia to see her children.

She died with grace.

Notes

This development of this paper from its draft form owes much to comments from Kenneth Gergen, Sue Kippax, Jerome Bruner, Rom Harré, Theodore Sarbin and Karl Scheibe.

1. *The Purple Rose of Cairo*, directed by Woody Allen, released in 1985.

2. For a more detailed explication of this argument see Murray (1987).

3. In early modern theories of narrative (see Shklovsky, 1965), the devices of the story were seen to permit the exclusion of habitual ways of making sense of the world. In making familiar objects strange, the plot uncovers the experiential world and thus introduces new ways of looking at things.

4. Other theorists who have employed these structures include Schafer (1976), White (1973), and Gergen and Gergen (1988). See Murray (1985a) for an argument for their usefulness as interpretive categories in the social sciences.

5. Sheehy's first best-selling book, *Passages* (1976), set out some prescribed routes through the life-course. This was followed by *Pathfinders* (1982), which more explicitly covered the demands necessary to become a fully realized individual. A comparison of Sheehy with other similar popular writers can be found in Murray (1986).

6. The particular marathon studied was the 1981 Melbourne Marathon. It attracted about 6000 partipicants in a city of 3 million people. The study examined the accounts of fifty first-time entrants who were over thirty years of age. (For more details see Murray, 1985b.)

7. Because theory about the narrative structures in designing one's life is not dealing in estimates of quantitative behavioural characteristics, the study of individual cases is more relevant than measures of larger samples. Our concern is not with statistical trends but with the sorts of possibilities in life granted by the narrative structures imposed on it.

8. Footscray and St Albans are lower-class areas of Melbourne; Kew is a respectable middle-class suburb.

9. The fact that the group is using the quality 'interesting' to determine what sort of person Nicola is indicates that she may not be necessarily a realistic person; yet, given that one of the main tasks in becoming a successful social actor is being an 'interesting' person, the way the group constructs this quality is far from irrelevant.

10. One of the members of the group observed that, in deciding to have a 'good' character, they risked avoiding some of the less idealistic problems that life contains. Nicola represents 'how we see ideal people growing up'. The apparent inattention to verisimilitude implied by this statement enables us to see more clearly how the function of narrative structures extends beyond the essentially mimetic purpose to its role in the realization of the moral order in the realm of experience.

11. The story of Nicola was far from an isolated instance of the discovery of personhood through the social group. Other characters constructed by groups found themselves in a social environment that permitted the free expression of their individuality. One more life is worth noting to highlight the regularity of this narrative. One can speculate that, because of the association between America and freedom, its narrative function in the lives of many migrants from other countries would be the same as it was in the life of Nicola: as a 'green world' in which the ties of the past are replaced by the promise of the future. America was given the same comic potential in a story constructed by a different group. Dealing with the life of an acrobat, the constructors decided to send her to New York to escape the IRA and attempt to realize her ability as a dancer.

J: So she's got a lot of money, right. This is her big chance to go wherever she wants to go.

S: So she picks New York.

C: Mm.

P: And signs up with the New York dance theatre or something like that.

J: Well, not necessarily New York.

C: But New York's really exciting, 'cos it's a place where expatriate [Irish people] go, and there's a lot of migrants there ... It's just a place where all sorts of people she'd identify with were, but were also strangers.

That New York contains people similar enough to the acrobat for her to identify with, yet remain strangers, indicates the possibility of close contact without any of the responsibilities normally associated with social relationships. It is in such a world that she is expected to discover her talent for dancing. However, her dream of being a successful dancer is treated cruelly by the acrobat's constructors. The reason for this was that the acrobat had spent her entire life on the outside of society, because of her mixed origins and her dream of dancing. Although New York appeared as a world containing people more like her than there were in Ireland, and thus promised to provide her with the support she was looking for, she is ultimately excluded by this world because of her status as an outsider in the story: her dancing is not fashionable. Although the moral vision of the world is tragic, New York still retains the same comic *potential* that it has for Nicola. Two other groups found utopic spaces for their characters in the university and a guerrilla camp in Brazil.

12. The growing theorization of these *unofficial* spaces for identity work includes psychosocial theories of friendship as 'ensemble' relations (Little, 1985), and the expression of folk identity through grotesque inversions of body symbology (Bakhtin, 1984).

13. Such a venture is broadly sympathetic with the concerns of autobiographical research proposed by de Waele and Harré (1979). Both attend to the social order that constrains the range of personas, etc., available to the individual, as well as the processes governing their eventual selection.

References

Bakhtin, M. (1984) *Rabelais and his World*. Bloomington: Indiana University Press.
Barton, R.W. (1985) 'Plato/Freud/Mann: Narrative Structure, Undecidability and the Social Text', *Semiotica*, 54: 351–86.
Berger, H. (1965) 'The Renaissance Imagination: Second World and Green World', *Centennial Review*, 9; 36–78.
Brooks, P. (1984) *Reading for the Plot: Design and Intention in Narrative*. New York: Vintage Press.
Bruner, J. (1986) *Actual Minds, Possible Worlds*. Cambridge, MA: Harvard University Press.
de Waele, J-P. and R. Harré (1979) 'Autobiography as a Psychological Method', in G.P. Ginsberg (ed.), *Emerging Strategies in Social Psychological Research*. Chichester: John Wiley.
Frye, N. (1957) *Anatomy of Criticism*. Princeton: Princeton University Press.
Gergen, K.J. (1984) 'An Introduction to Historical Social Psychology', in K.J. Gergen and M.M. Gergen, *Historical Social Psychology*. Hillsdale, NJ: Erlbaum.
Gergen, K.J. and M.M. Gergen (1988) 'Narrative and Self as Relationship', in L. Berkowitz (ed.), *Advances in Experimental Social Psychology*. New York: Academic Press.
Harré, R. (1983) *Personal Being*. Oxford: Basil Blackwell.
Harré, R., D. Clarke and N. de Carlo (1985) *Motives and Mechanisms: An Introduction to the Psychology of Action*. London: Methuen.
Hernnstein-Smith, B. (1978) *On the Margins of Discourse*. Chicago: University of Chicago Press.
Jameson, F. (1981) *The Political Unconscious: Narrative as a Socially Symbolic Act*. Ithaca, NY: Cornell University Press.

Keen, E. (1986) 'Paranoia and Cataclysmic Narratives', in T.R. Sarbin (ed.), *Narrative Psychology: The Storied Nature of Human Conduct*. New York: Praeger.

Little, G. (1985) *Political Ensembles*. Melbourne: Oxford University Press.

Murray, K. (1985a) 'Life as Fiction', *Journal for the Theory of Social Behaviour*, 15: 172–85.

Murray, K. (1985b) 'Justificatory Accounts and the Marathon as a Social Event', *Australian Psychologist*, 20: 61–74.

Murray, K. (1986) 'Finding Literary Paths through Passages', in T.R. Sarbin (ed.), *Narrative Psychology: The Storied Nature of Human Conduct*. New York: Praeger.

Murray, K. (1987) 'The Tall Man Reads Psychoanalysis and Finds Romance', *Southern Review*, 20: 49–68.

Price, M. (1983) *Forms of Life: Character and Imagination in the Novel*. New Haven, CN: Yale University Press.

Ricoeur, P. (1983, 1985) *Narrative and Time*, Vols 1 and 2. Chicago: University of Chicago Press.

Sarbin, T.R. (1986) 'Narratology as a Root Metaphor in Psychology', in T.R. Sarbin (ed.), *Narrative Psychology: The Storied Nature of Human Conduct*. New York: Praeger.

Schafer, R. (1976) *A New Language for Psychoanalysis*. New Haven, CN: Yale University Press.

Scheibe, K. (1986) 'Self-narratives and Adventure', in T.R. Sarbin (ed.), *Narrative Psychology: The Storied Nature of Human Conduct*. New York: Praeger.

Sheehy, G. (1976) *Passages*. New York: Bantam.

Sheehy, G. (1982) *Pathfinders*. New York: Bantam.

Shklovsky, V. (1965) 'Art as Technique', in L.T. Lemon and M.J. Reis (eds), *Russian Formalist Criticism: Four Essays*. Lincoln: University of Nebraska Press.

Turner, V. (1969) *The Ritual Process*. Chicago: Aldine.

Turner, V. (1980) 'Social Dramas and Stories about Them', *Critical Inquiry*, 7: 141–68.

von Cranach, M. (1982) 'Ordinary Interactive Action: Theory, Methods and some Empirical Findings', in M. von Cranach and R. Harré (eds), *The Analysis of Action*. Cambridge: Cambridge University Press.

Wegner, D.M. and R.R. Vallacher (1981) *Implicit Psychology*. Oxford: Oxford University Press.

White, H. (1973) *Metahistory: The Historical Imagination in the Nineteenth Century*. Baltimore: Johns Hopkins University Press.

13
Narrative Characters and Accounting for Violence

Margaret Wetherell and Jonathan Potter

In this chapter we examine the way self-discourse is used in acts of mitigation. When someone is excusing or justifying the purportedly aberrant behaviour of a group of people, how do they formulate the nature of those persons to facilitate the mitigating force of their accounts? What constructions of self and character provide persuasive excuses? Our investigation of this issue uses a form of systematic discourse analysis familiar from a number of other studies (Gilbert and Mulkay, 1984; Potter et al., 1984; Potter and Wetherell, 1987; Wetherell, 1986). Discourse analysis focuses on the constructed and constructive nature of language and on the functions and consequences of language use. The materials for this particular analysis consist of a set of accounts of 'violent police behaviour' during the South African Springbok rugby tour of New Zealand in 1981, and we look at how ordinary New Zealanders, interviewed about the police response to protests and civil disturbance, excused and justified police actions.

Narrative Characters in Psychology and Everyday Discourse

In a previous study (Potter et al., 1984, Ch. 7) we noted how traditional socio-psychological research on the self has focused on two principal self-constructions or narrative characters. Paralleling the images of self found in literary characterization, which also resonate throughout Western culture, psychologists have frequently chosen to see the self as a solid, unfragmented, coherent character or 'personality' and as a disintegrated, divided or split subject. These two possibilities are best represented in psychological trait theory (cf. Eysenck, 1953) and in socio-psychological uses of role theory (cf. Dahrendorf, 1973).

We argued that these psychological theories of the self can be seen as a form of discourse in themselves. Psychological theories of the self need not be taken as simple descriptions of an empirical reality discovered through observation and experiment, but rather as constructions evolved to achieve numerous pragmatic tasks, although generating their own problems in turn (cf. Gergen's Chapter 5 above). In this study we examine the way the characters developed in trait theory and role theory are used as resources in everyday discourse.

Simplifying greatly, the trait theory, or 'honest soul' model of the self as Trilling (1974) calls it, sees the person as a bundle of traits, attributes and abilities: the extrovert, the introvert, the kind, the submissive and so on. Individuals are simply the sum of their traits, and their behaviour is largely determined by these internal characteristics. Honest souls have a 'nature' and are driven by their type and temperament.

In this image, people are solid and unfragmented agents and the person is entirely synonymous with his or her dispositions. Trait theorists would never describe their subject as 'managing' the impression given to others, or as in the throes of an 'identity crisis'. This type of explanation is alien to the honest soul mode of self (Rorty, 1976) because in this case the individual is seen as having only one identity, their personality, and there is no ironic distance or separation within the self to produce the self-conflict implied in an identity crisis. The persons constructed in the discourse of trait theory are always authentic or true to themselves. The extrovert, for example, is not putting on a façade; their essential disposition is simply revealed in all their actions.

Role theorists, on the other hand, argue that the self is a social product. People have different parts to play in society which require different manifestations of self or different personalities. The individual is like a chameleon with not one stable consistent personality or set of traits but the ability to play many parts and assume many guises – one personality as mother, another as daughter, yet another to fulfil occupational demands and so on.

A very different type of narrative character is being posited here. People are not 'natural' characters, they are performers capable of dissembling. The individual is fragmented into a multiple set of possibly discordant identities; insincerity arises from being aware of the requirements of society. Whereas the honest soul is seen as unselfconscious in response and thus sincere to their disposition, the role player is capable of putting on a façade and hiding behind a mask or persona.

Role theory and trait theory, therefore, are two academic psychological images of the self which we kept in mind as we examined how ordinary people constructed character and motive in order to excuse aberrant behaviour.

208 *Drama and narrative in the construction of identities*

Background to the Study

All the examples we shall consider here are taken from open-ended interviews conducted with middle-class *pakeha* (white) New Zealanders (Wetherell and Potter, 1986). The interviews covered a wide range of 'controversial issues' including a number of questions concerned with events that happened during the 1981 Springbok rugby tour of New Zealand.

This tour was a highly controversial one. According to opinion polls, it was not supported by the majority of New Zealand population, although there was a sizeable minority of people who felt very strongly that the tour should go ahead, and it was strongly opposed by a large coalition of anti-apartheid campaigners who initiated protests and civil disturbance during this period. One of the scheduled matches was cancelled as a consequence of disturbances, and every game involved a demonstration of some kind, culminating in the final match of the tour where there was what has been described as a 'riot'. The conduct of the police during these protests was later called into question and became part of the debate surrounding the events of 1981 (Shears and Gidley, 1982). The following account illustrates the kind of accusation of excessive police violence that was made:

> The riot squad drew their batons, without apparent warning then started hitting people, injuring several. When they stopped about 30 seconds later, the command from the officer in charge was heard, 'move or you will be injured.' Nobody moved and more were injured. This happened several times. I was horrified to see the hungry look for violence on some of the policemen's faces. (letter, *The Star*, 2 September 1981)

The people we interviewed can be described as onlookers or spectators of this conflict, in the sense that none were involved in the protest movement, although all offered, generally strong, views about the events surrounding the tour, both pro and anti. In the interview the questions asked gave respondents the task of accounting for or explaining the conflict and violence to the interviewer and articulating their position. We will be concerned here solely with a particular subset of responses to a question about 'police violence' during the tour.

The interviewer's question, with some minor variations, runs as follows:

> I: Some people I have talked to, mainly anti-tour people, have argued that the police escalated the violence through their actions. Is that a view you'd have much sympathy for?

We split responses up into those that expressed agreement with this view, or gave 'symmetrical' accounts which stressed both police and protester violence, and those that expressed disagreement. Out of thirty-four interviews where this question was asked, eighteen gave responses that were predominantly excuses or justifications of the police behaviour. It is these that we will focus on.

Across the corpus of mitigating accounts, a variety of excusing and justifying components for police behaviour was drawn on. There is not space here to discuss all the mitigating accounts. We will concentrate on the most frequent types of mitigation, and particularly on those that utilize self-discourse. Thus, readers should be warned that the respondents used a number of less common but equally interesting techniques of mitigation. For each type of mitigation, we will indicate how many times it appears in the corpus of accounts.

The analysis will start with versions that do not use self-discourse to indicate some of the basic justifying and mitigating moves and then move on to examine accounts drawing on self-discourse. Except where missing material is indicated by square brackets, in each case we will reproduce the respondent's entire reply to the question.

How to Build an Excuse: (1) Without Building a Self

The first thing we need to think about is the nature of the question with which the interviewees were dealing. Although cast in 'neutral terms', it is a report of an accusation: a certain group of people have accused the police of escalating violence. To help us understand the way in which responses to the accusation are put together, we will draw, in the course of analysis, on Atkinson and Drew's (1979) work on the way accusations are managed in courts, and on Semin and Manstead's (1983) synthetic typology of excuses and justifications.

The first two types of rebuttal we will deal with do not involve self-discourse, but they illustrate some of the basic linguistic resources which can be drawn on to excuse and justify behaviour.

Version One: Causal Context (three instances)
The following is one of the simplest responses given. It provides a single mitigating component for police behaviour, namely, a causal context.

1. (1) Well, I wasn't there. (2) I couldn't really say, you know. (Mm.) (3) But I would say that, um, they would have been antagonized by the protesters anyway, some of them, you know, especially some of the hard cases up the front line using pretty abusive language and that. (Williamson: 13)

210 Drama and narrative in the construction of identities

This account mitigates by way of an excuse: the police have been *antagonized* by the protesters, and this antagonism is detailed as arising from 'hard cases' using 'abusive language and that'. The excuse works by providing a potent external cause for the police behaviour. The other instances of this version are very similar: extracts of this kind: '[the police'] were poked and pushed (Yeah) and bashed and then, finally, they were provoked into taking action' (Davison: 26), and 'they had women protesters that would go along and taunt the police and the police could not do a thing' (Jones: 11). In this version, then, the police did not *want to act violently – they were caused* to act in this way.

Interestingly, the police behaviour enters into the account in only a very minimal fashion – the one adjective 'antagonized' – and the account makes the protesters' nature and actions focal. This has the consequence of distracting attention from, and thereby downgrading the significance of, the issue of police violence raised in the question. Such downgrading of police violence has an excusing effect through what Semin and Manstead (1983) describe as 'minimization of the injury'.

Version Two: Rational Motivation (two instances)
As Austin (1961) and others have pointed out, there are two pre-eminent techniques for accounting for untoward behaviour: excuses, which normally offer factors that interfere with the actor's intentions, and justifications, which suggest 'good reasons' for acting in the apparently untoward manner. Version One takes the former approach, while Version Two takes the latter. In the following extract, 'good reasons' are offered for the violent police behaviour.

2. (1) No, I don't share that view. (No.) (2) No, I think that once, uh, well Mr Muldoon [the Prime Minister] I think in his defence of having the tour go on, he tried to, uh, emphasize that it was a law-and-order thing, after, once the violence was perpetrated at Hamilton (That's right, yeah), it was necessary for the police to meet force with force (Mmhm) to some extent. (3) But, eh, I think that's when the, eh, you know, that's when the sort of bitterness probably commenced. (Right.) (4) But whether there was any alternative, I don't know. (Ackland: 10).

Here we see a complex causal context of political strategies and the evolution of events deployed in (2). However, police action is represented both as a *response* to earlier violence and *necessary* in the current situation. In the other account of this kind the justification is made more explicit: 'police are well justified in the, in the history of, you know, how they handle situations ... the few things that they ... were subject to criticism of I think were quite minor in comparison with what they achieved.' Thus police behaviour is not caused, it is considered – it is not blameworthy because it was needed in this situation.

Extract 2 is also interesting because it shows another downgrading technique. The highly negative violent and bitter actions are described in *nominalized* form (Kress and Hodge, 1979; Trew, 1979); that is, they are processes or activities given noun status (cf. 'Strikers picket factory' transformed to 'Picketing'). One of the consequences of nominalization is that it makes it more difficult to recover tense and causal processes from the discourse. In this case, we have violence being perpetrated and bitterness commencing – in neither case can the causes be ascertained. There is information in the extract, especially in the sequencing of sentences (2) and (3), which suggests that police are responsible for the bitterness. The nominalization obviates the need to formulate this connection directly in a way that would cut down the mitigating effect of the account.

How to Build an Excuse: (2) With the Help of a Self

We saw in these first two versions two basic forms of mitigation. However, the majority of excusing and justifying responses (twelve out of eighteen) drew upon some kind of self-discourse, and it is these that we will concentrate on for the rest of the chapter.

Version Three: Rational Motivation, Universalizer (one instance)
This account is the same as Version Two in that it depicts the police violence as a consequence of rational and positive motivations. However, it goes on to introduce a new mitigating element.

3. (1) I believe some of the violence was pretty severe. (2) But I also believe it was warranted. (Yes.) (3) If, if it hadn't been, if it hadn't been as severe as as in some cases as it was, then a riot situation could have arisen. (Yeah.) (4) And nobody in New Zealand wants that (Yes.) (5) So I look up to the police. (6) It must have been a hell of a hard job there. (Yes.) (7) Uhum, they had to decide between, the fine line between do we stop or do we go in. (Yes.) (8) And, er, that would have been a decision which I wouldn't have liked to have taken. (Irvine: 34)

This passage stressed the *achievement* of police actions; that is, a positive goal is identified which gives the actions a rational basis. The speaker accepts that police violence was severe (1) but depicts that very severity as necessary for preventing a riot (2–3). The violence is thus justified by appealing to law and order.

Unlike Versions One and Two, this account does not downgrade the violence; indeed, it is described as 'pretty severe'. The mitigation works through depicting a very positive consequence in a very difficult situation rather than through minimizing its aggressive nature. However, there are some downgrading elements. In sentences (1)–(3) the speaker talks of severe violence, but in a nominalized form which depicts it as an object in itself rather than something performed by specific people, that is, as a kind of disembodied phantom. And when, later in the extract, a formulation mentioning the police is used, it deploys the highly downgraded description 'go in' (7) rather than repeating the 'severe violence' description (1-3).

Most interesting for our current discussion is the final section of this passage (6–8). The speaker stresses the difficulty of the decision the police had to make, the 'fine line' between 'stopping' and 'going in', and he says that this is a decision 'which I wouldn't have liked to have taken' (8); that is, he makes a direct analogy between his own rationality and that of the police.

This utterance seems to work in a number of ways. First, it fits in with the organization of the mitigation in terms of police violence being a rational and successful policy. Second, it emphasizes the difficulty of the decision: this is probably needed to keep the mitigation plausible, because even violence that has positive consequences will be seen as culpable if performed casually without serious consideration. Third, and most relevantly, the use of a self–police comparison works to universalize the issue: by implication, the decision the police had to make is one that *anyone*, exemplified by the current speaker, would find difficult. The job is not hard for the police because of any *special* characteristic they, as a category, might possess – poor decision-making, say, or a propensity to violence – it is hard because it would be hard for anyone.

The difference between this latter form of justification and that seen in Version Two can be seen if we think of an alternative formulation which accepts the rationality of the police actions but *only in their own terms*. We can imagine saying that the police acted in a certain manner because they mistakenly construed the situation in a particular way. However, in Version Three the speaker is explicitly aligning his everyday rationality with that of the police in the situation.

Here we see the first vestiges of self-discourse being used in this mitigation. The rationality of the police decision is compared with the rationality that might be exhibited by any rational self in this situation. Other sorts of potential police selves – violent selves, or incompetent selves – are excluded.

Version Four: Causal Context and Violent Self (seven instances)
The previous version deployed a rational motivation justification reinforced by a universalizing device. This was unusual in the accounts, appearing just once. A much more common pattern combined a causal context with a specific model of the self.

4. (1) U::m probably only 'cause they were human. (2) At the start, more at the start of the tour, I think the Australian reporters were amazed at how, um, how the police sort of held off and were so tolerant. (3) But, um, presumably their tempers wore a bit thin by the end of it. (4) And so they were presumably contributing a bit to the end. (5) But I think that, I mean, they stood, I [inaudible] the protesters putting all the Mongrel Mob fellows at the front, and the front lines and, uh, uh, motorcycle helmets and all this kind of thing. (Jackson: 8–9)
5. (1) I don't think so:. (2) We actually know two families, police families, very well, and it really did tear them apart. (3) In one the husband was away for about two months, um. (4) I think the police acted very well. (5) They're only human. (6) If they lashed out and cracked a skull occasionally, it was, hah, only a very human action I'm sure. (Bird: 11)
6. (1) Oh, I think they did alright. (2) I reckon if somebody got hurt they, they might have made a few mistakes. (Mmhm.) (3) But, you know, policemen are only ordinary people. (Mmhm.) (4) They must have had a lot of provocation. (Yes.) (5) And I don't blame them if at the last they were a bit rough, you know. (6) Well, well I guess I wasn't ever there. (7) The television people were pretty brutal. (8) Well a lot of them are probably anti-tour inclined, a bit of a biased view. (Owen: 16)

These accounts make up the largest subgroup of mitigations offered in the interviews. In each, police violence is downgraded by the use of an inexplicit descriptive style: 'tempers worn thin', 'contributing a bit' (4.3–4); 'lashed out and cracked a skull occasionally' (5.6); 'a few mistakes', 'a bit rough' (6.2–4). Such descriptive prose contrasts starkly with the detailed and florid prose in accounts blaming the police. The downgrade in extract 6 is further emphasized by characterizing the television coverage as biased against the police and even 'pretty brutal' (6.7) – a fascinating reassignment of blame for the violence.

Moreover, as in previous accounts, violent police behaviour is depicted as a consequence of circumstances. In extract 4 the precipitating circumstances are a 'front line' of protesters made up from New Zealand motorcycle gang members and people prepared for a fight (4.5). The police behaviour in the face of this is made more worthy by making an implicit positive comparison to the behaviour of Australian police (4.2). In extract 5 the precipitating circumstances are obliquely indicated by references to police families being 'torn apart' (5.2). In extract 6 reference is simply made to 'a lot of provocation' (6.4).

The novel feature of each of these accounts is that the police are represented as 'only human' or 'ordinary people' (4.1, 5.5, 6.3). The underlying logic of this form of description is that, given circumstances such as those that faced the police, the natural human thing to do is to behave violently. The sort of thing that humans do when under pressure or provocation is to 'lash out', 'make mistakes', be 'a bit rough', 'crack a few skulls'.

The mitigating component in these accounts, then, consists of a naturalized version of self. If persons *naturally* react in this way – violently – then they can hardly be blamed for it. Natural processes can be removed from the moral evaluative sphere applied to human behaviour: in Western culture volcanoes are not blamed for erupting or typhoons for destroying towns. Part of the mitigating effect, then, seems to arise from naturalizing the problematic police behaviour and thus questioning the relevance of the accusation in the interviewer's question. This police self is the honest soul described at the beginning of this chapter; he is blindly acting out his traits, in this case the propensity for violence which 'lies within all of us'.

Another part of the mitigating effect deriving from this self-discourse seems to derive from social comparison: everybody else acts equally badly, so why blame *these* people? As another interviewee put it, 'occasionally [the police] got out of hand but I suppose they're like anybody else' (Oates: 17). In other accounts the natural, expected nature of the police behaviour is implied more economically: ' [the police] were caught in very stressful situations and in those stressful situations some *of course* reacted and overreacted' (Waites: 11; emphasis added).

It is important to understand this use of self-discourse in context. As we have indicated, interviewees are responding to an implied accusation; the use of the '*only* human/ordinary people' construction suggests a contrast to something that is *more* than human or even *super*human. That is, the interviewee is implicitly characterizing the accusation of police violence as using too stringent standards or expecting the police to be supermen.

So far, then, we have looked at accounts that deploy a narrative character which has many features of the 'honest soul' discussed above. However, another narrative character was drawn on in other accounts which is more reminiscent of the role player.

Version Five: Doing the Job (two instances)
The following passage is preceded by a situational account of police violence ('in the heat of the moment I think probably the police used

force that wasn't necessary' – Mills: 15). After this it deploys a rather different form of mitigation.

9. (1) Having a friend in the police force that was involved. (Yeah.) (2) Er, in a way they didn't have much choice. (3) Because Muldoon [the Prime Minister] set the whole situation up. (4) That's what worries me the most. (5) And they were the blooming scapegoats who had to get out and police the thing. (Yes.) (6) Um, if the thing had been defused before it ever got off the ground they would never have been put in that situation. (Yes.) (7) I think it displayed the police in a different role than we in New Zealand have ever seen them, and I think that's scared a lot of New Zealanders. (8) It was like the Bastion Point thing [a controversial Maori land protest]. (Mmhm.) (9) Er, but then you've got to think of the individual men, and a lot of those individual policemen have really strong feelings, which I guess if they're going to stay in the police force, they've got to do their job, they can't take that into account. (10) I don't know if they were able to refuse to (Yes) to do duty, I mean in the Springbok Tour thing. (11) I don't imagine they were. (12) And I think a lot of people tend to forget that. (13) You know, they seem to think that the police were all getting at them. (Mills: 15–16)

In contrast to the previous version, which centred on the psychological reactions of a particular character type under extreme stress, in this version we see a complex narrative which places the problematic police behaviour in a sociological and political context. The police behaviour is excused as before by taking away their sphere of choice; however, instead of being caused by provocation, their actions are constrained by their role (9). The use of role discourse allows a split between the genuine motives and beliefs of the police and what they were required to do because it was their job. Thus, in this extract police are depicted as having 'really strong feelings' against the tour, which the nature of their job does not allow them to follow (8). At the end of the passage, the speaker explicitly formulates the implications of her account for the accusation of police violence: it is seen as based on the idea that the police wanted to get at them while forgetting that they merely had a job to do.

The same idea is deployed rather more economically by another interviewee: '[the police] were only doing their job, at the Springbok Tour and a lot of them didn't want to do it, but they had to because it was their job, and that's really sad' (James/Benton: 17). Again, the role discourse allows a separation to be made between the motives of the police as people and the nature of their occupation. A subtle combination of blaming–mitigating is permitted – the policy can be blamed, while the police who carry it out are mitigated.

It is notable that in both of these role accounts the actual behaviour of the police is formulated only in the most general terms. It is probably much more acceptable to present a general policy of 'being firm' as 'doing the job' than to use specific acts of violence. If the account is going to be more specific about police behaviour, then it may be necessary to connect the role account to other mitigating components. This, however, has to be done carefully, for there is always a danger of contradictions arising between police actions which are part of the job *as well as* an unfortunate but forgivable response to provocation.

Version Six: Causal Context, Violent Self, Doing the Job (two instances)

The final version combines role accounting with several of the components we have seen previously.

10. (1) No, I don't think so. (2) Ah, I think they had every right. (3) I mean the protesters, they were getting violent and they were virtually attacking the police. (4) I mean you're standing there, it's your job, you've been told to go out and keep the protest peaceful. (Mmhm.) (5) And somebody starts throwing rocks at you or starts hitting you an something like that. (6) I mean, personally I wouldn't stand there and take it! (Yes.) (7) I would have hit back. (Yeah.) (8) I do not blame them for their actions. (9) In fact I thought in some cases, uh, they were too reserved. (Mmhm.) (10) I mean, since I've got a violent attitude, ha ha. (11) I think the police had every right to put on a bit of pressure. (12) In the position they were in. (Yes.) (13) I didn't envy them one little bit, ha. (Hehe.) (Knight: 13)

All the individual components of this mitigation have been discussed above. It provides a causal context eliciting police actions (3, 5, 7, 12), and it describes the violence in downgraded form – 'put on a bit of pressure' (11). The account deploys a number of features which imply the natural, obvious, nature of the police reacting violently in circumstances of this kind (4–7). At the same time, it indicates that the police were doing their job (4); however, the role and violent self-accounting are kept separate. In this case the job is what places the police in the precipitating circumstances which lead violent selves to hit back.

Discussion: Selves for Mitigation

In this chapter we have examined a number of different approaches to the mitigation of the same potentially culpable actions. As we have seen, these mitigations have a complex and varied organization. Nevertheless, certain combinations of mitigating elements predominate.

Some of the interviewees placed the actions in a causal context such that attacks and provocation led the police to respond. To warrant this excuse, a particular model of the person is elaborated.

This person is flawed, with brutish tendencies. Most of the time his (!) uncivil nature is quiescent or restrained, but, given a sufficiently extreme situation or enough provocation, it will emerge. Such people are not managing or presenting their behaviour; for this self, the aggressive response is a natural product of internal dispositions.

Other interviews placed police actions in a rational context. The police are acting in a potentially culpable manner to produce a desired end, such as the prevention of a riot or a confrontation that is out of control. Seen in this light, police actions are justifiable. On some occasions this version is combined with a role account of police behaviour which stresses that they are only doing their job. The role account undermines accusations which question the motives of individual police by depicting their actions as following a general strategy. This form of accounting is particularly useful for interviewees such as Mills (extract 7), who want to maintain a positive view of police behaviour but condemn the general strategy they were asked to follow.

What we have done here, in a preliminary fashion, is to look at the way self-discourse is used by participants when faced with a specific practical problem, namely, the production of a mitigation. Instead of trying to read this discourse realistically, as a document of the way selves are, we have looked at the pragmatics of these self-versions. On the one hand, the honest soul–violent self enables violent behaviour to be naturalized, and universalized. On the other, the role model deflects blamings from specific individuals and translates the blameable issue into one of policy, strategy or politics generally.

It might, of course, be argued that this discourse should be read realistically. The argument would be that these interviewees are describing in slightly different ways a complex multi-faceted social event. However, both the broad organization of the accounts and the fine detail undermine this idea. In general terms, there are important contradictions between the basic strategies of mitigation. In particular, the claim that the culpable events are a causal consequence of protester violence and intimidation does not mesh with the claim that they are part of a necessary and thought-out strategy deployed to stop the events escalating, choosing to fight force with force. In terms of the detail of the accounts, interviewees recurrently talk of what 'must be' the case, what 'probably' happened, what 'would' have gone on and so on, indicating that they are offering a form of reasoning rather than a mere description. Indeed, they commonly disclaim direct knowledge, noting that they were not at matches, or did not see incidents, and they cast doubt on the veracity of media coverage.

We would like to end with one or two general points. First, we have looked at self-discourse in the context of a general analysis of discourse; we have not, that is, presupposed any fundamental

218   *Drama and narrative in the construction of identities*

difference between mitigations utilizing, say, ideas of constraint and ideas concerning the nature of persons. Such differences may, or may not, arise through further analysis – we do not wish to build them in before then.

Second, we have not been concerned with the effectiveness of these different styles of mitigation. The mitigations examined above are those that the interviewees considered sufficient in their responses. We might see a very different pattern if we looked at interactional material between people who disagreed about the activities of the police on the tour. One difference we might predict comes from Atkinson and Drew's (1979) work on courts. There, accusations led to defendants attempting to minimize the severity of offence, as we saw in the above accounts, but also attempting to minimize their disagreement with the prosecuting council. In the accounts examined above, the interviewees commonly gave responses that were highly discordant with the accusation and questioned its presuppositions. They were probably facilitated in this by the accusation being reported rather than directly offered by another speaker.

Third, we have not been concerned with the *motives* of the speakers. Some may have had a strong political point to make while some may have been simply concerned to make sense of a potentially order-threatening problematic claim: that the police have been violent. Nevertheless, the consequences of these accounts are more straightforward – they provide, in a number of different ways, mitigations of the police behaviour, and they question the motives of those making accusations of this kind. In this analysis, then, we have seen the way certain narrative characters are used as building blocks in accounts which, in effect, defend existing social institutions and arrangements against criticism.

Note

We would like to thank the UK Economic and Social Research Council for funding the research on which this chapter is based. We would also like to thank Quentin Halliday for helpful comments on the ideas discussed in this paper.

Appendix: transcription notation

The form of transcription used in this paper was developed by Gail Jefferson. A more complete description is found in Atkinson and Heritage (1984).

One or more colons indicate an extension of the preceding vowel sound, e.g.
    A: Yea::h, I see::

Round brackets indicate that material in brackets is either inaudible
or there is doubt about its accuracy, e.g.
　A: I (couldn't tell you) that
Square brackets indicate that some of the transcript has been
deliberately omitted. Material in square brackets is clarificatory
information, e.g.
　A: Brian [the speaker's brother] said [ ] its okay

References

Atkinson, J.M. and P. Drew (1979) *Order in Court: The Organization of Verbal Interaction in Judicial Settings*. London: Macmillan/SSRC.
Atkinson, J.M. and J.C. Heritage (eds) (1984) *Structures of Social Action: Studies in Conversational Analysis*. Cambridge: Cambridge University Press.
Austin, J. (1961) *Philosophical Papers*. Oxford: Clarendon Press.
Dahrendorf, R. (1973) *Homo Sociologicus*. London: Routledge & Kegan Paul.
Eysenck, H.J. (1953) *The Structure of Human Personality*. New York: Wiley.
Eysenck, H.J. and S.B. Eysenck (1963) 'The Validity of Questionnaires and Rating Assessments of Extraversion and Neuroticism and their Factorial Structure', *British Journal of Psychology*, 54: 51–62.
Gilbert, G.N. and M. Mulkay (1984) *Opening Pandora's Box: A Sociological Analysis of Scientists' Discourse*. Cambridge: Cambridge University Press.
Kress, G. and R. Hodge (1979) *Language as Ideology*. London: Routledge & Kegan Paul.
Potter, J. and M. Mulkay (1985) 'Scientists' Interview Talk: Interviews as a Technique for Revealing Participants' Interpretative Practices', in M. Brenner, J. Brown and D. Canter (eds), *The Research Interview: Uses and Approaches*. London: Academic Press.
Potter, J., P. Stringer and M. Wetherell (1984) *Social Texts and Context: Literature and Social Psychology*. London: Routledge & Kegan Paul.
Potter, J. and M. Wetherell (1987) *Discourse and Social Psychology: Beyond Attitudes and Behaviour*. London: Sage.
Rorty, A.O. (1976) 'A Literary Postscript: Characters, Persons, Selves, Individuals', in A.O. Rorty (ed.), *The Identities of Persons*. Berkeley: University of California Press.
Semin, G.R. and A.S.R. Manstead (1983) *The Accountability of Conduct*. London: Academic Press.
Shears, R. and I. Gidley (1982) *Storm Out of Africa!* Auckland, NZ: Macmillan.
Trew, T. (1979) 'What the Papers Say: Linguistic Variation and Ideological Difference', in R. Fowler, R. Hodge, G. Kress and T. Trew (eds), *Language and Control*. London: Routledge & Kegan Paul.
Trilling, L. (1974) *Sincerity and Authenticity*. London: Oxford University Press.
Wetherell, M. (1986) 'Linguistic Repertoires and Literary Criticism: New Directions for a Social Psychology of Gender', in S. Wilkinson (ed.), *Feminist Social Psychology*. Milton Keynes: Open University Press.
Wetherell, M. and J. Potter (1986) 'Majority Group Representations of "Race Relations" in New Zealand'. Paper presented at the British Psychological Society, Social Psychology Section Annual Conference, University of Sussex, September 1986.

14

Thriller: The Self in Modern Society

Kurt W. Back

James Thurber, in his delightful essay 'The Macbeth Murder
Mystery' (1945), introduces a lady who borrows a copy of *Macbeth*
when she has run out of mysteries during an ocean crossing.
When she returns the book, she has a 'solution'. Of course,
Macbeth could not be guilty (too obvious): it was Macduff, and
the rest of the action is explained by Macbeth and Lady Macbeth
trying to shield each other. Her companion, in exasperation, first
produces an even more intricate solution, and then suggests
that she read *Hamlet*, which has baffled the experts for four
hundred years.

This illustrative anecdote opens several themes, namely, the
contrast between the traditional and modern perception of fiction
and also the place of the mystery story in representing the
modern outlook. The transformation of literature in the period
of modernism is to a large degree a response to perceived
social change. For the traditional writer, the character's selfhood
was given. Individuals were put into plot situations where they
acted according to their personality; sometimes they were simply
identified by their temperaments alone. In addition, their actions
were frequently determined by their social background and their
station in life. Heroes behaved heroic, villains villainous. The
modern position makes the self problematic in two ways: individuals
do not know each other, and they are constantly surprised by the
different identities of their fellows. The self is not seen as unified
but is fragmented and unclear. Art and literature of the modernistic
period constitute the supreme expression of this new self; style as
well as content represent this condition. This chapter will discuss
the conditions of this change in society, and its representation in
the literature of modernism, expressed in writing for mass audiences
(mysteries and spy-thrillers) as well as in the art and literature of
high culture.

Modernism and Society

The rise of the modernist movement is generally dated as beginning about 1910, with the post-impressionist exhibitions in London and New York; for some, these events can be taken as markers to identify the start of the movement (Hodin, 1973). In the years around this time, Forster and Virginia Woolf published their first novels, Ezra Pound and his friends edited *The Vortex*, T.S. Eliot started writing 'The Love Song of J. Alfred Prufrock' and 'Sweeney Agonistes', and James Joyce wrote *Dubliners* and started on *Ulysses*. Within a few decades the movement expanded, and reached in literature its strong representatives in Joyce, Gertrude Stein, Proust, Thomas Mann and Pirandello, with parallel development in painting and sculpture encompassing Picasso, Matisse, expressionists and surrealists. Modernism spread into other forms of art and even amalgamations of different art forms, creating new combinations and affecting the general culture.

This wealth of manifestations and dispersion into different movements can lead to the neglect of common aspects, or even of the fact that modernism can be called one movement. As a conscious rebellion, which modernism had in common with other movements, several features stand out which derive from an intense questioning of all assumptions. In form, it rejected the tradition of representation or, alternatively, ornamentation. In content, it rejected the assumptions of unity – not only the Aristotelian unities of place, time and action, but even the unity of the actors, corresponding to a unity of the self.

Here we shall be concerned mainly with this rejection of the unity of the self in its manifestation in different forms of presentations. This form may be innovative, for instance in the stream-of-consciousness technique. It has also infiltrated those aspects of cultural production that remained impervious to stylistic innovations, but preserved the outward form of the nineteenth-century novel. Here, in mysteries and thrillers, the modernist view of the self stands out against a background of traditional style.

The dissolution of the self in modern art was conceived as a reaction to social conditions. The forces that led to a unity-of-the-self concept are weakened or counteracted in mass society. Heterogeneity of life in metropolitan areas may lead to tolerance and enrichment of stimulation, but it also leads to ambivalence in norms, even in norms of perception. Taking the place of the other, morally as well as perceptually, becomes a desirable trait. In the development of the self, inconsistent influences impinge on the child. They are not even regular according to the situation and might destroy the systematic arrangement-of-self concept; for instance, 'I am indulged by my parents, but competed within the playgroup.' Different clues may be given at the same time, a condition that some psychologists have exalted as the protean (Lifton, 1976), or oceanic, self (Zurcher, 1977). The ability to adapt to short-term relationships and to keep the life-course compartmentalized has been praised as a new achievement for modern man (Rogers, 1968), but it also exacts its price. The family is changing in composition and influence. The parents themselves are subjected to a variety of standards from personal contacts and mass media, and they are not able to enforce norms of which they are taught to be doubtful. Discrepancies in norms or between spoken norms and behaviour are unintentionally transmitted to children and obstruct the development of a united self. A fragmentation of the self is perhaps functional to a social milieu that exalts change.

Social Science and Modernism

Scientific development during this time reflected in part the new state of affairs and then became an influence in itself on the changing social conditions. We face here three interacting conditions: first, the nature of the human self and self-concept changed during this time; second, the scientific investigations of the time started to advance new concepts of the self; and third, the cultural representation of the self changed as well.

The principal change in the organization of the self was from single to multiple, according to Gordon and Gergen's (1968) classification of different perspectives on the self. Psychological research raised questions of the unity of the self. Enquiry into dissociated states in psychosis or induced through drugs or hypnosis drew the attention of early medical psychologists such as Charcot.

This concern about abnormal states led to depth-psychological research and especially to psychoanalysis. Freud moved from work with drugs and hypnosis to the analysis of different parts of the self by techniques that approximated normal human interaction, and he also showed that equivalent processes occurred in the normal person. Thus, the multiple self was no longer looked at as exceptional and threatening, but as part of the normal course of life. Different layers of the person were distinguished, such as Freud's super-ego, ego and id, with sometimes intense combat between them. Freud's own presentation follows that of a mystery story in picking up diverse cues and forcing readers into accepting the sleuth's or researcher's interpretation; we find not a consistent character, but virtually a battlefield on which remnants of old experienced and current concerns are fought out. Freud himself was a mystery story fan (Fish, 1986).

Other theorists arranged the self differently, but accepted the idea that the unity of what we call a 'person' is only an arbitrary construction. In particular, William James (1892) described the self as consisting of several layers that were not necessarily consistent with each other. In a significant chain in intellectual history, Gertrude Stein, one of the early modernist writers, completed her PhD dissertation under James's direction on automatic writing, a dissociated phenomenon (Mellow, 1974). Her own writings emphasized discontinuity in style as well as in choice of subjects. The stream-of-consciousness technique and the ambiguity and self-contradiction of characters in modern writing testify to the dissolution of the self.

The problematic unity of the self became the cornerstone of the work of the school of symbolic interactionists (McCall and Simmons, 1978). Their main approach has been to attribute the development of the self to the effect of the reactions of others. The 'looking-glass self' (Cooley, 1902) consists of the incorporation of other people's responses, the so-called 'significant others'. We may note the neutrality of this term, indicating no socially determined other on whom this responsibility rests. This term, significant others, has even entered common language to indicate intimate relationships without commitment to social meaning. Social interactionists do not see themselves as representing an historical change in self and identity, but try to discover an historically constant view of the self. An historical view of the self would have to take into account changes in the self-concept as shown by available records which include contemporary scientific and conceptual statements. In this sense, popular literature can be used as evidence of a change of the self and documentation of a process in Western society from the Renaissance to the modernist age (Verhave and van Hoorn, 1984).

Complementing this array of different influences on the self which eventually created very differentiated selves is the discovery of the self as a precious possession. This possession is guarded jealously, and the maintenance of the worth of the self, of high self-esteem, becomes a primary goal throughout the life-span. However, the possibility of dissonant sources and a resultant splitting of the self is always present. These circumstances lead to a special effort to maintain the continuity of the self, to preserve the essential 'me' throughout the vicissitudes of social life.

This may become clear to the person, but is easily hidden from others.

The self is seen as created and maintained through social inter-action, but some individual self is subjectively preserved. People try to influence others to contribute to a desired self-image, and this self-presentation is achieved partly through behaviour and expression. The work of Erving Goffman (1959, 1962) on self-presentation and stigma is significant in this regard. Goffman studied the signs that people use to manage self-presentation and the social cues that are used to obtain insight into other people. Stigma can be defined as the inference of moral worth from outward signs. Control of stigma becomes an aim of the individual; self-disclosure is conditional and a subject to be investigated in its own right (Jourard, 1964).

Questions of unity of the self and of self-presentation become crucial in a mobile and multi-faceted society; the emphasis among social scientists to study these phenomena is a measure of the importance of this labile self-concept in the society. It is unlikely that this line of thought would have become popular in a caste society. At the same time, this work also served to legitimate such adaptive processes of splintering of the self and of self-presentation. Concurrently, a new virtue was created, namely sincerity, the value of acting according to one's feeling and social status (Trilling, 1971; Back, 1983). Discovering insincerity and finding the real self became a new task in social life.

The leading protagonists of modernism accepted wholeheartedly both the new breakdown of form or style and the dissolution of the self. The many ways in which the new forms could be created led to the many different strands within modernism; the current century cannot be easily allocated to any one style. Novelists, dramatists and poets have tried to create new forms to accommodate their new insights. They seem to be particularly fascinated by the division of the real self, the presentation to the audience by author and actor. In *Enrico IV* and *Six Characters in Search of an Author*, Pirandello used different levels of illusion to show the different, even contradictory, aspects of a person in madness or hypocrisy. O'Neill used the ancient device of masks in *The Great God Brown* to distin-guish the different levels of the self. In the accelerating drumbeat in the successive scenes of *The Emperor Jones*, he involved the audience in the regression and breakdown of the hero's self-concept. Techniques of distinguishing different aspects of the self and of making audiences part of the artistic process become the hallmarks of the artistic movements and their leading representatives of which modernism is composed. Shocking the audience, making it partici-pate or being so unclear that the audience has to make a special effort are different ways in which modern artists and writers try to abolish old forms of communication and representation in order to dissolve the self.

The murder mystery can be seen as a form of counterpoint to the development of modernistic literature. In the latter we see an intensive striving to abolish the unity of the self in the author, in the subject matter as well as in the audience. The search for techniques of breakdown have created a variety of different schools within the modernist movement and ultimately the development of the avant-garde position. Avant-garde artists, as the name implied, were the first to attempt in their work to represent the new conditions. They typically welcomed the new era and tried to revolutionize the whole artistic enterprise to do it justice.

Avant-garde and Mystery Stories

In contrast to the avant-garde work, the mystery story has remained mostly within the confines of traditional form. In fact, the continuing production and popularity of the classic mystery may be considered a continuing manifestation of the nineteenth-century novel in the present era. Within its structure and style, the central attraction is the penetration of unsuspected possibility of the other person.

The attraction of the mystery story during modern times had been the object of much puzzlement among literary critics and cultural analysts. Perhaps the strongest indictment of the form was pronounced by Edmund Wilson. The title of his essay, 'Who Cares Who Killed Roger Ackroyd?' (1950), expresses the tenor of his indictment. Other critiques have condemned the style of writing, the one-dimensionality of the characters and the lack of plausibility of the plots. In spite of these mainly justified strictures, the genre has flourished. This vitality is likely to represent a definite need in society – or at least among readers. The murder mystery and allied genres preserve the accustomed forms in new social conditions. The processes of creating a self in modern times are acknowledged, but the forms of intertwining the selves of the artist and audience are not accepted. On the contrary, readers are distanced from the action, which is presented as an intellectual puzzle. This distancing is aided by a number of conventions, for instance not presenting the victim as a person with whom readers should sympathize. In this regard, Wilson's question, 'Who Cares Who Killed Roger Ackroyd?' is justified; however, this is not the point of the genre. The non-involvement of the reader is an artifice. L.A. Morse, in *An Old-fashioned Mystery* (note the title!), shows that ultimately the reader is the murderer: without the reader's interest, the murder certainly would not have occurred.

The mystery story deserves attention as a cultural phenomenon, especially as its development parallels the development of modernism. Both had their roots in early Victorian writing, although these beginnings were not followed up for some time. Both started to rise during the beginning of the century; the towering Sherlock Holmes stories of Conan Doyle continue to be popular. Both reached their peak during the interwar years and had a second flowering during the middle of the century. And if the future of both is problematic, their transformations could be decoded as portents of changes in society.

Background of the Mystery Story

Generally, the first writers of mysteries seemed unable to handle the ambivalence of character, and their solutions, while often ingenious, seem extreme. Wilkie Collins's *Moonstone*, celebrated frequently as the first mystery novel, can solve the character of the criminal only by having him act under the influence of a hypnotic drug; his criminal act – stealing the moonstone – is thus outside the course of his real personality. Stevenson used the same device in *Dr Jekyll and Mr Hyde*. The self is not inherently ambiguous for these authors; only extreme dissociation through drugs, corresponding to current work in medical psychology, can explain criminal acts in a respectable member of the community.

Poe's two short stories, which are also credited with initiating the genre, introduce the model great detective, but still Poe avoids the problem of the character of the criminal. In the *Murder in the Rue de Morgue* we escape thinking that an undiscovered citizen, who could commit a brutal double-murder, walks the streets of Paris by learning that the murderer was not human at all. The celebrated *Purloined Letter* revolves not around the identity of the criminal but only around the discovery of the letter.

We may note here that the concentration on murder, while standard today, took some time to evolve. The extreme uncertainty in understanding the self and other would be best represented by the extreme and rare act of killing another. Recognizing someone as a murderer leads by necessity to a complete re-evaluation of character. Few people will kill even under the greatest provocation. A military historian has estimated that, even in battle, only one-third of all soldiers actually try to kill an enemy (Keegan, 1976).

Unmasking a murderer is therefore the ultimate representation of the uncertainty of the self.

Several of the major Victorian novelists touched on some aspects of the crime novel, but not of murder mystery. Dickens is sometimes taken as another ancestor in the field, but he did not deal with crime as mystery of character. His police tales, offshoots of his work as a reporter, are principally procedural stories of police work; the identity of criminals is neither puzzling nor important in the plot – the work of detectives is the story.

Similarly, when Dickens uses crimes as a plot device, the identity of the criminal such as Uriah Heep, is completely in character. It is significant that his unfinished novel, *The Mystery of Edwin Drood*, has left puzzles in the mind of critics who tried to finish it, and a favourite solution has been to resolve the mystery of self by recourse to some oriental drug or secret order. Trollope also used crimes and detectives in his plots, but again, the discovery of the real story only confirms the impression of the character that he had proposed in the first place. The modern mystery had to wait until opaqueness could be introduced into the personalities of all characters. Correspondingly, reverting in the present era to extreme personality dissociation and amnesia is considered to be a clumsy plot device, unless it is used in an exceptional, well-constructed story, as in Margaret Millar's *The Horizontal Man*. And, of course, nobody would fault Hitchcock for *Psycho*, although the use of the same device in less skilful hands would be seen as objectionable.

The essence of the murder mystery, which is important here for our purposes, makes it distinct from stories in which crimes are committed or solved. If one wants to give a long ancestry to the mystery story, one can trace it back to *Oedipus Rex* (Grossvogel, 1979) or, with Thurber's companion, to *Macbeth* and *Hamlet*. These stories all deal with crimes that are discovered in the course of the action, but they have little to do with a modern mystery. Two main features distinguish them: typically, in the old crime story it is clear to the reader or audience who committed the crime, and the main emphasis is not on the process of discovery and the exciting surprises that the discovery brings. The Greek audience would be well informed of Oedipus' guilt from the beginning and would only be concerned with how the different characters react to its revelation. In fact, the irony of much of the dialogue depends for its effect on prior knowledge of Oedipus' deed. Similarly, it is rather clear to the audience who killed Hamlet's father. The famous mystery of Hamlet is not the discovery of the crime, but the nature of Hamlet's reaction. If it were a modern thriller, Hamlet might be unmasked at the end as a Norwegian agent; we would not be sure of his basic loyalty.

Dostoevsky's novels, *Crime and Punishment* and *The Brothers Karamazov*, may be seen as a transition towards the more modern outlook. In the first, the murder is described in detail and the subsequent detection gives no surprise to readers. However, the lengthy interrogations of Raskolnikov look like models for similar interrogation scenes in modern thrillers. In *The Brothers Karamazov* the identity of the murderer is not revealed until late in the story, but the discovery itself is somehow of minor importance to the plot, overshadowed by the personalities of the brothers. As in many other ways, Dostoevsky points the way to modern literature, but here he cannot be said to have created a new genre.

The innovator and outstanding figure in the founding of the modern mystery story was, of course, Conan Doyle. Sherlock Holmes has become an important hero in our society. It is interesting to note that Holmes was modelled on a medical researcher; the procedure of the detective fiction and of other enquiry into the human mind ran parallel with Freud. Doyle's creation of the great detective overshadowed the other characters in the mystery, and most literary analysis of the mystery story has followed this lead and centred on the character of the detective. The nature of the person of the detective, the outsider, the intellectual giant or other character who symbolizes a role in our culture, has fascinated most scholars and commentators on the nature of the mystery story (Most and Stowe, 1983).

Looking beyond the detective, we can see other ways in which Doyle mirrored the modern sensibility. Just as Prufrock wandered through the fog of Boston, Bloom navigated through the Scylla and Charybdis of Dublin and Marcel tried to make sense of his varying impressions of French society, so Sherlock Holmes sat in his rooms in Baker Street and had different representatives of metropolitan life drift by and reveal facets of their lives to him. It is significant that he is situated off the centre of London, which was then the main metropolis, with people coming from everywhere, both spatially and socially. Persons coming into Holmes's rooms could have practically any kind of background; what they chose to reveal to him was not necessarily a correct or complete description of themselves. The real identity might be tied up with conditions far away, for instance events decades ago in the Utah desert ('The Scarlet Room'). Conversely, identities might easily be created out of minor characteristics ('The Red-headed League'). Holmes cannot, and does not, assume a transparent self or the kind of stable characters put into difficult situations that would exist in a settled society. Watson does so frequently, and this is where he goes wrong.

The Classic Mystery Story and the Self

It was his approach to the character of the criminal – and the falsely accused – that placed Doyle into the mainstream of his own time and made his style so popular. The subsequent development of the murder mystery retained these features and continued to stress the instability of the self. There are two traditions that have elaborated this genre, sometimes called the English and the American. The American tradition sustained Doyle's use of the metropolitan city. American mysteries typically take place in locales of high migration – California, Florida and the major cities. The history and real self of all the characters are unclear; they are presented in a new incarnation. The great California writers Raymond Chandler and Ross MacDonald are exemplary; the latter in particular has practically a standardized plot, which reveals changes in all the characters (only the detective stays stable). The solution is found through relationships between a number of seemingly unrelated characters which occurred decades ago, typically in a mid-western city where the stable self resided. The great mystery writer Dashiell Hammett even obscured his personal history. His biography and real character have become a matter of active speculation.

The American tradition derives the uncertainty of the self from high mobility and the resulting uncertainty of knowing a person. The English tradition goes further and shows that, even in relatively stable places, there are aspects of other persons which do not fit the unitary picture that they present to the world. In this tradition we find a group of people connected in some way or living in a small community in which a crime occurs; the recesses of everybody's motives and circumstances are explored until all personal secrets are revealed and the identity of the murderer is thus discovered. This form, represented in the first half of the century by such authors as Agatha Christie, Hammond Innes, Dorothy Sayers and Ngaio Marsh, created a series of great detectives. It also created the tradition of standardized cues as shown by Thurber's heroine's travel companion.

Somewhat submerged under the emphasis on the character of the English detective is the recognition of the ambiguity of the personality of all participants. It is interesting, however, to notice that frequently the spouses of the detectives have special abilities and occupational training to assess the hidden selves. Roderick Alleyn's wife (Ngaio Marsh) is a portrait painter, Appleby's (Innes) is an explorer, Peter Wimsey's (Dorothy Sayers) is a writer, all with special experience to look at character under the visual surface or to estimate the self under stress. Increasingly, the centre of interest shifts from the spy-glass and clues to the complexities of character. One way of doing this is to use the conventional stereotypes about social backgrounds to mislead the reader. Christie's use of this device has been especially noted (Grossvogel, 1979). It is not always the dark foreigner who must be the villain. For instance, in both *The Mysterious Affair at Styles* and *Evil Under the Sun*, stereotypes are expressed which are not borne out by the more subtle identities of the villains.

The increasing emphasis on the complexities of the self is shown in some changes in plot devices. Two telling instances can be mentioned. The first is the mechanism by which the self is concealed by outward signs. The classical use of disguise has fallen increasingly into disuse, even into disrepute. No more does the detective pull off a wig or false beard from his face or that of a villain at the crucial moment; disguises are more subtle, established through fake identity cards or fabricated biographies. Disguises are faintly comic for today's reader. Taking a role involves today more and less than putting on a mask. Even in the context of the theatre, method acting goes from the inside out and requires the aspiring actor to change the self-concept to adapt to the new character, while costume and make-up become quite superficial. The popularity of the role concept and symbolic interactionism, especially in the USA, may lie in their representation of these aspects of modern society. Neither the detective nor the criminal must disguise himself in obvious ways; their position in the plot depends not on visible markers, but on the separated identities which become apparent only in the struggle for information control and revelation.

The fascination exerted by the criminal who trades on his easy change of identity has transcended the detective fiction genre. The confidence man is a symbol of modern society, from Herman Melville to Thomas Mann (Blair, 1979). Changing one's total identity according to the requirements of the situation is an ambivalent ability of the modern hero, useful in some ways but pathological in others; the danger was put to an extreme use in Woody Allen's film *Zelig*. The confusion of identities and the resulting threat of loss of identity has been a familiar ingredient of the spy thriller; a spy must play with several identities and is at great risk if the wrong one manifests itself. Extreme mechanisms of dissociation have reappeared here, from Richard Condon's *Manchurian Candidate* to Robert Ludlum's *Bourne Identity*. The affinity of the spy with the confidence man has frequently been acknowledged, but it is most clearly stated by John Le Carré in *The Perfect Spy*.

If the ease of assuming another identity has aligned the plot of the mystery story with the diffusion of the self in modern society, the quest for real identity has remained as a second important issue. However, in this case the emphasis has shifted. One aspect of identity is family origin and ancestral connection. In older stories, regular novels as well as mysteries, this was usually defined as social connection, and the long-lost heir would appear to assume his rightful place. The modern version goes deeper into the self, into the genetic heritage. Here origin matters not for economic and social purposes, but to establish an essence of the self. This topic appears with increasing frequency: P.D. James has used it in novels (*An Unsuitable Job for a Woman* and *Innocent Blood*), Michael Z. Lewin used similar plot devices in *The Enemy Within*, and Gertrude Bell's *Question of Inheritance* uses biological inheritance to explain an important character. The latter plot was given special prominence originally by William March in *The Bad Seed*. The two developments – playing down superficial changes in the self in disguises and looking for a basic, genetic, self – reveal a striving for diversity and continuity which forms the modern dilemma of identity.

Spy Thrillers

The indeterminateness of the individual self has been expanded to a world-wide condition. Interpersonal understanding is no longer restricted to small definable units: the scene of understanding and of crime exists on a transnational basis. Much of the difficulty of understanding another person and even understanding oneself has been transferred to the spy thriller. Here a similar progression has occurred. The traditional, nineteenth-century spy-adventure placed the well-defined hero battling against villains whose personalities were also quite clear. A good example is *The Scarlet Pimpernel*, where the main emphasis is on the action, the disguises, climbing in and out of buildings and hand-to-hand fighting. There is never any question about where the reader's sympathy is to lie; the unity of the protagonists, their loyalty and the reader's loyalty are taken for granted. This simple plot development has established its own tradition: its origin can be traced to Erskine Childers's *The Riddle of the Sands*, which was practically written as a propaganda story warning England of Germany's intentions. But even here, the ambiguity of the modern self appears: Childers was executed in 1922 for suspected treachery during the Irish Civil War. The tradition of this type of thriller was extended by John Buchan and reached its climax with Ian Fleming's James Bond stories. But here the unitary perspective on self begins to clash with the modern outlook: these stories cannot be read, and certainly cannot be produced, in visual media without a certain amount of self-parody.

The novels in this genre, which are now taken more seriously, have had a development parallel to the murder mystery. They have moved away from the means and ends of action, to the unmasking of the potentially real nature of each protagonist. One must say 'potentially' because the widening of the scene leaves the question of the real self indeterminate. In many current spy thrillers the loyalty and the aims of the participants remain ambiguous even after the final unmasking. It is sometimes difficult to see what the intelligence organizations are after: they seem to be engaged primarily in the recruitment of agents and purification of their agencies, that is, in finding out who they are and who the enemy is. In many British novels of this type one can see the influence of the real trauma of the McLean–Burgess affair, but this also is an example in real life of the splintering of the self.

The medium of thriller also had its origin early in the century with Joseph Conrad's *Secret Agent*. This story stresses the ambiguous identity of the protagonists, but also the ambiguity of the causes they serve. Thus, the balance between the plots with clear identities and those with a more modernist point of view swings in part with political conditions and the polarization of friends and enemies. Ambiguous identity is more easily expressed by those writers whose own point of view clashes with the official position. Thus, Graham Greene can express his own opinions within the plot of his novels. There may be a parallel in detective stories proper with periodic social changes in views of law and order.

The model writer of this genre at the present time is John Le Carré. His characters come in and out of the cold, and readers are exposed to shadowy organizations and ambivalent characters as opposed to well-defined intelligence organizations trying to find out something important. The characters are more actors then persons. The extreme of the dissolution of the self is the title heroine of *The Little Drummer Girl*, a professional actress. She is recruited although she has no inclination for intelligence work or any particular sympathy for the cause she is to work for. She is so malleable and without a core that she adheres to her assignment and, in addition, accepts for herself the

history that she is given. She appears as a real person, but
without any steady self-concept. *The Little Drummer Girl* shows
another limitation of this kind of spy thriller. Here the action is
directed not inward to the intelligence organization, but outward
towards a real conflict. Leaving the problems of individual and
organization and entering the real world of political conflict
has made Le Carré vulnerable to broad ideological criticism.
For the genre of the spy thriller, this kind of argument is
pernicious.

In his next novel, *The Perfect Spy*, Le Carré remains closer to
the identity problems of the spy, practically dissecting the self. The
psychological mode is aided here by the autobiographical sources
of the novel. His character is forced to a complicated dissembling
scheme as long as he feels bound to his father as a role
model. We can also notice that this model is the confidence
man. The intrapersonal organization of the self has joined the
world organization of international affairs; neither level provides a
secure anchor.

Current Trends in Mystery and Spy Novel

Murder mystery and spy novel started from the opposite extremes,
the mystery dealing with individual conflicts between murderer,
victim and detective, and the spy story describing action between
large social units. In the latter genre murder is not a problematic
action: James Bond's code 007 means licence to kill. The two
extremes meet, however, in the current overwhelming attention
directed to the power of institutions. Detective and intelligence
agent worry as much about their organizational problems as
about the case at hand. On a world-wide base, the spy thriller
reflects the dissolution of the individual self into a part of an
autotelic organization. The murder mystery proper has moved
towards the same point from the other side. This is indicated
by the rise of the so-called procedural novels, which show the
work of a whole police department in action. Although one or
several officers may be especially distinguished, the emphasis is
on the organizational action, the attention to details and the patient
accumulating of evidence. The criminal is, in many cases, shown
only at the end at the point of discovery (thereby violating a
rule of the classic story that the criminal has to be part of the
whole action). The identity of the criminal is not important: the
chase, the work of the organization, supplants the interest in the
person–detective for the criminal. This genre seems to follow the
early writing of Dickens. In neither the procedural novel nor the

organization spy story is personality delineated; whether steady or unclear, self ceases to be important. Suprahuman units are fighting each other.

Thus, in the murder mystery, routine series about police departments have followed the charismatic writers and detectives. The new detectives are no longer lone heroes, but have become chief inspectors in different settings, worrying about promotion and pension plans. The emphasis is more on the setting itself – country towns, metropolitan neighbourhoods or occupational routines; the character studies of different suspects lead eventually to the murderer. The tradition now has led towards a balance between: considerations of social change (new town, new commuters, decline of the gentry); the effectiveness of established institutions (private detectives decline in importance); and the resulting importance of the study of characters as a necessary supplement to police routine and the search for clues.

The emphasis on police procedure and the standard reliance on motive, opportunity and means emphasize also the loss of the criminal character; anybody, given the circumstances, can be the culprit. There is no longer a criminal personality. Significantly, again, the representation of the criminal in the murder mystery runs parallel to current developments in criminology. Criminal opportunity theory claims that crime rates are dependent on the development of criminals not through social or developmental conditions, but through variations in criminal opportunities. Crimes are consequences not of criminal selves, but of criminal settings (Cohen et al., 1981).

The apex of this story of mutual influence between the community, the police organization and the self is reached with George Simenon. Standing outside the Anglo-American tradition, his Inspector Maigret uses the resources of the police and his understanding of the different sectors of French life to understand the hidden personality of the murderer and thereby solve the case. Maigret's technique of empathy and absorption of atmosphere becomes a metaphor of the interpersonal relations in a complex society.

Many current writers in this genre have more or less openly looked at Simenon's style and Maigret's personality as valid models. As examples, we have Alan Hunter's *Gently*, Nicholas Freeling's *Van der Walk* or Bartholemy Gill's *McGarr*. The last of these shows also how difficult it is today to separate private murder from international conflict; several of Gill's investigations can easily merge both. Spatially and temporally, the self and the social environment have become indefinite. A desire for more definite boundaries may be seen in the renewed popularity of the classic mystery stories, although supplemented by the same unclarity of the modern self. The old omniscient detective, if revived at all, is taken with more than a grain of salt.

Outlook

Changes in content within the traditional frame of storytelling may furnish sensitive indicators of social change. The trends in thrillers seem to overcome the dissolution of the self, but do not portend a return to the old definite self. They point to a stability in the attention to social forms and a questioning of reality within these organized social units: within the police, within the gang, within intelligence organizations, within literature itself. How can we identify the individual at all or the truth of individual perceptions and beliefs? These may become the basic questions of the post-modern period.

References

Back, K.W. (1983) 'Compliance and Conformity in an Age of Sincerity', pp. 50–76 in M. Rosenbaum (ed.), *Compliant Behavior*. New York: Human Sciences Press.

Blair, J.E. (1979) *The Confidence Man in Modern Fiction*. New York: Barnes and Noble.

Cohen, L.E., J.R. Klugel and K.C. Land (1981) 'Social Inequality and Predatory Criminal Victimization: An Exposition and Test of a Formal Theory', *American Sociological Review*, 46: 505–24.

Cooley, C.H. (1902) *Human Nature and the Social Order*. New York: Scribners.

Fish, S. (1986) 'Withholding the Missing Portion: Power, Meaning and Persuasion in Freud's "The Wolf Man"', *Times Literary Supplement*, 29 August: 935–8.

Goffman, E. (1959) *The Presentation of Self in Everyday Life*. Garden City and New York: Doubleday-Anchor.

Goffman, E. (1962) *Stigma: Management of Spoiled Identity*. Englewood Cliffs, NJ: Prentice-Hall.

Gordon, C. and K.J. Gergen (1968) Introduction to their *The Self in Social Interaction*, Vol. I. New York: John Wiley.

Grossvogel, D.I. (1979) *Mystery and Its Fictions: From Oedipus to Agatha Christie*. Baltimore: Johns Hopkins University Press.

Hodin, J.P. (1973) *Modern Art and Modern Man*. Cleveland: Case Western Reserve University Press.

James, W. (1892) *Psychology*. New York: Henry Holt.

Jourard, S.M. (1964) *The Transparent Self*. Princeton: Van Nostrand.

Keegan, J. (1976) *The Face of Battle*. New York: Viking Press.

Lifton, R.J. (1976) *The Life of the Self*. New York: Simon & Shuster.

McCall, G. and J.L. Simmons (1978) *Identity and Interaction*. New York: Free Press.

236 Drama and narrative in the construction of identities

Mellow, J.R. (1974) *Charmed Circle: Gertrude Stein and Company*. New York: Praeger.

Most, G.W. and W.W. Stowe (eds) (1983) *The Poetics of Murder*. New York: Harcourt Brace Jovanovich.

Rogers, C. (1968) 'Interpersonal Relationships in USA 2000', *Journal of Applied Behavioral Science*, 4: 208–60.

Thurber, J. (1945) 'The Macbeth Murder Mystery', pp. 60–3 in *The Thurber Carnival*. New York: Harper and Bros.

Trilling, L. (1971) *Sincerity and Authenticity*. Cambridge, MA: Harvard University Press.

Verhave, T. and W. van Hoorn (1984) 'The Temporalization of the Self', pp. 325–46 in K.J. Gergen and M.M. Gergen (eds), *Historical Social Psychology*. Hillsdale, NJ: Erlbaum.

Wilson, E. (1950) 'Who Cares Who Killed Roger Ackroyd?' pp. 356–63 in his *Classics and Commercials*. New York: Farrar, Straus and Giroux.

Zurcher, L. (1977) *The Mutable Self*. Beverly Hills, CA: Sage.

Index